To one of the most
Inspired & inspiring
teachers I know.

Much love
Jessica

WELCOME TO THE AQUARIUM

WELCOME TO
THE AQUARIUM

A YEAR IN THE LIVES OF CHILDREN

Julie Diamond

THE NEW PRESS

NEW YORK
LONDON

Requests for permission to reproduce selections
from this book should be mailed to:
Permissions Department, The New Press, 38 Greene Street,
New York, NY 10013.

Published in the United States by The New Press, New York, 2008
Distributed by W. W. Norton & Company, Inc., New York

LIBRARY OF CONGRESS CATALOGING-IN-PUBLICATION DATA

Diamond, Julie.
Welcome to the aquarium: a year in the lives of children / Julie Diamond.
     p.   cm.
Includes bibliographical references and index.
ISBN 978-1-59558-171-6 (hc.)
1. Kindergarten teachers.   2. Classroom management.
3. Curriculum planning   I. Title.
LB1733.D53 2008
372.1102—dc22   2008024221

The New Press was established in 1990 as a not-for-profit alternative to the large,
commercial publishing houses currently dominating the book publishing industry.
The New Press operates in the public interest rather than for private gain, and is
committed to publishing, in innovative ways, works of educational, cultural, and
community value that are often deemed insufficiently profitable.

www.thenewpress.com

Composition by dix!
This book was set in Walbaum MT

Printed in the United States of America

2   4   6   8   10   9   7   5   3   1

For Eqbal Ahmad and Dohra Ahmad

CONTENTS

FOREWORD

Not that I remember, but I bet I had a kindergarten teacher like Julie Diamond. Kindergarten was my one good year in school; after that, it was all downhill. I can recall my mother dragging me off to P.S. 77 in the Bronx, crying, terrified, begging for a reprieve from this alien world to which I was about to be abandoned.

Kindergarten was my introduction to the unanticipated sci-fi elements of life: my first contact with THEM, THE OTHER, the unfamiliar universe of rules, structure, and enforced socialization.

Most of the kids I didn't know, most of them I didn't want to know. And what I also didn't want to know was the internal chaos that came with forced entry into this strange new world. Involuntary servitude in a regimented society where you had to line up here, march there, hang up your coats—all together now!—on the same pegs in the same closet at the same time, sit at the same desk next to the same kid who didn't seem all that interested in me but was so much quicker at getting it, figuring out the system, playing the game.

But even I, who was bad at games, found that by the end of the first week—or certainly not long thereafter—it was OK. I was no longer scared. I understood. I belonged. THE OTHER had been assimilated. I was going to be fine. I was five years old, too young to have a shrink, so it must have been the teacher.

Julie Diamond is my kind of kindergarten teacher and she has written my kind of book on her years in the public schools of New

York City, primarily at P.S. 87, the very school my daughters Halley and Julie attended. And it came to pass that Julie (Diamond) taught Julie (Feiffer) in kindergarten, so how could I not be interested in what she has to say about her life as an educator?

Julie is an innovative survivor in a system that likes to assure us that its heart is in the right place, but what place that would be is hard to know because the language in which the system prefers to express itself is a virtual anti-language and would pull a failing grade if it were a paper your child had turned in.

So what is a teacher to do? We learn from selections from Julie's journals, her moment-by-moment classroom observations, reflections, doubts, and resolved doubts. Her humanity and her humor: "Long ago, when I was beginning to teach, I had a very hard time bringing a group of children in from the yard one afternoon. As I saw it at the time, they just wouldn't listen. I was furious, and yelled and threatened—they finally came in. One girl railed back, in full five-year-old disdain, 'Julie, you know about teaching, but you don't know about children!' "

But she learned. Oy, did she learn, and now she rewards us with a page-turner on how and what she learned, simply and gracefully written, with so much clarity, such focus, such pride, such little intrusion of ego.

"At these moments, which come often enough, I look around the classroom at the work layered on walls and surfaces: loops of patterned necklaces made from dyed and strung pasta shapes . . . little drawstring bags; drawings of sea creatures, a seahorse with its tail wrapped around seaweed; saved Lego constructions. . . ."

She cites and quotes her many exemplars, the community of teachers out there, here and abroad, mentors and role models who form a bond of sanity, reason, determination, and goodwill.

Time and again we encounter the engaged teacher circling around myriad obstacles set up by the pod people who represent the system, but obstacles set up no less by herself. Follow along on the suspenseful odyssey of Henry and his aquarium, where child, parents, and teacher cannot seem to get it right, miscommunicate monumentally, and pull in different directions toward a conclusion you cannot help but be moved by, so rich is its sense of inquiry, observation, mission, and self-examination. It brought tears to this reader's eyes.

Not all Julie's self-examination is accurate: "In the school's hallways, when the first-graders whom I taught the previous year catch sight of me, they jump up and down; they shout to the others who were in my class—'It's Julie!' The second-graders are still excited, they wave and smile, but more sedately. By the end of second grade, I've receded into the past; I'm far away, and am undoubtedly smaller."

No way.

—Jules Feiffer

PERMISSIONS

ACKNOWLEDGMENTS

P.S. 87, where this book is set, mirrors its neighborhood: lively and fast-paced, multihued in population, its culture celebrating creativity and difference as well as accord. (I have changed names and identifying details to preserve privacy.) It is rarely entirely quiet. Jane Hand, the principal who hired me in 1994, seemed to know the names of every one of the school's almost one thousand children. The teachers work exceptionally hard and help each other out; my kindergarten colleagues and the teachers on my hall could be counted on. The parents, besides donating time and resources, are warmly appreciative of the work teachers do. No school is perfect, but I felt at home at P.S. 87 and could teach according to my beliefs.

My beliefs about teaching were formed at Bank Street College of Education. When I attended, it was still located on Bank Street, and many professors—Barbara Biber, Dorothy Cohen, Lois Wolf, and others—had known an earlier generation of progressive New York City educators. The grounding in child development that Bank Street provided was a base for everything I learned subsequently.

My teaching was a group project. For almost two decades, I was fortunate to be connected with the Teachers College preservice program. Their energetic student teachers, and student teachers and interns from other institutions, added to the classroom in distinctive ways. I benefited, too, from the talented paraprofessionals and assistants with whom I worked over many years—Magda

Kamal, Sayma Begum, Aris Puente, Arshea Hall, Henny Matias, Jesenia Zambrano, and Natasha Torres.

I want to give credit, too, to the colleagues who influenced my teaching and to those who—once I'd begun writing—read chapters and commented: Kay Campbell, Ruth Charney, Eleanor Duckworth, Beverly Falk, Hollee Freeman, Mary Frosch, Theresa Furman, David and Jacqui Getz, Betsy Grob, Ginger Hanlon, Naomi Hill, Linda Kasarjian, Gwyn Kellam, Eva McKeon, Deborah Meier, Aisha Ray, Joanna Uhry, Mary Weaver, and Michael Ziemski. Ruth Charney's generosity, questions, and comments benefited me immensely. Several art educators commented on the chapter about art: Kirsten Cole, Andrea Kantrowitz, Ann Schaumberger, Amy Snider, and Jenny Snider, artist and friend. Librarians at Bank Street College and at Donnell Library were extremely helpful. At P.S. 87, Phil Firsenbaum's documentation of children's journal writing informed the section on writing. A visit to the schools of Reggio Emilia as part of a Wheelock College study tour made the approach real, and deepened my thinking about the purposes and context of teaching.

The faith of friends spurred me on. Janet Wolff offered encouragement at the beginning. Other friends also read chapters and offered suggestions or moral support: Emily Abel, Connie Brown, Helen Hopps, Rayna Knobler and Martin Popps, Harriet Luria, Annie O'Neill, Anne Roberts and Peter Boothroyd, David Sperlinger, Zina Steinberg, and Phyllis Trager and Ed Mufson. Hanna Moskin and Ann Sullivan listened through indecisive moments; Roberta Guerette and Elly Shodell offered perfect advice. I gained insights about teaching relationships from Nettie Terestman and was heartened by David Rappaport's confidence in my writing. I want to thank Jenny Allen and Jules Feiffer for their responses to the chapters on literacy. I found quiet for writing, away from the city, thanks to Hanna and Jeffrey Moskin, Margaret Burnham and Max Stern, Noosha Baqi and Grego Marcano, and Ruth Wald.

My parents, Abraham and Sylvia Diamond, teachers in the New York City school system, bequeathed to me humanistic values. My sister, Cora Diamond, edited and encouraged. I'm grateful to my late husband, Eqbal Ahmad, another teacher, for his insistence that I was a writer, and for his love. To my daughter, Dohra Ahmad, I owe much—for her consistent backing, help, and humor. My son-in-law, Orin Herskowitz, and granddaughters, Eliya and Melina Ahmad, contributed to my welfare in essential ways.

When I first thought about this book, I talked to Ellen Reeves at The New Press. I'd thought of the book as a diary. No, she said, you have to *write* it! I did, aided by her questions and commitment. My thanks also go to Jennifer Rappaport and Sarah Fan for shepherding the book to completion, to Gary Stimeling for his thorough copyediting, and to The New Press. Finally, I thank the children I taught. My ultimate purpose is to recognize the worlds they created.

WELCOME TO THE AQUARIUM

INTRODUCTION

When I was growing up, my elementary school was full of older teachers, women in their fifties, sixties, seventies, who had gray or white hair and excellent posture. Since that time, the feminist movement has opened up career choices for women. Of the young women who now become teachers, many of the most energetic and ambitious soon leave the classroom for administrative or supervisory positions. Classroom teaching is something to do for five or ten years; a lifetime in the classroom seems old-fashioned. At age sixty, I was the oldest classroom teacher in my school: I was a dinosaur.

Looking back at almost three decades of teaching, I see a column of years, each one stamped with successes and failures, constraints and possibilities. As fewer and fewer teachers have this perspective, is nothing important lost? Is there anything irreplaceable that veteran teachers offer schools? I believe that veteran teachers' knowledge is not, most deeply, a matter of accumulated techniques and teaching methods. What I gained, I believe, is an increased ability to know children, to apprehend and appreciate the world they inhabit and are engaged with. I see the work of *knowing* the children we teach as the teacher's central task.

This view of teaching isn't an automatic benefit of longevity. It grows out of a progressive approach to education, the conviction that learning is something a learner *does*, not something *done to* the learner. At graduate school, I was exposed to the idea that learning is not imposed from without, that we teach the "whole child," who is an active agent with an "urge to learn."[1] I began teaching in the late 1960s, a period of social activism, when hopes for the schools were tied to dreams of social justice and racial equality. Many of us wanted our classrooms to be informed by the "lives of children."[2] We wanted school to be a place for children's thinking and stories, their real selves. We were inspired by reports of educational reforms in England and by new curricula based on children's exploration.[3]

Progressive principles remain relevant and exciting for me: the respect for children's modes of inquiry that characterized the British schools of the 1970s is alive today in the schools of Reggio Emilia, Italy; the honoring of human experience and commitment to documenting children's work that motivated twentieth-century progressive educators motivates many current teacher-writers. But our public schools are increasingly inhospitable to progressive values. Testing rules the schools; and just as progressive education has a history, there's a history to the idea that subjects should be taught in the same way for all children, without regard to what children bring to school. Our national priorities are those expressed by Dickens's character Thomas Gradgrind in *Hard Times*: "Facts alone are wanted in life. Plant nothing else, and root out everything else."[4]

In contrast, the children in K-104 made an aquarium in their classroom. K-104, the kindergarten class I taught (104 was the room number), was in a public school on New York's Upper West Side, a school with a racially and economically diverse population. In the course of the year, the twenty-four children became a *class*, with a unique identity and culture. I played a part in moving them toward this goal, one that's intangible but consequential. The culture of a classroom provides a context for, and shapes, students' individual achievements. The children come to see themselves as individually powerful *and* connected to others. Citizenship in a class is, I believe, essential to the children's future as educated adults. The classroom's myriad details—its organiza-

The Aquarium
Photo by Julie Diamond

tion, curriculum, and relationships, the teacher's pondering and decision making—spell out the reality of social ideals.

The themes of participation and connection are nowhere more visible than in the story of Henry. In the fall, Henry had resolutely kept to himself. By the spring, he was prolific, making signs and works of art for the room. When the class studied undersea animals and made models of sea creatures, the children invited the parents to visit the aquarium they had built in the block-building area. On his own, Henry produced a sign of welcome for the classroom door, WELCOME TO THE AQUARIUM, his words surrounded by sharks, eels, and swirling seaweed. Writing about him, I saw him *in* the classroom environment, adapting to it. The classroom, like an aquarium and the sea itself, is a common, shared space, as well as a space for differences and individuality. Like an aquarium (but unlike the ocean), the classroom is both real *and* invented: classrooms are real places, inhabited by real people, but the meanings that children—and adults—find there are meanings they create themselves.

Signing up to study different animals
Photo by Julie Diamond

The book's time frame replicates the structure of a school year, but each chapter takes up a specific topic. The fall chapters describe the classroom environment and its communication of values; the rituals and routines that initiate a sense of community; art activities that introduce a model of student work and achievement; and the roles of teachers and children in developing curriculum. The winter section includes two chapters on literacy, one on its purposes and one on the teaching of literacy-related skills. A third chapter looks at how I took into account students' patterns of engagement as well as my own; it examines the sources of teachers' authority, and the values and beliefs that underpin my daily encounters with children.

The first spring chapter maps Henry's growth from isolation to greater engagement with others, and recounts my struggle to work with him and his parents. The next chapter takes place at the end of the year. It focuses on how children use metaphors to grasp concepts of growth and change, and how metaphors crystallize ideas and feelings for teachers as well. In the last chapter, I write about the personal motivations behind my choice of a classroom life and the qualities I brought to teaching. I analyze the effect of teachers' material and human environment on their ability to work, a topic of particular importance because schools are often expected to ameliorate race and class inequities. I write about the obstacles that teachers face as a result of educational standardization, and the human resources available to teachers who hope to maintain a commitment to children and teaching.

Other adults were actively present in K-104. Arshea Hall, my wonderful assistant teacher, was caring and talented. I've had many wonderful assistants, but I was beyond fortunate in being able to work with her; we planned, compared notes, laughed, and generally appreciated and encouraged each other. David Vitale-Wolff was an enthusiastic and committed intern from Bank Street's Urban Education Semester, and one of many student teachers to whom I've been indebted. The "we" in the book often refers to the three of us, but the book presents my own thinking about the class, the year, and teaching.

The subject of the book is also the teacher. Years ago, I read Sylvia Ashton-Warner's *Teacher*. Its impact on me was derived partly from the power of her voice. Her voice was that of the person I wanted to be as a teacher: strong *and* self-critical, hectoring *and* humorous, realistic *and* optimistic, wholly committed to the children she taught. Reading *Teacher*, I could hear her, talking back to the children and arguing with herself.

I wanted my voice to be as distinctive. Now, that result seems inevitable; I was there in the classroom as myself. In describing K-104—attempting to make the classroom come alive, to be precise about details and also capture the impression of things in constant motion—my writing reflects my perspective. I appear in the foreground at times for another reason as well. In laying out the "subject matter . . . in all its complexity" (as Eleanor Duckworth describes the teacher's task),[5] I can't omit my mistakes, confusions, and good guesses.

Complexity doesn't lend itself to a clear moral. It strikes me as significant that in telling the story of Henry, which is at the heart of the book, I don't draw one clear-cut, conclusive lesson. But this *is* the conclusion: we work to see who a child is and to make a place for that child in the classroom. We confront our limits and make whatever use we can of our strengths. The central story is continuous, not heroic or definitive. In learning who children are, we learn who we are, as teachers and people. This is the challenge of teaching, and it's also the reward. In the long run, for me, it was enough.

1

◌ℐ◌

August: Beginning the Year

Opening Up the Room

The rituals of beginning are very satisfying—the sense that I know how to do this. At the start of the day or the year—opening the door, looking around. Bare walls, empty floor. It's my room, even today, with everything packed away.*

For the last thirteen years, I've taught kindergarten in the same classroom. My school year begins in late August, one week before teachers are officially due back. *Ate breakfast with Linda, who's teaching second grade this year. We didn't talk about school, but about other things—her family, mine.* The hallways are dark and quiet, although a number of other teachers are back. I open the classroom door; I use the wooden window pole to open all the windows. I plug in the fan, the radio, and the clock, set the clock to the right time, and hang it back on the wall.

This week is my own. Sometimes I just sit and look around the room, deciding what to do next. I move boxes and crates off the countertops, look in the closets for the coffee can in which I keep the "teacher pens." Repeating these acts every August, opening up the room, I conjure up the teacher self I'd left behind in June, the person who occupies this classroom: *I have to change back, from having what I see as my own life, to being the teacher.* Begin-

---

* Italicized sections are excerpts from a journal I kept during the school year.

ning at this slow pace is a luxury, but an essential one. *I'm relaxed: I forget how hard the job really is.*

For the next week and a half, I get the room ready. Certain assumptions govern my thinking about the arrangement of the room: I want it to have a spare appearance, because the children's work will fill it; I don't want either the organization or decoration to be fussy and distracting. When children enter the room, I want them to feel—in their bones—this is *their* room. The room must be open enough to allow for a degree of flow of activities and materials, yet not so open that it erases all boundaries between areas. If the spaces *work*, the organization of the room will ground me, too.

The stages in getting the room ready are always the same: first, an empty floor with everything stacked on the countertops, then I spread things out. I pile stuff up on the tables and floor, wash the plastic baskets, bins, cubes, and block animals. I make a list of the areas of the room and the activities that children will be pursuing:

math
journals
writing folders? writing materials
science exhibit, science books
art
music?
games
blocks
pretend
rug and library
children's tables
my chair and table.

How will these fit in the room? Which areas should be adjacent, which separated? Although I've set up this room for years, I start by making a plan on paper. Certain activities demand to be in certain places: the rug and class library are in one corner; the block-building area gets the opposite corner; both need space and protection. Art activities near the sink. Shelves for plants go near the window. Where to put the rabbit's cage, turtle tank, listening center? I build on last year's plan, but change details, enlarging the science area this year: I add chairs and a bookcase just for science books. I want the science area next to the wall, so there's a place for children's science drawings. But when I change one thing, everything else has to shift.

From the hardware store, I get paint for the bookshelves and traps for the mice, who multiply over the summer. I paint the bulletin boards and bookshelves dark blue. I think about the functions of different pieces of furniture. A low table that borders the rug is used for writing, drawing, and puzzles, and children sit on it at meeting time. A low shelf, made from milk crates and a board, faces the block area and holds block accessories; it doubles as an extra table or bench for children playing in the adjacent pretend area, a space for their dramatic play. The shelves that separate the pretend area from the tables are open at the front and the back, permitting materials to be taken from either side.

I think about how children will move around the room. There's more than one pathway to the rug, so it can be approached from different directions. Paper and writing materials are accessible in several places: there are paper trays, markers, and pencils in the art area and also on a set of shelves near the low table; there's a basket with clipboards and writing pads in the pretend area; and later in the year, I'll add index cards and markers to the block area. The organization of the room is simple and uncluttered; it is easily comprehended. I want the children to be able to read the environment, to find what they want, to know where to put things away. I move things and then switch them, and at various moments of indecision ask colleagues from down the hall to come in. They'll see things with fresh eyes and give me good advice. I'm decisive about certain choices, when my reasoning is a result of my goals and my experience: I leave space around the rabbit cage, because I know children will want to sit or stretch out next to the cage. Finally, I put the rug down, move the last pieces of furniture into place, and the room is pulled together.

I search for the right-size basket to put materials in. The room should *look* good—balanced, colorful, appealing, with enough but not too much stuff—baskets of crayons, containers of markers, cans of sharpened pencils, paper in paper trays, games, some puzzles, a few tubs of brightly colored math and construction materials. In the block area, trucks, toy zoo animals, and Duplos; in the pretend area, dolls in newly washed doll clothes, trays with cups and saucers, and telephones. Baskets of books on the library shelves that rim the rug.

All that I add by way of decoration, along the walls at the back and front of the room, and on the bulletin boards on the coat closets, are large photographs from calendars: sea shells, parent and baby animals, reproductions of Amish quilts. No charts, posters, computer-generated pictures: nothing "cute." In time, the room will reflect the children themselves, their interests and purposes. This is a place for children's work; that's the message. If we need a chart, later in the year, the text will be their words, and it will be illustrated with their drawings. In many classroom, walls and bulletin boards are plastered with charts and posters; the rooms are filled with images and text even before the children have arrived. If I've done a good job, the organization and simple decor of the room will be enough.

I'm committed to a definition of the classroom as laboratory, workshop. The room should function as a setting to "stimulate the active inquiry of the children themselves," in the words of the twentieth-century British psychologist and educator Susan Isaacs.[1] In order to study children's social and cognitive development, Isaacs ran a school in Cambridge, England, in the 1920s. Her extensive daily records of children's actions and talk, which form the heart of her books *Intellectual Growth in Young Children* and *Social Development in Young Children*, constitute perhaps the first qualitative school research project. Although

Isaacs's interest was theoretical, of great practical usefulness for educators are the sections in *Intellectual Growth* that describe the school's environment and educational aims; these provide a vivid picture of what school can be.[2]

In this kind of classroom, the goal is the development of children's intrinsic interests. The *stuff* that's made available—the books, the science, math and art materials, the animals—as well as the organization of space that allows children to use the stuff, are intended not only to teach a specific bit of knowledge (rabbits are mammals, and mammals are born alive), but to give children perspectives on the world. Children arrive at their understandings through actions, through representations and discussion, undertaken as individuals and as a group, with the active participation of the teacher. If I believe this, the room will announce it, as much because of what it doesn't have—its emptiness—as for what has been made available. It's a stage set, waiting for the actors.

Names

On the way to school, Linda and I talk about this period of time before school starts. She says, Right now we know nothing; she's "a blank slate"—because of not knowing these particular children. It's all anticipation, all getting ready. Like the line in Hamlet, "Readiness is all."

I get my class list from the office. Last name, first name, boy or girl, date of birth, ethnicity. I look at the list, struck by the mystery that these names represent. The first thing I do is rewrite the names in alphabetical order by first name. This is how I'll write the names on my class list, and this is how I'll see the names in my mind all year. Soon enough, a face and personality will go with each name. As I get to know the children, it will be impossible to imagine those names *not* associated with those personalities.

I'm always eager to get the class list. My future is there, in those names. I may know a name or two—siblings, whom I'd seen

before as babies. But for the most part, the names are all I have. I
rewrite them a second time, this time by month of birth, seeing
how many "old" children I have, those born January through
April, how many young ones, born September through December, and how many in the middle. From one year to the next,
there can be great variation in how the birthdays are spread out: I
remember one year when thirteen children—mostly boys—were
born in September or later. Thirteen children (around half the
class) who'd entered kindergarten at age four, and who—the
boys, particularly—naturally loved rolling around; it was physically impossible for them to come to the rug without at least one
tumble.

It's intriguing to know the names but not the children. Some of
them may not turn up (the no-shows), and I may get other children. As we get closer to the first day of school, I print the names
on yellow oaktag. All these preparations, around a central core
that's missing: *Getting the room physically ready, sharpening the
pencils, labeling the cans. As I'm setting up the room, I'm aware of
my state of mental readiness, of being, as Linda put it, a blank slate.
Tolerating readiness.* Tolerating, because anxiety is a component
of this state. My dreams wake me with anxiety: school opens, and
I've got eighty kids in the room; school opens, and the room is totally unready. But anxiety is part of not knowing, and not knowing is essential: *I have to make a space, I have to not be my summer
self—active, occupied with my own interests. Emptying myself, in
a way.* Being a blank slate is work, takes effort. I'm struck by
Linda's analogy. Traditional education pictures children as the
slates, teachers doing the writing. If *we're* receptive—to children,
to what they bring to school—the relationship is reversed. We're
the slates, they do the writing. Just as I create a space in the room
for the work children will do, I have to find it in myself.

This isn't to say that I don't prepare. I may be a blank slate, but
I also leave nothing to chance. I carry with me whole textbooks of
knowledge, everything I've done at the start of other school years,
years of workshops, and everything I know about five-year-olds. I

check my notebooks from previous years. I make decisions about what materials will be out, choosing some things that will probably be familiar to the children from nursery school (puzzles, play dough, games that are easy to play), and a few things that may be new (the math materials). I'm thoroughly, emphatically organized: I have plans, a schedule for the first few days; I get the materials ready. The books I choose to read the first week are simple and repetitive: a simple folk tale—*The Three Billy Goats Gruff*—or *Little Blue and Little Yellow*, with its theme of separation and reunion. I decide which songs and chants I'll teach, choosing, again, something probably familiar from preschool (the fingerplay Open Them, Shut Them), and something that will probably be new (the chant Crackers and Crumbs). With all this in hand, I'm prepared to be flexible. I know that I don't know exactly what will happen. During these days before school actually begins, before the kids appear, I carry around this absence in my mind. It starts when I get the names and only ends when I meet the children, when they come into the room with their parents, and I hear who they are and finally get to put faces to names.

Taking Time

On Saturday I go in for two hours of final chores, setting out seashells, sea glass, and a bird's nest on trays on the science table, taping up a list of the supplies I'm asking parents for (tissues and liquid soap). I bring in a big pot of purple chrysanthemums and put it on a bookshelf by the window.

Teachers are officially due back on the Tuesday after Labor Day, the start of a week that allows no leisure. Staff meetings on Tuesday and Wednesday last all morning: *A different week—mandatory, not voluntary. Each A.M. begins with hours of sitting and listening. Voices in the air.* The meetings go on too long, and I resent them for taking time that I want to spend in my room. I stay late Friday, and go in Saturday, to do last-minute jobs—making a large masking-tape X across the block shelves and adding a sign, CLOSED, because the block area won't be open right away. I don't get everything done, and at some point, I just put everything extraneous out of sight.

I'm in bed early on Sunday night. *But I can't sleep; I'm no less anxious than the children probably are. It's the first morning I'll wake up with an alarm since June. In unconscious rebellion, I set the alarm for 6:45 instead of 6:15. I end up having to hurry to school.* Teachers in the city system no longer have to punch a time clock, but time continues to impose itself. All year, the institutional timetable makes its demands: the children must be in the cafeteria at 11:05, out to the yard for dismissal at 2:45. Schools run on tight schedules: I try to arrive promptly at the classrooms of the teachers who give me "prep" periods. Being on time is a perennial struggle for me; on too many afternoons I'm the last teacher out at dismissal, once more apologizing to waiting parents and babysitters. It's not just a time-management problem, but also a desire to give children the time for whatever they're doing. When they're productive and happy, I think, *I'll give them a few extra minutes.* I often have the feeling—it's something teachers complain about all the time, and I suppose nonteachers feel it too—there's never enough time.

I want to give the children time to think, time to make decisions; to give them the same luxury that I took for myself in setting up the room. Just as I want to give them the floor space to stretch out in front of the rabbit's cage, I want to give them time to develop an idea or project, time to develop friendships. I want time for myself to observe them, time to figure out what questions to ask.

The luxury of time is not, in fact, a luxury. It's not only a practical need but a necessity required by the ultimate purposes of education. The relationship between classroom time and educational values is described by the Italian educator Carlina Rinaldi, writing about the educational philosophy of the municipal preschools of Reggio Emilia. An innovative approach to learning and teaching has been developed in these schools, one that has become well known to educators around the world: children and teachers essentially collaborate on extended explorations of subjects being studied. Looking at the principles behind the approach, Rinaldi states that "for a school to be a place of life, then it needs the time of life, and that time of life is different, for example, to the time of production. . . . In a school what is important is the process, the path we develop. The educational relation needs to be able to make time. . . . It needs empty time. It is . . . about having the courage to rediscover the time of human beings. [It is] not only . . . a right, but . . . a social and cultural value." [3]

American educator Patricia Carini discusses time in a similar way, stressing the relationship between the time that teachers give children and the values that underlie education. She writes about the time for children's "telling and re-telling" [4]—time that allows children to develop ideas, and to see their connections: "To let meaning occur requires time and the possibility for the rich and varied relationships among things to become evident." [5] For Carini, time is also important because it allows children to develop intentions, to work with purpose, on their own and with others: "To let *choice* occur requires time and the possibility for discernment, taste, and perspective to develop; to sustain *purpose* and *commitment* requires time and the possibility for discipline to occur." [6]

For teachers to protect children's right to time—to *empty time*—requires courage, especially at this moment in history. Our lives, adults' as well as children's, are overprogrammed, without occasions for something unplanned. There's a benefit when teachers don't pack each moment. Time allows children to develop as people with broad interests and capacities; it allows them to gain a sense of conviction about their choices.

Walking into my classroom after two months away, I notice two things that I'd left tacked up on the corkboard of the teacher's coat closet when I'd packed things away the previous June. One is a print reproduction of a quilt, a bold, symmetrical red and black design; the other, a small red felt heart that a student made years ago. These two spots of color welcome me back; I'd forgotten about them. Who made the heart? I'm not certain—it's from over a decade ago.

They're stuck up casually, side by side, part of the environment. But like pieces of work in a museum's permanent exhibit, they also comment on the environment, telling a visitor something about this place and what goes on here. To me they say this is what school is about. They're samples of work, produced by individuals (one a real object, the other a reproduction). They make the point that children's efforts—their art, their thinking, their building and construction, their investigations—are *human* activities. They are versions of what adults do. Yet children's efforts are also—because, again, they are human efforts—valuable in themselves. The aesthetic pleasure I feel in looking at them is partially related to the circumstances of their production: both of these were made with concentration and industry. Whoever made them worked with *purpose*, made judgments. In what they are, they communicate something of the value they must have had for the people who made them. The purpose with which they were made is visible and adds to their value for me, and this says something to me about this classroom and my job as teacher.

I want children to take from this year an attitude of respect toward their own capacities: for *having* purposes, for making things, for thinking. I want children to take themselves seriously while having fun. Some children enter kindergarten with an extraordinary ability to concentrate, to work with commitment; others are distractible, and only by the end of the year do they become fully engaged. This is my goal, to whatever degree I can achieve it in this one year: to guide children in concrete, practical ways toward conviction, toward the knowledge that who they are and what they do *count*.

⤢

2

Routines and Rituals: Making the Room Theirs

The Need for Routines

What was the discussion today? The topic was some animal—and so many of them had something to say. The continual problem for me, for any teacher, is organization: how the mechanics of a classroom allow these discussions to occur.

The routines and rituals that are a part of classroom life echo the routines and rituals that we adults use to ease our way through our own daily tasks and responsibilities. We associate the word *routine* with dull repetition, yet without routines, we'd be in a bog of continual decision making. When educational purposes dictate classroom routines (not the other way around, as is sometimes the case), routines serve many functions. In addition, teachers can encourage the development of rituals that customize routines, that stamp routines with the personality and individuality of a particular group of children.

By and large, routines are imposed by the teacher and by the environment that the teacher creates; rituals are generated by children as they respond to this new physical and social environment. Through the introduction of routines and the generation of rituals, teachers ensure that these twenty-four or so new students become oriented as members of this unique group. Through routines, the environment shapes the children's behavior; through the rituals they in turn enact, children shape their environment.

The initial function of routines is to provide children with a sense of comfort and familiarity in a strange new place. In the first weeks of school, the predictability of class routines translates into a sense of safety. As children learn the routines, they come to know the room, and what will be expected of them. To the extent that the room becomes *theirs* and to the extent that events are predictable and familiar-seeming, children become more able to separate and are more at ease when parents or caregivers say good-bye.

During this transition period, which lasts about two months, the teacher must plan so that every activity incorporates a way of doing things. Ruth Charney, who taught for many years at the Greenfield Center School in Greenfield, Massachusetts, analyzes the role of routines in her thoughtful book *Teaching Children to Care.*[1] Charney argues that the first months of school are crucial in terms of the transmission of routines. The teacher's commitment to the *teaching* of routines is essential; this is not something that should be left to chance.

In this period, I ask myself numerous questions. Which materials will I set out in the first days and the first weeks? How will I introduce them? Are all materials ones that are relatively easy to put away (and to pick up, since containers will certainly be knocked over)? How clearly are expectations stated? New teachers, wanting to be creative, may have a hard time being slow and deliberate with the introduction of materials. But when details are left to chance in a classroom with young children, things slide quickly into chaos. If enterprising children spot sponges next to the sink, they may decide to clean the tables. Wetting the sponges, they happily squeeze water on the tables, and before the teacher notices, water is flowing over many surfaces, and children at the sink are fighting for sponges. The teacher's ability to teach and reinforce expectations—to "see everything," as Charney puts it—provides the basis for whatever fancy stuff happens later in the year. The simplicity and explicitness of expectations during this transitional period can affect children's functioning throughout the entire year. In well-organized rooms, routines may not be apparent to the casual observer. But although routines may be hidden, they exert a decisive influence on behavior, the sense that "this is how we do it."

The mechanics of a room and its educational content are joined; curriculum requires a smoothly running classroom. Discussions can't take place if no one's paying attention; children won't develop the ability to work in a consistent and committed way if their work is misplaced or damaged; and efforts to work on more complicated projects are problematic when class materials and tools are hard to find. The year I began teaching in the New York City public schools, I took over the classroom of a teacher who had retired. Clearing out the junk took months. I found math and construction materials mixed together—wooden pattern blocks and plastic Unifix cubes, Legos, pegs, odd puzzle pieces, broken objects—all jumbled together in miscellaneous bins. What do children make of this kind of disorganization? What do they learn in this kind of environment? They *don't* learn to put things away; they *don't* learn that things have places where they belong and can be found. Not only do they learn to treat tools and materials carelessly, but their desire to pursue specific objectives may be stymied. Those children who haven't yet developed focus and commitment are more likely to engage in repetitive play, e.g., crashing toy cars together. There is an additional benefit for teachers once routines are learned: the functioning of the room demands less attention, and teachers are freer to focus on students and the work they are doing. *Routines are the room's infrastructure, the railroad tracks—how we get from here to there.*

Signs and Labels

End of the first week, only three days, because the schools were closed for the Jewish holidays, but we got a huge amount done. Self-portraits for the door: Michael's stick figure person, only head and legs, one color; Lila's clouds and tree with branches; Denay's colorful mother and child.

When children are involved from the very beginning in *establishing* routines, they see for themselves how their intentions and purposes help form the environment; through routines, they claim the classroom for their own use. This process begins as soon as children walk into the room. The first day, I have an hour with half of the group and another hour with the other half. (Beginning the year with shortened days is extremely important in helping children start school; ideally, children would not have a full day of school until the second week.) When the children arrive, I give them time to walk around the room with their parents; some of them are tentative, sticking close to parents, others exploring more adventurously. I find a minute for each child: we go together to the coat closet and I show them where coats will go later in the year; we peel off a label with the child's name and the child sticks it on a piece of colored construction paper next to one of the hooks. They try the puzzles, use play dough, or draw; after a while, I warn them and their parents that in a few minutes I'll be asking parents to go. The advance notice and the chance to play a little longer are usually enough for the children to say good-bye without strong protests. Some children like extra assurances that the parents will return soon and are not far away. Occasionally, if a child seems deeply upset, a parent may stay, but for the most part, the children are interested in seeing what comes next.

A few minutes after the parents have left, we put things away and have a short meeting—singing a song, hearing each other's names for the first time, learning the name of the classroom and the names of the adults. I give them squares of paper and ask them to draw whatever they want, and (if they can) to write their names. As they finish, they choose cubbies, and I use a bit of tape to stick the squares down in individual cubbies; later, I'll cover the squares with clear contact paper. Before children go home that day, two places in the room—coat hooks and cubbies—have been marked with their names. My big goal that first day: to make sure they want to come back.

In the next few weeks of school, we set up the room together.

The children make signs, set up the class library, make a wall alphabet. As they do this, they help put in place routines that will be part of classroom life, while at the same time beginning to see that responsibility for the room is theirs. This process not only assumes their competence, but also places children's ability to represent and write at the service of a group goal. Through this process, they make the room *theirs*.

One of the most important projects at the start of the year is making signs. We need schedule signs, door signs (to indicate the whereabouts of the class), and signs for areas of the room. The schedule signs are used immediately; the schedule is posted every day, and the class reads the signs aloud at our morning meeting. (Toward the end of the year, the children change the signs themselves if I've neglected to.) I start with signs for meeting, work time, story, snack, and home, making more signs as we need them. To make signs, a small group works at a table with the student teacher or assistant teacher; the *children* decide how to illustrate each schedule card. For meeting, a child draws a blue square to represent the blue rug, and then adds a single figure; for work time, a child draws blocks. What will illustrate snack time? A child draws a circle and a square: a juice cup seen from the top, and a cracker. To make the door signs, the children draw the pictures *and* write the words: WE ARE AT LUNCH. They copy one word at a time, cut each word out, and glue the words in a row, a table of sign makers copying words and cutting them out. All of this takes more time than if I used computer-generated pictures or drew the pictures myself. Yet the effort is worth it, because when children make signs, their work has practical meaning. When the signs are finished, I mount and laminate them and add Velcro to the backs. One sign goes outside the classroom, the rest go on the back of the door; two children change the door signs whenever the class leaves the room or returns.

To organize the library, I sit on the rug with a small group of children and a large pile of books. We sort the books, figuring out what categories make sense: animal books, books about children,

ABC books. We make labels; the children draw the pictures and I write the words. The books go in the baskets, and the baskets go on the shelves. At the next meeting, the children who made labels show them to the class. I add more books as the weeks go by, and the children and I decide, Do these books belong in existing baskets or do we need a new basket? This continues all year as the library grows. Sometimes a child insists we need a new basket: Lila asks for a basket for Dr. Seuss books. Problems arise as children see that a book could belong in two (or more) baskets; the discussion is more interesting than the outcome. I create some of the categories through my choice of books—like Folk and Fairy Tales, one of my favorite categories.

During these first weeks, children also make a wall alphabet. I draw the outlines of upper- and lower-case letters on shiny finger-paint paper, and the children color the letters with markers: some children make neat patterns of dots or flowers or hearts; many draw stripes; some make monochromatic scribbles and say, "I'm done." Letter by letter, the alphabet goes up. Later in the year, the children will make pictures to go with each letter.

Children's participation in the process of establishing routines allows them to imbue routines with personal meaning. Nowhere can this be seen more clearly than in their use of the class calendar. To make the calendar, I buy a large heavy-duty plastic board, on which I rule a calendar grid in permanent marker. The calendar is introduced in October, around three weeks into the school year. Using a sponge-off pen, I write in the days of the week and the dates. At the end of the month, the calendar is sponged off, and dates for the next month are filled in. By December, children take over the job of writing the days and numerals.

The calendar quickly becomes a central source of information. Children write "no school" on weekend days and holidays. They draw cupcakes on their own birthdays and mark the birthdays of parents and siblings. They may mark parents' out-of-town trips by drawing planes, trains, or cars on the dates; when their parents travel frequently, marking departures and returns gives children

Writing on the calendar
Photo by Julie Diamond

a feeling of control in relation to circumstances they don't actually control. As a group, we use the calendar to count the days until a coming event, Halloween or Christmas or a class trip, counting backward and recording the numbers with increasing excitement as the event gets closer. In a sense, the calendar is a book: it is "read" and conveys information that matters. As children refer to it—which happens constantly—they develop common understandings and associations. Thus, an ordinary class routine of keeping track of dates on a calendar is opened up by children's participation; and as they make it *their* calendar, they also integrate a symbol system into their own world.

There are numerous educational implications when routines are opened up in this way. For example, as five-year-old children make signs, copying and cutting words, they see concretely how each written word equals one spoken word. Children may also

begin to draw conclusions about the correspondences between letters and letter sounds. In upper grades, sign making allows older
children to impose their own notions of useful classroom organization. For both younger and older students, the process of making signs incorporates skills of reading, writing, and math as tools
for the children's own purposes. Most significantly, in making
signs and in producing other classroom materials, children see
that meanings are not arbitrary, imposed by an unknown higher
authority: meanings are created through people's actions. The
reasons for routines, the ways in which they function, become accessible to children and connected to their intentions.

Where Does This Go?

*Cleanup, that most mundane of tasks. I move around the room, I
badger and harass, calling them back, reminding them: throw your
scraps of paper away! We learn these things through action. Responsibility, accountability—these are demanded by group life.*

Routines make active learning possible. Organization and structure are especially necessary in classrooms where teachers value
student-initiated activities. By communicating an expectation that
the care of room and materials is children's responsibility—to
whatever extent is realistic given the age of a specific group—
adults convey a message about their belief in children's capacity
for responsibility, their vision of children as capable, and their
understanding of education as a social process.

From the first day, my plans include teaching children to *know*
this new room, to know where to find things and where to put
them away. We play treasure-hunt games: I give out objects, and
children work in teams to find one of the same things, or to find
where the objects are put away. As children learn where things
belong, they are also being introduced to the division of space into
areas that have distinct functions. The rug is the social (though
not the physical) center of the room, the place the class returns to
at intervals throughout the day, the place where the class gathers

for any important discussion. As the year progresses, the rug becomes the area where certain kinds of group construction projects arise, projects that mix materials and allow for participation by a diverse group of children.

When the teacher asks children to clean up, everything that the children know about the room and materials comes into play; and everything the children do, as they clean up, tells the teacher who they are, how they function, and how they see themselves as part of a group. Despite the seeming confusion, the cacophony of voices, the hectic swirl of movement, much of importance goes on that teachers can constantly observe and assess. Which children get into the swing of things and move with focus and efficiency? Which children jump in but become distracted? Which children are unable to function in the openness and relative freedom of a cleanup period? Which children consistently ignore requests to stop working?

At the beginning of the year and periodically throughout the year, I demonstrate the "how" of cleanup: constructions are to be taken apart, not knocked down; materials are *put* in bins, not tossed. The arrangement of the room and the organization of supplies can facilitate cleanup. When a problem occurs repeatedly, I look for routines to deal with that problem: because the children frequently have to hunt for missing marker tops, I keep a basket just for "extra pen tops."

The adult's expectation is crucial: children who work in an area are responsible for that area and for the materials used; no one walks away. A child who complains, "I'm the only one cleaning," is asked to round up the others who were in that area. Jobs are *distributed*: "Who's putting the scissors away?" Everyone helps: the statement "It isn't my mess" is not given a hearing; it's everyone's room. When a child asks, "Where does this go?" I turn to other children, "Who knows where this goes?" Teachers pitch in, too. When some children continue working, reluctant to end their drawing or block building despite repeated requests, the adult's physical involvement and statement—"Look, *I'm* helping!"—contribute to an atmosphere of participation. As children work together, getting the room ready for the next activity, they gain the experience of organizing tasks: sorting objects, putting away objects that go on the same shelf, throwing away scraps. They work with a sense of purpose and accomplishment—a sense of what they can accomplish as a group. Yes, "routine" implies the dull and dreary, the opposite of the unexpected, the impromptu, the conscious, the expressive. But when children fully engage in routine tasks like cleanup, these activities can have their own expressive quality, their own energy: they mobilize the group, pulling everyone together to create order.

Organizing the Day

Amina has just said good-bye to her mother. Amina still doesn't talk to me, but we sit together on the rug and look at Alphabatics, *that great alphabet book where the letters turn into things—the H becomes, in three pictures, a house with a chimney. Adam joins us. After a while, I reluctantly tell them to put stuff away. The beginning of the day is often so lovely, I hate to end it.*

The organization of the day is another way that routines make children's experiences manageable. On the first day, the children are introduced to time divisions that continue throughout the year. Each of these times has its own character, and it is through manipulating the differences that a day can have wholeness, balance. By this I mean that the divisions of the day reflect the distinct ups and downs of children's energy and focus.

Every morning, when children come in, there is a time to put their things away, look around, catch up with friends. After several weeks, perhaps by late October, I introduce "assignments," tasks that require attention but also allow for a certain flow. When children finish assignments, they can draw, do a puzzle, sit with a book. These assignments differ from day to day: Monday, guessing the number of objects in a jar; Tuesday, writing numerals; Wednesday, decoding a "secret code" word, and later in the year, signing out class library books; Thursday, doing a journal entry; Friday, finishing work that's piled up in the work basket. By late fall, these first ten to fifteen minutes can have the appearance of controlled chaos, as children eagerly rush in to greet friends, to see what the assignment is, to check out something from the day before. In the first half of the year, the parents bring children to the room. This time helps me catch up with them and gives them a chance to tell me something. The looseness of the period allows me to observe the children, or to sit with someone I might not find the time for later in the day.

Morning meeting is the day's official start. Meeting is an anchor in the day: the children begin together. Meeting alerts children to the day's events, and allows for the introduction of topics by teacher or students. Much of the *business* of meeting has to do with divisions of time: looking at the schedule, at the calendar and events to come, keeping track of the number of days of school. It's also the time of day when children air individual concerns or topics: a child exhibits a loose tooth, tells the others about an ill grandparent, shows a beehive found over the weekend.

Meeting talk can range widely: *We have a discussion of ice/ snow/water—because they have seen ice outside—it is the first day of temperature in the twenties, and streets have frozen puddles. A few say, the ice melts, and that makes snow. I write down their comments and also suggest that we can bring in some ice and watch it melt.*

The day proceeds, alternating periods in which children's choices are fewer, when they must accept limits and directions or listen to others, and periods in which they expend energies outward, imposing their will on materials by building, coloring, or gluing, periods in which they can collaborate, disagree, argue, start something new. Big muscles, small muscles; action, containment. This rhythm was described by Sylvia Ashton-Warner, who taught young children in New Zealand schools for decades. In her book *Teacher*, first published in 1963, she writes of time for children to "breathe out" ("conversation, painting, crying, quarrelling, creative writing, blocks, clay, sand, water") and time for them to "breathe in" ("key vocabulary . . . standard reading").[2] The patterns that teachers impose can complement the rhythms of children's engagement. However, teachers will do well to remember that any schedule imposes hardships: children normally prefer to continue a given activity until they deem it completed; they prefer not to be interrupted; and they don't like having to sit still and listen to others for any length of time.

The making of time-space distinctions points toward a further educational function of routines. In carrying out routines, children continually search for and find pattern and order; they discern similarities and differences. Routine classroom actions— lining up, finding materials and putting them away, changing a door sign—all necessitate the making of categories. When, for example, children hang their jackets in the closet, they are utilizing such categories as right, left, top, bottom, small, large. Categorizing is a primary intellectual function, a base of cognition in all fields, according to Hubert Dyasi, who for many years directed the Workshop Center at City College of New York, which focused on science education. Dyasi defines science, in part, as "a continuing search for underlying commonalities in apparently disparate phenomena."[3] Thus, through their physical actions as they carry out routines, use things in the room, and move through their day, they think and make decisions, sort and create categories. These experiences aid them throughout their school lives when they confront more strictly intellectual tasks, when they write up science experiments, learn rules of punctuation and grammar, or grasp mathematical patterns.

Protecting Group Life

Much of what I plan is intended to help children make sense of their world. I assume the world is knowable, at least enough of it; I assume agency—that individuals can be active, can think, conclude. I as-

*sume that the world is ultimately social. My planning has as its goal
children's development of the ability to govern themselves.*

In thinking about routines, teachers should be concerned not
with maintaining classroom order per se, but with engineering a
social space in which certain activities can be pursued. This formulation of the teacher's role has a theoretical basis in the ideas
of the American philosopher John Dewey, particularly as laid out
in *Experience and Education.*[4] Dewey wrote extensively about education and was associated in the early part of the twentieth cen-
tury with the Laboratory School of the University of Chicago. He
describes education as "essentially a social process"[5] and goes on
to define *social control* as the many ways in which a group regu-
lates the behavior of the individuals who are part of it. The
group, Dewey asserts, has "common purposes" that lend it power
to regulate social behavior and enforce norms: "It is not the will
or desire of any one person which establishes order but the moving spirit of the whole group."[6]

Illustrations of this process are found in the work of Vivian
Paley. Paley, who taught kindergarten for many years at the University of Chicago Laboratory School, produced vivid narratives
of classroom life in books including *White Teacher,*[7] *Wally's
Stories,*[8] and *The Boy Who Would Be a Helicopter.*[9] Paley writes of
Tanya, a child who could be "tyrannical." When Tanya disrupts
the playing of a recording, Paley asks the other children for solutions. One child suggests, "Keep changing the record until you
find one Tanya likes." Paley comments, "In the record corner the
children said: we like you, Tanya, and you can stay. They did not
withhold friendship or impose hardships, and Tanya stopped
teasing."[10] It is worth pointing out that Paley steps in here to discuss the matter with the children. On another occasion, Paley in-
tervenes more directly. Tanya has splattered paint on another
child's picture, and Paley sends Tanya out of the area. Reflecting
on the incident, Paley sees no useful result of her involvement:
"I . . . made her leave the art table. . . . [Tanya] shouted, 'I'm
never going to paint again!' . . . After lunch she returned to the

painting table and repeated her mischief. . . . I had excluded
Tanya from the art table and achieved little besides temporary
peace and quiet." Yet Dewey argues that intervention *is* justified
when "it is done in behalf of the interest of the group." [11] Dewey's
only proviso is that teachers limit their interventions: "The
teacher reduces to a minimum the occasions in which he or she
has to exercise authority in a personal way." [12]

As is true for social control, teachers' enforcement of routines
protects group life at the same time that it protects the individual.
To put it concretely, routines make it possible for these twenty-
odd children to achieve their goals. While Paley didn't succeed in
making Tanya care more about others' feelings, she took a stand
on the side of respect for others' work, protecting Tanya as well as
her victim.

The teacher's responsibility for safety, for putting in place and
monitoring routines that protect the group's interests, is, in fact,
as necessary for the more impulsive children as for the child who
might be the object of willful aggressive behavior. These individuals, the children whose internal controls are less well developed
(children who may be labeled "mean," "bad," "sneaky"), need
the teacher's protection from their own impulses.

This more psychologically complex description of the teacher's role is found in Susan Isaacs's outline of the educational
principles that governed her school. What's relevant here is her
formulation of the adult's responsibility in relation to children's
behavior: "One general maxim with regard to the social education of young children is that the educator should act for the
child, where the child cannot act for himself." [13] By accepting responsibility for children's safe and purposeful functioning, Isaacs
concluded, the teacher enlarges rather than diminishes children's
responsibility for what *is* within their control: "In general, we
tried to use our parental powers in such a way as to reduce the
children's need for them." [14] In other words, adult support of children's exercise of their powers must not come at the expense of

adult monitoring of behavior, which is a necessary function we serve *as adults* in relation to children.

By setting out the environment's expectations of behavior, routines function as a bridge to children's development of internal controls. When adults create routines that support children's activity, social expectations are tied to practical concerns. The general functioning of the room and the teacher's enforcement of routines is not a matter of the teacher's personal preferences but of practical considerations, which adults can point to when they regulate behavior. Isaacs gives numerous examples of the ways that adults in her school aimed at helping children govern their own behavior: "we made even the necessary social sanctions always quite specific. 'If you hit John with the spade, I shall take it away.' "[15] By and large, Isaacs predicated the framework of routines and adult interventions on "concrete grounds, either of a practical or educational nature."[16] For example, she avoided using language that would be confusing to children, not telling them they "must" do something when she in fact meant that it was something she was requesting that they do, with certain consequences if they failed to do it. In addition, she avoided morally loaded terms: "We never used general categories such as 'naughty,' 'good' or 'horrid.' In other words, we wanted to help the children to realize and adjust to other people's wishes as everyday facts rather than as mysterious absolutes."[17]

While Isaacs justifies her admonitions on practical rather than moral grounds, moral matters are implicitly at stake. The records of conversations in Isaacs's school make clear that the adults valued children as individuals; and adults were truthful and trustworthy in their dealings with children. Ruth Charney is more explicit in seeing, in the details of classroom organization and management, a way of giving real and practical form to her ideals and principles. The title of her book, *Teaching Children to Care*, lays out the ultimate issues here: the teacher has the opportunity and responsibility to teach children concern for others. In general, routines have an impact on children not only because they provide structure and safety, but because, more deeply, they embody social and moral values.

Charney gives an example of the relationship between a teacher's values and her way of communicating expectations. What's at stake is the value of trust—her trust in the children, and the children's trust in her: "Ms. Thompson had just handed out sharp scissors for the groups to share. She carefully demonstrated how she wished to see them held: point down." Charney describes the teacher going over her instructions, reminding the children of other things they needed to know before letting them begin. Observing the class, Ms. Thompson saw one child walking with scissors held carelessly. "Ms. Thompson beckoned to Michael. She quietly reached out her hand. Without a word, Michael placed the scissors in her outstretched palm. He had lost the right to use the scissors for the rest of the period. . . . It was not only the safe handling of the tools that was at stake, it was the true handling of her words. Her class believed her. The students . . . learned something about the value of words when they're used to say important things." [18]

This is the ultimate rationale for the teacher's active role, an activism that may also take the form of listening intently to children as they attempt to justify behavior, of sympathizing with a child who's been "tyrannical," and of creating the structures that allow for children's mistakes as well as their productive and cooperative activity. Young children naturally identify with others and are capable of sympathy and kindness, even if only intermittently, even if their ability to work and play with others is, at times, limited by less social impulses. By identifying with children's learning, and by placing learning in a social setting (for example, by making groups), teachers help children develop a more consistently social outlook, one that can stand up to more purely selfish desires. This role has a moral dimension: we hope that through our attention to individual children and the social environment, and through their identification with us, children will develop values of concern and attentiveness, toward themselves and others.

Dilemmas

A great discussion yesterday as we read a John Burningham book, Hey, Get Off Our Train. *It all started with this digression, on what animals/things you take to bed to help you sleep.*

Ideally, routines should exist to protect children's learning and activity rather than to make life easier for teachers. In practice, this isn't always the case. Teachers base decisions about routines and acceptable behavior on numerous considerations, not least their own comfort and their wish to feel in control. Who decides what level of noise is acceptable? What message do teachers send every time they ask for the class's attention, flicking the lights or ringing a bell? Which routines are connected to safety concerns, and which are a function of the teacher's desire to keep a group in line, to *manage* a group? Seating twenty-four children in a small space means that forty-eight elbows and knees are pressed closely together, an invitation to squabbles; hence my insistence that hands and feet be "parked," so that fingers can't get stepped on and feet can't trip up children walking past. Still, I wonder at times if I'm insisting on these seating requirements partly as a matter of form, a way of policing children's physical selves.

What's the teacher's role, for example, if we want to encourage truly open discussions? If teachers don't moderate discussions, how do we prevent the more aggressive and confident children from drowning out the slower and quieter ones? If we want to avoid intervening, what do we do about the voices that seem never to be heard in public? Yet in stepping in to moderate discussions, teachers may be motivated more by the wish to protect *themselves*, fearing that things will spin out of control. Teachers may wish to maintain control of the traffic of ideas and knowledge to protect themselves against the unsettling sense that they're in the backseat. They may worry about the result of too much

spontaneity—children's straying off topic, their side comments
to each other, their possibly anarchic hilarity. When do teacher
interventions protect the group against monopolizing or boring
speakers, and when do they rob the group of the opportunity to
develop social norms?

In general and on a daily basis, teachers have a dilemma in
terms of routines and behavior. Principles govern decisions about
when to intervene, but no rules cover all cases; decision making
is difficult because each situation is unique. As Charney notes,
"There are no perfect arrangements."[19] Perhaps teachers' conflicts about when and how to intervene reflect the necessary and
inevitable conflict between group needs and individual needs.

I want to conclude a consideration of routines with a plea for
occasional inconsistency. Consistency is generally a good thing:
children feel comfortable when they know what to expect, and
they are disturbed by unexpected changes in routine. When a
teacher is forced to switch things around after routines have been
established, there is a price to pay in children's unsettledness, and
certain children may become distressed. Children are also likely
to protest if adults seem to apply shifting standards of behavior:
"You said . . ." But changes in plans can't always be helped, either
for reasons outside a teacher's control or because for some reason a
teacher decides to do things differently on a particular day. A
teacher may also make an exception for one child (e.g., by adjusting an assignment that would present an overwhelming challenge for the child, or adjusting behavioral expectations). The
yardstick here is whether inconsistency in standards has a basis in
competing educational goals rather than favoritism. Children
allow exceptions when they see the reasons for them, when it
doesn't seem that one child is getting away with something generally not allowed.

Inconsistencies are inevitable: *I'm inconsistent at the end of the
day: I'm running late, my energy is low, all the frayed bits seem to
catch up with me, and I let routines slide.* There are also the in-

evitable differences between the expectations established at school and those at home. Children admonish their parents, "That's not how we do it at school!" and may also complain to their teachers, "But my mother lets me!" As long as the differences are not too great—e.g., when parents' code of behavior calls for children's physical defense of themselves and teachers require children to "use words" or get adult help—children learn to live with different standards.

Overall, negotiating differences is helpful to children. When teachers are *rigidly* consistent, children don't gain the experience of confronting conflicting goals. They don't develop tolerance for inconsistencies; they don't gain flexibility; they don't learn to make well-reasoned judgments. Human experience is fluid. We want children to be able to tolerate ambivalence and doubt when the situation calls for it. Teachers, too, must be prepared to do things differently on occasion, and to reflect on whether inconsistencies are justified.

The Click Club: Sharing Power

The children use markers on the very first day. I show the class where the markers go, and demonstrate how to close the marker: listen for the click! The word click *is an aid to memory. In the first weeks, as the class is drawing pictures and designs, I say again and again, "You remembered to click!" When I find a marker with the top off, I sometimes stop the class: "Look up! What do you see here?" Denay loves these demonstrations, and comes up to me frequently to show me a marker with its top off. I let Denay make the announcement: "Look up! Denay has something to show everyone!" and she holds up the marker. Soon others are bringing me markers they found left open. One day I say, "Denay, you always remember; you are in the Click Club!" Soon others tell me, "I'm in the Click Club." This is around the same time that the children are making name lists, copying names from the name cards. Denay takes a clipboard and writes CKCB (Click Club), and she goes around to everyone asking, "Are you in the Click Club?" They sign their names on her list.*

Routines help us remember what to do and how to do it. Rituals, on the other hand, have elements that are not purely practical. The example above has layers of meaning: shy Denay finds a way to make a place for herself in this new classroom. There is a bit of showing off for the teacher, and attention from the teacher for model behavior. Eager to please, Denay makes her mark (so to speak) by taking on the teacher's role as she goes around the room with her clipboard, writing down names. There's drama too, and words that are alliterative and onomatopoeic, which cement the whole thing.

Rituals have complex meanings and are often connected with power and participation. By giving Denay room to take this role, I share power over the enforcement of standards of behavior; I diffuse power *through a ritual* that Denay helped invent. If routines reflect the teacher's wish for a classroom environment in which productive learning can take place, children's rituals can be seen as responses to the teacher's hegemony over the environment. Rituals often have a moral core: they communicate information about values, about what's right and wrong.

I am looking here at rituals that children initiate; I am not interested in rituals that are imposed solely by teachers. Classroom rituals can include the distinctive use of a particular material—children's use of clipboards to make lists or do surveys; songs or chants that children associate with a particular time of the day; their idiosyncratic phrases or ways of writing or drawing: *Adam is writing in "fat letters"—block letters—Philip is doing it too; who else? A kind of contagion, everyone is trying it.* These classroom rituals take two forms: a ritualized form of a routine or activity, in which children *interpret* the activity in a repetitive and personalized way (and by doing so, also see themselves as initiators); and a ritual that is, in effect, an antiroutine, in which children's version of the routine is slightly skewed or even outrightly defiant. Rituals answer back adult authority, with its multiplicity of demands and limitations on children's activity. Rituals are a way that children reconcile themselves to the very real limitations on their power. When children invent a way of interpreting the teacher's expectations, they save face, complying without being *merely* compliant. They submit without being submissive.

By sharing power, the teacher strengthens the commitment of the group as a whole to a system of classroom governance that has legitimacy. When teachers endorse rituals that arise spontaneously, a class culture is formed that accommodates adult goals and children's inventiveness. There may be holdouts—children whose involvement with other children is tenuous, children who act surreptitiously rather than publicly (e.g., scribbling on tables)—but the group appears to act in concert. This can be true even when rituals are energetically transgressive:

One year, in the fall, I accidentally held the name cards upside down as I took attendance. The children were gleeful, and the next day, asked me to do it that way again. They were, perhaps, seeing what they could get away with—what they could control in this new classroom. This became a frequent request. One day, some children wanted the cards held upside down, and other children objected. We had a vote. The results struck me: with the exception of one girl, all the girls voted for right side up; with the exception of one boy, all the boys voted for upside down.

The incident is fascinating and certainly encourages speculation: did the split along gender lines represent the girls' preference for tradition and continuity? Were the boys favoring adventure and challenge? Whatever lay behind the vote, the outcome satisfied both sides: after some discussion, we decided I would hold the name cards upside down on some days, and right side up on other days, a routine that continued throughout that fall and that the children accepted with the occasional protest. They learned they could make an innovation, a spin on routine, and the teacher accepted their power to do this. In addition, they had seen how, through discussion and voting, a plan of action could become institutionalized within the semidemocratic world of this classroom. They learned that they themselves could play a role in shaping class routines, and they'd also learned a process of decision making. These were valuable lessons, although I hadn't planned them.

When children's natural playfulness takes the form of innovation, and teachers allow this innovation to become institutionalized, children develop a stronger sense of belonging, of commitment to their place in this classroom. The social role of rituals in general is to aid in the development of a group's identity, whether the group is religious or secular. Rituals mediate the relationship between the individual and the group, between personal preferences and group demands for adherence to recognized behavioral norms. (Perhaps for this reason, rituals are often concerned with transitional periods in human lives and in the cycles of time; many classroom rituals arise during times of transition from one activity to the next.)

Classroom rituals create group feeling as children gain power and a sense of identity and solidarity through the enactment of common actions and meanings. Dewey's concept of social control is relevant in explaining the contagiousness of children's rituals. He describes children as "cooperative or interacting parts" of a "whole situation."[20] Thus, the classroom itself changes as children introduce rituals.

What Rituals Tell Us

Brooke said to me, You have to remember, kids read to the class on Wednesday. I've been forgetting—weeks ago, I began a routine of letting a child read the story to the class every Wednesday. They would either really read some simple book or hold the book and pretend to read, mimicking me, retelling the story, often hilariously. But I keep forgetting. I said, Brooke, write a note so I'll remember. She wrote it on a Post-it, KID REDS, and I put it up at the top of the wipe-off board, where the days of the week are written. Brooke's particular qualities—her steadfast determination to be master of details, of classroom rights and wrongs—are given an outlet, and at the same time, they influence and help form class culture. Not only better adherence to our Wednesday kid-reading routine, but a new idea: you can write notes to Julie.

Ritual making is a creative act—that is, children *invent* rituals. For this reason, the forms that rituals take reflect children's individual motivations, involvements, and characteristics.

The rituals that catch on, that give the class a discernible group identity, give the teacher material worth thinking about. When teachers look closely at the rituals their students suggest and implement, they learn who their children really are. Is humor the dominant note? Defiance? Playfulness? Rituals can be negative as well as positive: a class can develop a rash of writing on tables, or children can take to disrupting the teacher or other children by yelling out certain mocking phrases. Tattling can become a ritualized response to any perceived injury or infraction: "I'm telling!" one student barks at another, a threat put immediately into effect. The tattling child struts toward the teacher, and the offending child chases after, tearfully shouting, "I said I'm sorry! *I said I'm sorry!*" The ritualized nature of this interaction makes it harder to stop, irritating as it may be to the teacher. Nevertheless, it makes clear to the teacher what's at stake for these individual children. No matter how many times the teacher says to the tattling child, "Talk to the other child first, before you come to me," for this child, something else matters more, perhaps the immediate gratification of getting the teacher on her side when she feels injured, indignant, and righteous. The teacher's job is to look for some other means by which a child can gain a sense of being in the right, one that doesn't come at another child's expense.

When negative rituals gain ascendancy in a classroom, teachers must examine various aspects of classroom life. It may be that children's energies have been pent up and that more time is needed for exploration, project making, music, and movement. It may be that individual children are seeking more power, a way to be leaders. To the extent that a negative ritual interferes with classroom functioning, the teacher can make it the subject of discussion with the class as a whole. Yet it is wise to remember that rituals may die out, especially if a teacher can gain some understanding of their genesis.

Which actions or bits of behavior are likely to be turned into rituals? What catches on? Because their function is not primarily *practical*, rituals matter in a way that is not rational or obvious. Rituals have a *magical* utility, a meaning that's not always apparent but that is accessible to children, which they pass on to each other without explanations. Ritual elements may exist as part of various ordinary classroom activities. Why do children write in block letters? There is a ritualized quality in many of the activities that children repeat in classrooms. It's as if children must take up some everyday classroom routine or material or activity and imbue it with a meaning that they themselves intuit.

Rituals transform an act that might otherwise be ordinary. Children often master the printing of letters by the spring of their kindergarten year. They begin to write in some fancy way, making fat block letters, or writing their letters in alternating colors, or pretending to write script. Confident in their printing ability, they must wring some change in the skill, must transform the act of writing. In some cases, rituals are more obviously concerned with power relationships: *Linda tells me what's been happening in her second-grade class. She's been reading chapter books aloud to the class, and she always sits on a table on the opposite side of the room from the blue chair that is her usual seat. Whenever she is about to read, she moves a chair around for her feet. Now, the children check out the schedule, and at the end of the period before she's going to read, someone shifts the chair around for her, and someone else gets the book the class is currently reading and places it on the table. This, of course, was never discussed, never planned by anyone.* The children in Linda's class, by turning the chair and getting the book for her, were, in a small way, making a power grab: *we'll* do it, we'll take over this job.

Children like repeating certain words or phrases. "Questions or comments?" they ask after sharing their journal pages, and the ritual question turns them into the leaders of the discussion. Other ritual phrases arise as children play with words and sounds. Shouted out and repeated, these phrases transform classroom social relationships, as children's chanting in unison draws them together, or makes outsiders of other children or adults. Susan Isaacs describes the children in her school initiating a ritual around the towels used to dry lunch dishes. The children were responsible for their own washing and drying, and the towels hung on towel rails. "Every day before lunch, they rush to the towel rail and take one of the towels up, touch it, and hold on to it for a few minutes. Today, about the middle of the morning, they rushed to do this, and each hung on to his towel, saying, 'Save, save, save!' Mrs. [Isaacs] asked them, 'Please don't hang on to the towel rail— you may break it.' 'All right, we won't, but we want to *save* it for a bit longer,' repeating the gesture and the word, as if these made the towels belong inherently to them thereafter." [21] The children here seem to be reveling in their recognition of a shared possessiveness, but their repetition of action and words points to the powerful function of ritual in cementing group feeling.

Perhaps some children are especially adept at apprehending which actions or communications have potential as rituals. These children develop a way of doing things—they move a chair or shout out a word ("Save!"), which is repeated by child after child until it has become an authentic element of the environment. Rituals spread mysteriously, gathering significance as they are shared and even altered by different children. Which rituals will take hold in a classroom depends on the group itself: the more widely a ritual can be shared and the deeper its common meaning, the greater its power and appeal. Although the values these rituals impart may come to define the classroom community, the exact meaning of the values may be obscure, even impossible to pin down. This is certainly true in the case of the nonsense words that somehow catch on. Yet rituals, whether their meaning is transparent or opaque, perform a powerful function, communicating to each child a sense of solidarity with the others in the class, the specialness of belonging to this classroom, this group. Out of their shared ways of doing things, the children produce a distinctive culture to which each child feels loyalty.

Rituals have rhythm, a capacity for expressiveness. They are like catchy tunes. For this reason, if a teacher notices children's uses of rituals and allows them space, rituals can immeasurably enrich and energize classroom culture. Watchfulness and an ability to accept the openings offered by children give a teacher access to this layer of meaning. Rituals cannot be planned for, except in one important sense: a teacher's experience brings knowledge of what to look for, the ability to recognize a good thing. As discussed earlier, teachers share power when they accept rituals, and that in turn enhances their own authority. We are ultimately the people responsible for our classrooms, for planning routines, and for judging the contribution of rituals to classroom life, but the children can participate. When they do, they are more likely to see us as allies and to move into a life as students with a feeling of being at home in the classroom.

3

⚭

Collages: Making Art

Painting, and Painting Over

The children take something, absorb it, find variations. They've come up with the idea of cutting out diamond shapes and adding yarn or ribbon for "kites." Lizzie uses short lengths of yarn, all different colors, threading the pieces through holes she's punched all around the diamond. Caroline makes a happy-face kite and a sad-face kite and a plaid kite. Graham sees Alyssa's paper with pop-up shapes, and he makes one, too. A few children still seem peripheral—Sam, Henry—but I'm beginning to see, in all this action at the long table, a sense of the group.

Art: eight children are squashed around the table near the sink, leaning over each other to sort through piles of colored construction paper, reaching for a hole puncher or a marker. Art—collage and construction in particular—has become a focal activity for this class. If a class is to come together, it must come together around something that students genuinely care about.

Art resists adult judgments based on right and wrong; an infinite number of possibilities exist in every medium. One child may be "talented," may display precocity—an intuitive feel for decoration and design, a strong sense of color, an uncanny ability to observe and draw. Yet *all* children are capable of producing work that is *felt*, work that displays their individual strengths. Art *is* work, a process that engages children's capacity for understanding, one that culminates in a product that can be shared, and that communicates that new understanding. A study undertaken by the Guggenheim Museum found, in fact, measurable improvement in the critical-thinking skills of children who participated in an art program sponsored by the museum, compared with skills of children who did not participate.[1] Children can come to see themselves as insiders in the world of art, rather than mystified outsiders. This happens when schools encourage children to produce work that is truly theirs, alongside others who are similarly engaged, and when schools provide children with opportunities to look at and talk about the work of exhibited artists (whether through museum trips or use of reproductions). When children participate in these sorts of experiences, they not only gain a vocabulary, but they learn to take for granted their ability to understand the meanings and values inherent in art. They see art as work, produced *by people*, and *for people*.

Art is one of the first activities I plan every fall. I put out fat markers and crayons, and large heavy-duty plastic shape templates—squares, triangles, diamonds, circles, and rectangles. The first few days, children trace and color; one of them will discover you can use the templates numerous times on the same paper, superimposing shapes and creating new forms. As children continue to explore and gain control, I add, over several days, scissors, tape, hole punchers, ribbon, yarn, and eventually glue sticks. The slow introduction of these tools and materials gives me a chance to demonstrate their use. The first lesson, every year, is a demonstration of how to put the marker tops back and—as described in chapter 2—listen for the click. I make sure children hold scissors the right way, show them how to tear tape and screw a glue stick up and down, and watch to make sure they put materials back when they're finished with them. So while art is arty—expressive, free—it has another side; teaching it carries a load of skill and routine and necessitates a focus on learning good habits of care and use of materials. It includes reality-based conventions and techniques (remember to wipe your brush) at the same time

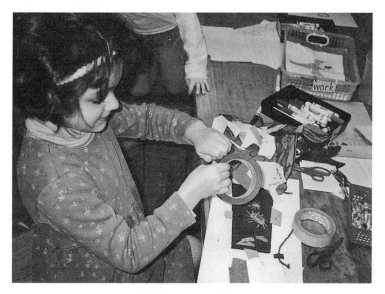

Working on a collage
Photo by Julie Diamond

that the central focus remains, the requirement that children put
their seeing on paper.

Art, by its nature, suits young children's expressive needs.
Young children, like babies, find pleasure in movement for its
own sake and produce art through physical motion. Their art is
often full of circular shapes—swirls, spirals, arcs—created as
they swing their arms back and forth and around. They love in-
venting and repeating forms. They love the sensuous pleasure of
mixing colors. Children often apply colors with great concentration and care, only to paint over the entire surface, creating
a monotone and murky surface. While adults find this incom-
prehensible, the process of adding layers of paint gives children
immense satisfaction and a sense of power, as they make colors
and forms appear *and* disappear. (It is the same pleasure and
power young children feel when they "crash" a block building

that they have worked on with energy and commitment.) For the most part, children who have had plenty of painting experience as three- and four-year-olds are less likely to paint over; they are more interested in producing bold and deliberate explorations of line and form. Using paint (or crayons or other media), they organize their visual world. Children have, I believe, an innate sense of design, and without any instruction will spontaneously make use of pattern and symmetry.

As children move toward representation, they begin to give concrete form to themes that are highly personal, e.g., by drawing themselves and family members. They articulate particular motifs—child, house, flowers, sun—that have both real and symbolic meanings; year after year, children all over the world repeat these themes. In representing actual things, children create a world of their own desires, integrating this world of fantasy and imagination with the realities of technique and mastery of materials. By serving all these purposes, art deserves its position in early-childhood classrooms.

"How Did You Make That?"

The point for me, as the months pass, is to see how certain themes recur with each child, and to see the way that some projects—projects they have essentially invented themselves, through collective action—take hold of the class.

I studied painting and drawing when I was young, and more recently began making prints. Perhaps because art is a primary means of expression for me, I was predisposed to give it a significant place in classroom life. In other classrooms, teachers' interests or predispositions may lead them to support other kinds of experiences that help shape the identity that a class develops. Vivian Paley and Karen Gallas, two teacher-writers, have written extensively about the stories and plays children make up, and the jokes they tell. Paley and Gallas describe how children's narratives snowball and create elaborate and ritualized class tales and themes. For *this* class, it was art that contributed significantly to the class's identity and gave the class a theme; art that threaded itself through the day, with each child influencing others as they tried out and interpreted others' ideas. It was art that gave a role to certain children, a way to contribute to the class—children who would otherwise probably have been outsiders.

In addition, art introduced this group of children to *work*, or rather, to the kind of work they would continue to do all year, work that was both exploratory and disciplined. Children's work, as I see it, is a formulation of their experience, something that grows out of their involvement with content and materials. It's easy to see this when a work of art expresses an idea. I remember, from years ago, a four-year-old's drawing of a bulb, after we'd planted bulbs. He had drawn the bulb, a round brown shape, and then covered the entire paper with brown crayon, explaining that it was the earth covering the bulb. The work of drawing, of representation, was an extension of what this child understood. But I see this quality of thoughtfulness whenever children are fully involved with art materials—they make judgments and express concepts as they find out what they can do with the stuff they're using. In this way, art establishes the power of children individually and *as a group* to claim content. It establishes their (relative) freedom to define their work for themselves. As they do this, they gain confidence in themselves as capable and committed makers of objects.

A critical component of art work, as I understand it, is an acceptance of the unknowability of the end product. I've had to learn this for myself, as I've faced struggles with my own art work. Whenever I've held on to too definite an idea of the image I want, I've resisted the changes that occur as I work. I've had to learn about the inevitability of mistakes; again and again, I've learned to give up any notion that it's possible to control the process. I've had to learn that mistakes are not only inevitable but necessary and useful, and that dealing with them—untangling some knot—takes us somewhere unexpected. Nothing beats the pleasure of producing something that did not exist before, something that my own manipulation of the materials brought into being. Yet the process is certainly daunting, and perhaps it is the very unknowability of the outcome that scares those teachers who are determined to control what happens in their classrooms.

Significantly, not all teachers see art as real work, as an integral element of children's intellectual development. For many teachers and administrators, art is an extra, allowed only after children have finished their "work." For these teachers, children's desire to draw is something to be used as an incentive to motivate children to complete other assignments.

In many classrooms, what's called "art" is something else entirely. It is all too common to walk into classrooms to see twenty-five identical egg-carton caterpillars. Children are shown a model and given a set of instructions in order to "create" the product; the closer the resemblance between the student's product and the model, the more successful he's been—in the teacher's eyes, and his own. There is no room for exploration, discovery, independent thinking. Teachers hand out photocopied sheets, e.g., showing the life cycle of the frog. Children color in, then cut and glue the pictures in the right sequence. What children learn is that their own efforts to conceptualize and represent are inadequate. Power to conceptualize lies with adults; children's "work" is to—literally—color in. Grade after grade, children's confidence is sapped, and they come to say, "Oh, I'm not artistic," or "I can't draw!"—having lost faith in their expressive capacity.

When children engage in art as I understand it, they are also being introduced to a set of relationships that concern power and authority in a classroom. If children are to be "in charge" of their work—making the important decisions, and doing the thinking that lies behind the decisions—teachers must trust them and be willing to share authority with them. The teacher's role shifts, without diminishing in importance: someone who can provide additional materials, ask probing questions, make comparisons, or find a relevant resource, a dictionary page when a child wants to draw a particular animal. The teacher also ensures that work is shared: *I make the decisions about time and space—I allow public space for their work.* By taking time for the whole group to look at and discuss work, the individual child's insights, knowledge, and thinking are made public, something others can participate in and build on. *We all listen as Graham talks about his block building the "Lincoln Memorial." Afterward, Sam draws it; thus we (they, with my aid) create a class culture, something necessarily unique, from these shared projects.*

Through their art experiences, as children crowd around the table near the sink, they are, in effect, creating a group ethos of work. They are defining work as something powerfully personal that at the same time arises in a social context and connects them to others. When someone shares work, a child will inevitably ask, "How did you make that?" The child who's been questioned goes into a long explanation, "First I drew the face, then I . . ." Teachers dislike the question, as they wonder how long to let the child go on; to them, it's unnecessary, but to the other children, it's *the* question.

As children help each other, the role of one child or another grows, depending on that child's knowledge of methods and materials: *Alyssa was having problems making things stay attached and I sent her to Rosie. Of course, making Rosie an expert is a great thing for* her. At any point, a child's power depends on what that child can offer to others in the group. Thus, the social nature of their work together changes classroom relationships: the teacher is no longer the sole authority, and children's shared problems and solutions engender a sense of community.

Yellow Skin and Orange Hair

There's a huge amount of energy in projects of their own devising: today, at the art table, this work with toilet paper tubes and pen tops, which Rosie had started, in a modest way, a week ago. They work on mat board or shirt cardboard. Brooke made a great building, with lots of stuff, Rosie a four-story construction. Graham made faces, clever and symmetrical.

As the children make aesthetic judgments, they do so in myriad ways. One child likes symmetry, another loves action and movement. If children are allowed access to art materials, encouraged to work with seriousness and conviction, they develop a style that can be instantly recognized. Through their judgments and decisions, their idiosyncratic use of materials, the way they put crayon or paint to paper, children not only define the material, they define themselves. *Philip draws minipictures, packed with information. One of his drawings shows an amusement park he went to with his family, with three different rides, one for children the age of his little sister, one for children his age, one for older kids and adults. Another of his drawings shows the Amtrak station, with luggage on luggage carts and boards with train arrival and departure times.* Philip's love of information, his intellectual organization, comes through clearly in his art.

By age five, when children arrive in elementary school, they have evolved definite *selves*, amalgams of innate temperament and lived experiences. They have their passionate interests, concerns, topics, humor: a style that is theirs. They move through the classroom in distinctive ways. When Henry walks around the classroom, his shoelaces are loose and he bumps into things. He writes his name illegibly; his drawings are hard to read. Yet he frequently chooses to draw or make constructions, and his drawings are complicated and full of action.

Henry worked on one drawing for all of work time, then explained it to me. I was quite amazed—I'd forgotten this is exactly his style. The drawing reminds me of Philip's train station drawings; it's a whole world.

By the spring, Henry is reading fluently. Marcus, Henry's opposite in certain ways, moves with grace and rhythm, never walks if he can dance, either across the room or on line to lunch. He, too, loves drawing, but his drawings are easy to read. He makes clear outlines and colors them in, adding rainbows to everything he makes—rainbow boats, rainbow dinosaurs. He is not as well prepared for academic work as Henry and doesn't even know all the alphabet letters. For Henry, art slowly becomes a link with others in the class. For Marcus, art was from the beginning a tie to others, always an indicator of his social involvement.

The distinctive manner in which different children use the same materials tells me about *them*: *I see children's selves in the way they pace themselves—Caroline's crashes, her enthusiasms.* Caroline, with her production of kites, each one made in a fast and furious way, defines herself through sheer quantity of production: her work is quick, sometimes sloppy. I'm likely to find half-begun pieces of work, abandoned, while she's moved on to the next piece of paper. She never has a fallow phase; I am always pushing her to come back to finish something. In the course of the year, I see change, as Caroline becomes more able to push one piece of work to completion without losing her ebullience.

Looking at one piece of work, teachers sometimes misread its meaning. Some misjudgments are a result of the expectation that development proceeds at a uniform pace. But growth does not occur evenly: *Rosie did a great face, bright yellow skin and orange hair, loopy circling lines. This level of work seems to come out of nowhere: months of drawings that seem disorganized and wispy— then this, confident, competent.* Discovering a misinterpretation can be helpful; it's a sign of the teacher's struggle to see children fairly, without prejudice. If we come to a conclusion about the meaning of a piece of work, can we confirm it? Do we find the time to ask children about their work? If we find ourselves caught short, surprised, the chances are that we are coming closer to describing work accurately: *Today, Henry drew page after page in his art class sketchbook. It may have been that he wanted to get to the last page, in order to take the sketchbook home—he'd asked when he could take it home. On one page, he'd drawn something and was going over it again and again, with these attacking lines. It looked to me like a destructive impulse. I called him up and asked, Can you tell me about this? He said, It's popcorn popping.*

The more a child's personal qualities and predilections inform the process of making art, the greater the child's motivation. When teachers impose decisions, and negate or minimize children's choices, they find themselves battling against children's energies. There is, of course, an underlying and inevitable conflict between school as an institution and young children. Young children feel things with immediacy, and group settings always impose some restraints on children's individual impulses: "Wait!" we say, "Not now!" Yet to the extent that classrooms can channel and engage children's unique selves, to that degree their energy will enrich classroom life.

Mixing Media

Art work is a way of playing with shapes, materials. Play engages children, allows them extraordinary flexibility, the possibility of invention, of trying out endless ideas, because there is no linear right-wrong, no label of "better."

Young children's ability to think "as if," to place few limits on imagination or on the transformation of objects and materials, can be observed in all their dramatic play, their sensibility and their view of the world. They easily cross the border between what they want to believe and what's factual and verifiable. A piece of cloth can be a baby; a pencil, a rocket. Yet while children are animists, with the ability to give things life and to turn objects into other objects, they are at the same time realists. Fantasy, for young children, often serves some practical, real-world purpose. Their ability to move without a passport between these countries—the inanimate and the animate, the real and the wished-for—is one of their great resources.

Several years ago, a rather rigid art teacher came every week to my kindergarten class. The lessons were highly prescriptive; each lesson had one aim. One week, children were introduced to "form": shown how drawn lines could enclose space to produce forms. The teacher told the children to use the forms to make animals, which they would then paint. One very independent boy had drawn and painted his animal; he was clearly pleased with himself and finished with the piece. The art teacher wanted him to paint in the background, and he, equally insistent, refused. Teachers, validly, wonder about how to move children forward; but this teacher's strategy was an example of how *not* to proceed, an example of a teacher imposing *her* idea. She pestered him until he finally said, "This animal lives at the North Pole, and that [pointing to the background] is the snow." With that, he'd won, using his creative powers to defeat her decisively (on her own turf, so to speak, as an artist) and to hold on to his right to make his own work.

Certain materials don't allow much play for the imagination; they permit only one use or interpretation. With these materials, children's work is excessively product-oriented; children have no opportunities to judge, ponder, and make decisions. At the opposite end of the spectrum are materials like play dough or clay, which allow children a range of transformations. Collage, using found materials, is an art form that is extremely well adapted to children's imaginative uses.

First, there's the *stuff* itself. Torn paper, paper that's shiny, rough, or smooth, all sorts of textured materials (corrugated cardboard, burlap, sandpaper); materials that are thick or thin, fat or skinny; found objects of all sorts (tops of markers, tops of juice or milk containers, bread tags; tiny beads; pebbles, bark, and shells; metal bits)—all of these *things* appeal to children's senses directly and immediately. These are the things children notice lying on the ground, things they pick up and pocket. At the end of the school day, feeling like an archaeologist, I empty my pockets and find these. As children choose and arrange these objects, their decisions are both aesthetic and personal.

For this class of children, collage had a very strong appeal.

Looking back, I would say that their work with collage defined the class. Collage found its way into everything we did. I introduced collage in October, after the class had explored the use of the shape templates, and had also begun to learn about care of materials. I gave the children pieces of mat board, cut into different sizes, as a base for the materials glued on top.[2] I set out a variety of collage materials. As children finished their collages, I let them paint around or on top of the glued forms, so that the work was produced in two separate stages. This process was extremely popular. Children welcomed the opportunity to go back into a piece of work and add more color. The layering of work gave them even more choice and artistic freedom. It allowed for an especially rich construction of the surface of the work.

All year, as the children continued to make collages, I continued to add new materials—popsicle sticks, cardboard tubes and boxes, straws, coffee stirrers. As the year proceeded, children began to work on pieces for several days. They built longer, larger, more complex pieces that were, essentially, constructions. They would tape two pieces of mat board together to accommodate their expanding work; sometimes friends would work together on a piece.

We used multimedia processes, in varying combinations: crayon or Cray-Pas with watercolor on top, collage plus Cray-Pas plus watercolor, printing techniques with added watercolor or Cray-Pas, and construction with collage and paint. The practice of combining different media invited experimentation and playfulness. Further, the *layering* of materials, the adding on of diverse elements, is a metaphor for learning itself, for what occurs when children integrate new experiences with what they already know and make accommodations that redefine the whole. Whatever the causes, when children are involved in multimedia projects, their commitment is impressive, and they produce some of their most vivid and compelling work.

A Path That Doesn't Go Any Place Special

Teaching art has to do with the difference between trusting children and believing you must teach them everything about a subject or they won't know it.

When I came to P.S. 87, every class received art instruction. A parent at the school had developed the lessons, which were taught by parents whom she'd trained. The lessons were highly struc-tured and technique-based. Children made color wheels in order to learn to mix colors. To make self-portraits, they drew ovals, which they then bisected vertically and horizontally, so that the features could be positioned correctly. The results were hung in the hallways, and I found the resulting work disheartening—the color wheels, the nearly identical oval faces, the stiff drawings de-void of personality.

When my kindergarten classes had their art classes, I was an unhappy observer. For their first painting lesson, children were given containers of red, blue, and yellow paint. They were shown how to mix orange, then green, then purple, one color at a time. After this, the children were allowed to paint using all six colors, but they had to listen to different pieces of music and paint according to the kind of music they heard. Instead of trusting children to explore, allowing them the excitement of their own discoveries, the lesson directed their every move. For children with extensive painting experience, it was overdirected; for those with little experience, it was frustrating. The musical "motiva-tion" was a distraction.

Lessons like these put children's expressive abilities in the backseat. George Szekely, an artist-teacher who describes himself as "a student of the children's world," critiques this approach in his book *Encouraging Creativity in Art Lessons*.[5] The criteria he proposes include, centrally, whether lessons help develop stu-dents' understanding of the creative process. He asks, What are the student's choices, how much room is there for individuality? When a specific lesson produces results that are "illustrations of [the teacher's] plans," then too much of the "creative decision-making was controlled by the teacher." The discovery and exploration that should be a component of the art experience was the teacher's, when the lesson was shaped. These lessons take children's art as a stage on the way to adult art.[4]

This year, the school administration had decided to make a change: the kindergarten classes would be taught by Andrea Kantrowitz, an artist from Studio in the Schools, a nonprofit organization. Andrea worked with us for eleven weeks in the late winter and spring. She was a great match for the class: she was genuinely interested in children's art. She met with me first, before coming in to teach, wanting to know what kinds of work the children had been doing and what they would be studying; she set her lessons in the context of the class's prior experiences.

Andrea's carefully planned lessons introduced specific artistic elements but allowed for maximum exploration; they were, in a sense, highly revisable, provisional encounters designed to spark children's involvement. Exploration was guided; its parameters were set by the materials and their uses, yet it was open enough to permit each child's experience and unique preferences to inform the approach to the materials. Andrea believed art could be taught but that it shouldn't be taught prescriptively. Her goal was to help children develop their abilities to see, design, use color; to help them extend their visual vocabulary; to help them gain clarity and conviction, while making something that was authentically theirs.

Children, Andrea told me, "naturally have their own likes and dislikes." We had been discussing how she worked with children on wood constructions: "I talk to them about balance, about height, and about bridging. How can you make the piece tall? How can you support something? Then I let them work." She said she watched how the children work, and took note of their distinctive styles and methods. For some, she said, narrative elements are strong—the piece tells a story. They'll tell the teacher, "and *this* is . . ." For others, design is central: pieces display symmetry, or elements are placed in sequential series. Others *build*: one girl had used the whole period to discover engineering principles, figuring out how to cantilever the pieces of wood.

Creative expression, Andrea said, isn't limited to the emotions. Mathematical ideas can be expressed in art as well. Andrea sees ideas repeated as children work together at a table, observing, adapting, influencing each other. At the end of the art period, the children look at each others' work and comment on what they see. Andrea's focus on children's engagement with the task—her sensitivity to children's *level* and *method* of engagement—helped her look at a piece of work with them; it helped her plan. As Andrea's visits continued, I saw her use her repertoire of activities, adapting lessons to the class rather than expecting the children to adapt to the lessons. She also gave the class sketchbooks, in which they drew at the end of art periods. Sometimes they drew what they'd made—and these representations of their own artworks were marvelous. In the course of our time with this program, the sketchbooks became increasingly used and valued.

In the spring, the issue of how art should be taught was brought up at a staff meeting. We had to decide whether to continue to fund the parent-taught program. Many teachers defended the program; others criticized it. The heated debate forced me to clarify my own ideas about teaching art: *There are things you train kids to do—wiping brushes, looking at the whole paper— things you want to become ingrained, automatic. But you don't need to give them a lesson in looking at the whole paper; you don't need a lesson to teach children to think about rhythm, contrast, movement of line. They can learn to see those aspects of art as they work. Then it gets woven into their thinking about the work they're making. A high school art student can validly be asked to produce a piece of work using only one color and black and white. But for elementary school students to make something that revolves around a narrowly set problem is a waste of an art period, too scarce a thing to waste. To whatever extent young children study art, their work should be inspired by their own desire to create art.*

• • •

Two out-of-the-classroom experiences contributed to the children's feelings about art, and their ability to talk about art. Denay's mother offered to arrange a visit for the class to the Whitney Museum, where there was an exhibition of work by Romare Bearden. A painter and collagist, Bearden's works are accessible in subject matter but still somehow mysterious. I made an appointment for the class, and one February day, off we went to the Whitney, accompanied by many parents. The museum was closed when we visited, and we had the galleries to ourselves. Jane Royale, from the Education Department, met us, and she chose three works for the class to focus on. As she talked with the children, they sat very still and concentrated on the work. Her questions were specific yet open-ended, and sparked long, intense discussions: *We looked first at a painting of a family. What objects were included in the painting, and why had they been included? What could the children say about the gestures the people were making? Why had he painted what he painted—who were the people? What could we guess about how they were feeling?* The children were so precise about what they were seeing: "I think he is angry because of the way his hand is." The next day, the children dictated a thank-you letter and made collages to include with the letter.

Another February day, overcast and gray: out again, this time to Central Park. Christo's *Gates* project, huge orange curtains hung at intervals along the paths, had turned the park's winter landscape into a bright, gigantic public sculpture. The class bounded along the paths. Returning to the classroom, the children talked about what they'd seen. Their comments showed their ability to think for themselves. *Michael: it's like a path that doesn't go to any place special. Vanessa: I didn't like them because there was no painting. Max: it was boring because it didn't do anything. Lizzie: I liked it because Central Park didn't have any color.*

What elements did our two art trips add? There is a difference, I think, between making art and talking about it, between having art as part of your everyday life and knowing that it can be something out of the ordinary, something you go to see. The discussion at the museum contributed to their belief that they could talk about art. Both trips showed the children that they could bring what they had learned about art in the classroom to their thinking about art that was out in the world.

Art in the Curriculum

I watch Rosie draw animals for her alphabet book. She starts with the feet and draws an outline. The parts end up totally out of proportion, and she gets discouraged. I have to help her see what she knows about the animals she's drawing.

In the fall, a number of children worked on art projects with concentration and interest, but the work of most of the others was quick and slapdash. By the end of the year, all the children drew constantly and with intensity; they taped their drawings to the walls; they hated it when I told them to put away their sketchbooks. The change in the course of the year resulted, to an extent, from the way art was taught: both Andrea and I always put children's expressiveness first. Art activities were valued, as well, because the class environment was rich in art. Art was part of everything the children did, part of all content areas: they illustrated poems, drew the classroom animals and plants, printed with the leaves we'd collected in the park, and made collages to illustrate information about the animals they were studying. They used math materials to make elaborate and beautiful patterns, which they then copied; they drew on wipe-off boards. They did "food color experiments," mixing food colors in water, writing the equations (2 blue + 3 red), and saving the resulting colors on coffee filter papers. The children brought to the various experiences a sense of joy and a high level of personal involvement. They had complete confidence in themselves as producers of art, whatever their actual degree of skill. They communicated ease in *making* art and *thinking* about art.

Display of children's drawings
Photo by Julie Diamond

Toward the end of the year, the class undertook a study of undersea animals. The children chose the animals they wanted to study, and as the weeks passed and the children engaged in research on their animals, they drew incessantly. Drawings, with text, were displayed: colorful jellyfish, starfish, sharp-toothed sharks, and playful dolphins. A group of boys who were studying octopuses and squids made numerous beautiful pen drawings of giant squids, the squids floating alone, trailed by clouds of ink, or grappling with sperm whales. One result of the study was a book about undersea animals that the children wrote and illustrated. The children also made fish prints, painting a flounder and pressing paper to its scaly body.

With Andrea, they made undersea-animal mobiles, a project that took several weeks. They drew and cut out animals from oak tag, then collaged burlap onto them. The next week, they printed from the collaged shapes. Next, with parents' help, we made mobiles from the painted animals, which were hung in the school lobby for the Studio in the Schools exhibition. On their own, children made paper sharks, dolphins, jellyfish, and starfish, which we hung from the lights.

Our last class project was a K-104 aquarium, which the families came to see as part of our end-of-year celebration. All the children made models of sea animals. They first used plasticene for practice and then made models with a hardening material, which they painted. Several children constructed an aquarium from blocks, with areas for different animals. They labeled their animals and placed them, on pieces of cardboard, in the aquarium. Overhead, the jellyfish waved their tentacles, the dolphins leaped, sharks exposed their teeth—*a sea of creatures, hanging from the lights.*

What energized the class in all this work over many weeks, what drew the children in, were not only their feelings about sea creatures, deep as those feelings were, but their commitment to producing art. The commitment grew out of a year of making art; it was fueled by art-related trips, by their work with Andrea, and by the class environment. They had gained a sense of themselves as proficient in art, and further, their art experiences gave them a model of what *work* can be.

They had come to translate their feelings as individuals into a thorough valuing of their role as contributors to the class. Their individualism had not been lost or submerged. The aquarium was something they had truly created together. Working with confidence, as a group, they had transformed the world of the classroom. At the end of the year, they had created an environment that reflected not only what they had learned but whom they had become.

✐

4

Finding Curriculum:
A Study of Squirrels

Tooth Marks: Children Observe the World Around Them

Yesterday, after a few days of talking about squirrels, one came and hung on the window grill. We watched, described what the squirrel was doing—then Caroline asked, How does he balance like that?

Every fall, I've studied trees and leaves with my class. The city sidewalks, playgrounds, and streets are awash with fallen leaves, seed balls, acorns, and maple keys. Young children often walk to school with eyes on the ground, searching for finds that they will proudly present to teachers. I bring in acorns and twisty honey-locust pods, letting students sort through them and break open the pods to find the shiny seeds. We exhibit all of these on trays, in containers, on the science table. The children write labels, using junior tree guides. They start collecting more leaves and nuts, looking at the varieties of leaves and observing the differences. They make leaf rubbings and leaf prints. I make a photocopy of ginkgo, oak, and sycamore leaves and reproduce it for a home-work assignment: children are to look for these leaves, which are distinctive and easily found in the school's neighborhood.

This year, for the first time, I decided to study squirrels. David, our student teacher, was interested in studying an animal. I made the choice to study squirrels. We'd already begun studying trees, and had a collection of acorns. Examining the acorns with mag-nifying glasses, the children had noticed tooth marks. It was an easy leap from trees to squirrels.

What lends itself to study? With young children, the environment provides a wealth of topics: the children themselves and their families; the physical and social environment of the school; the neighborhood of the school, street signs, shops, banks, fire stations, restaurants. Children are also curious about physical aspects of the environment: weather, weeds that grow in sidewalk cracks, shadows, ice and snow in the winter. Young children are incessant investigators, particularly about real things in the world. Teachers do not need to wait for questions to arise, but can initiate studies. We can find and display resources—real objects, books, photos—that will pique interest, *if* the subject is inherently engaging. When a study begins with something that is already part of the children's world, their involvement can be immediate. One year when I taught first grade, the cardboard Halloween skeletons that appeared in late October sparked an interest in bones that resulted in weeks of study of human and animal bones.

Children invest certain topics with meanings that resonate for *them* at a certain age. When the first-graders studied bones, it was a natural extension of their interest in their bodies. Young children will talk endlessly about their injuries and show them off with enthusiasm. Blood fascinates them. "Did it bleed?" they'll ask when someone describes a fall. "Did you get stitches?" What is at issue for them is not only their safety but their identity. When their bodies' borders are breached, will everything stay safely inside? What *is* inside? Similarly, four- and five-year-olds' fascination with dinosaurs often revolves around issues of aggression and defense: what can one dinosaur do to another, and how can the other dinosaur protect or defend itself? These questions arise at a period in their lives when young children are finding themselves less closely supervised by adults, as they play in the schoolyard at recess, or in a park playground. What is allowed? What should I do if someone pushes me? When is it OK to push back? Will I be able to defend myself? The issues of right and wrong that parents might bring up are set aside in the child's search for safety *and* autonomy, and dinosaurs are certainly creatures un-troubled by moral qualms.

My choice of squirrels as a topic was based both on their being very much part of our environment and on my knowl-edge that five-year-olds enjoy observing animals, particularly animal movement. I've always had class animals—rabbits, guinea pigs, snakes, turtles—and have noticed, over the years, that children's most frequent comments are about the animals' movements.

In deciding to study squirrels, I was also influenced by what I know about how five-year-olds learn. My years spent in their company, as well as my reading of educators Jean Piaget, Susan Isaacs, and John Dewey, have made clear to me that young chil-dren learn best through *concrete experiences*. They learn through their bodies and their senses: they look closely at things, poke at them, smell them, and shake them to see what sounds they pro-duce. Is a topic one that lends itself to the provision of concrete experiences? In the case of a squirrel study, we could easily plan activities that involved children's firsthand observations. The children would also bring to the study a knowledge of squirrels acquired from previous observations of their environment.

After we noticed the tooth marks on the acorns, I brought in books about squirrels. I planned our first trip, to the sidewalk right outside the school building, where there is a row of oak trees. We would look for evidence of squirrel activity and see what we could collect.

Investigations

Today we took them out to collect acorns. Found acorns, noted "bird poop," and found some kind of berry. Back in the classroom, when the children drew what they'd found, they were totally absorbed. Each of them had a plastic box for their finds. We made the mistake (we'd planned this, but it was a bad idea) of letting them use crayons, but many of them didn't, and the pencil drawings are the best. Most of them got the idea of really looking.

In the first weeks of school, the children had made "science drawings." It was something I actively encouraged, providing paper and pencils. The children drew the things on the science table: seashells, starfish, rocks, sea glass, birds' nests. Some children had drawn the class rabbit, noticing, for example, the length of his body when he was lying down. Magnifying glasses had been set out on the science table, and we talked at meeting about how to focus them. Their drawings were date-stamped. I would ask them what they'd noticed about the object, and I'd write down what they said. At class meetings, children would show the others their science drawings, as well as the objects, and say whatever they wanted to about what they'd done. Other children could ask questions. Afterward, the drawings were put up on the wall next to the science table. The drawings began to form a class resource, a library of images. I took photographs of each child holding his or her drawing and the object drawn, and these photographs were put up on the wall too, next to the drawings.

From the beginning of the year, I was introducing children to a protocol. I was saying, implicitly, this kind of drawing is different from other drawing; you are doing something different. Drawing was being used as a tool for the children to learn about, to *investigate*, some phenomenon. When they draw an object from life, children notice more: the swirl in a shell or the jagged edge of a nut. Drawing something makes them feel proprietary; it gives them a sense of ownership of the object or process observed. The use of drawing as a tool of investigation is natural for young children; in the classroom, their purpose can become more conscious. It should be added that sometimes children will attempt to trace an object rather than drawing from observation, or will say they "can't" draw it. This may occur either when they have not had a lot of experience with the free use of drawing materials (for example, if they have only had the use of coloring books, or have had limited access to blank paper, crayons, and markers), or when they have experience but have become self-conscious about their representational abilities (for example, if older siblings have made fun of their drawings). I have found that learned inhibitions about drawing can be overcome if a teacher actively helps a child look at an object to be drawn (e.g., asking, "What do you notice about it? Do you see any lines on it? How do the lines move?").

As was true when the children shared artwork, the sharing of the science drawings added to the knowledge of the class as a whole and reinforced the idea that knowledge exists in a social context. Children's thinking, in the form of drawings, was made public. Last, photos documented the work of observation. Drawings and photos together create a record of the development of children's observational abilities. The records can be part of a science journal, or can be put in a file for students to look back on later in the year or for teachers to share with parents.

In using drawing as a tool of investigation, I was influenced by the approach of the municipal preschools in Reggio Emilia, Italy. I was first introduced to the work there when I'd seen an exhibition of photographs and children's work called the Hundred Languages of Children over a decade ago. I'd been struck by the quality of the work, the careful observation, sophistication, directness, and clarity, as well as the sense of joy that the drawings expressed. What had produced this level of work?

In Reggio Emilia preschools, children investigate the world around them, using paint, clay, paper, natural objects, and the manipulation of light and shadow to organize their knowledge. They explore various themes with the active collaboration of adults who document the work and help define the projects. Each school has an atelier in which children work in small groups with an artist-teacher. Teacher collaboration is an integral element, as is the schools' integration in the community. Reggio methods are rooted in the city's social and political values, and developed over several decades.

I saw that the approach shared philosophic roots with the progressive pedagogy in which I'd been trained, but I also knew I couldn't remotely duplicate the schools' physical and social environment. I could incorporate individual elements, however: I could use drawing as a way for children to gain knowledge, particularly knowledge about the natural world. I could use discussion, photographic documentation, children's dictated words, and displays to continually make their insights public. I could ensure that their aesthetic sensibility was given a central place when I planned. I have found that the example of Reggio Emilia has produced a gradual shift in my understanding of the teacher's role. I have grown more and more to see teaching as the job of understanding children's thinking.

Questions and Answers

Max insists that babies don't open their eyes at birth. It isn't this particular belief that interests me right now, though I should think about that, but the quality of his persistence, his certainty, despite the fact that we'd looked at a photo in one of the baby books, a newborn with its eyes open. The next day, Max repeated it: newborn babies can't open their eyes. I see it as a fact about him, this sticking to what he believes, a holding on despite evidence, a need to shift slowly, to struggle to integrate new information; it's something important about Max.

Looking back at this journal entry, I see what I missed. I notice now what Max noticed, what he *insisted* we recognize. He had concluded—from our study of squirrels and his own knowledge of rabbits (from his perusal of books in the rabbit book basket)—that the eyes of these small mammals are shut at birth. If people are mammals too, he may have reasoned, shouldn't *our* eyes be shut at birth? What mattered, for the class as a whole as well as for Max, was not that he was wrong but that he'd had a powerful insight: newborn mammals are similar in certain ways. *How* are newborn mammals alike and how are they different? What might explain the differences? These are productive questions, which I didn't think of. The underlying question for me was whether my focus on Max's wrongness prevented me from following his thinking process.

The teacher's conception of the teaching role is at the center of everything that happens or doesn't happen in a classroom. We bring to teaching who we are, I remember Dorothy Cohen saying. Dorothy was my advisor at Bank Street College. She was also the author of *The Learning Child*, a work that summarizes child development in the preschool and elementary years and examines the implications for educational and parenting practices.[1] My good fortune in having had her as advisor was something that became more apparent the longer I taught. She was tough and uncompromising, smart, and extremely knowledgeable about children and teaching. Observing me as I student-taught, she told me, "You don't trust them." I puzzled over that remark, and it took me decades to see what she meant.

Trust in kids is not easy to practice. For both new and experienced teachers, it's hard to avoid being didactic, hard to leave children the room to theorize. We love knowing, we love telling. We go into teaching in order to teach, and in a deep way we believe that teaching *is* telling. We focus on what we know and what children *don't* know.

In her book *Talking Their Way into Science*, the educator Karen Gallas has a different way of looking at what children don't know. She sees their self-invented explanations as theories.[2] Gallas was a classroom teacher in Brookline, Massachusetts, who took a detour to obtain a PhD, but unlike many with higher degrees, she went back into the classroom. Gallas documents and analyzes children's talk, concluding that their "misconceptions . . . are the result of observation, imagination, and logic." Her commitment to children's theory making leads her to be concerned that teachers' interruptions cause children to "believe that their ideas are always being judged."[3] She proposes, "Rather than viewing misconceptions as cause for . . . intervention, we should carefully elicit them and work with the children to uncover the kinds of data upon which they have based their theories."[4]

David, our student teacher, worked to gain this point of view. *David and I talked after he'd worked with a small group. Lila had said, Squirrels lay eggs. He'd asked, What makes you think that? So he was getting it. But I pushed him, asking, why do you think Lila might have thought that? He saw that she might have made an analogy to birds, extending her thinking, applying something she already knows—with the common element that they both live in trees. I'm thinking now—it's proof that Lila is learning something new. This is proof also of what we can find out about children's thinking . . . if we don't correct, or dispense knowledge, but have ideas about where the discussion can go.* Rather than asking ourselves what Lila was thinking, how much easier to rush in and correct: "Squirrels don't lay eggs, they're mammals!" *If* we step back, while remaining present, we allow children their excitement, the intensity of feeling, which feeds their identification with the *stuff*—squirrels, trees, ice and snow, whatever it is that has their attention. It's this identification we aim for, and it's made possible when we trust children's learning.

The stance of being present but holding back requires *our* engagement, first of all with the children we teach, and second, with the content. We must feel connected to the subject, know about it, care about it, and want to learn more; we, too, must be curious. We must know and care about the subject, so that when we listen to children, *we'll know what to listen for.* We'll know what to ask, we'll know where to head.

A Theory of Curriculum

Adam came up to me and asked, Are there really powers? Any question with "really" or "real" is automatically interesting. I wasn't at all sure what he meant, and asked, Do you mean do people have powers? He seemed to mean powers that are inexplicable. The point

is how interesting the questions are and how unexpectedly they bub-
ble up. This year: Are skeletons real? Are dinosaurs real? Another
year: Is snow really real?

These questions are useful; they provide information about
children's thinking. For example, four- and five-year-olds often
ask about whether things are "real": they have been told tales for
a number of years, and some of these have come to be seen as un-
true. The adult's authority is no longer enough for them; they are
slowly becoming skeptics as they learn to rely more and more on
data they collect for themselves or pick up from friends. Curriculum can gather up the questions that have special resonance for
children developmentally and in terms of their experiences.
Those questions can spur them to extend their thinking and can
generate discussions, experiments, research, and the drawing of
conclusions.

The curricular approach of this squirrel study has been termed
emergent curriculum. The difference between this approach and
traditional methods is sharp. Teachers are often handed curriculum packets that they are expected to follow; these may be used
year after year, with few changes. When teachers follow predetermined programs of instruction, the important connections are
made *by* adults *for* children, and indeed, the classroom teacher's
involvement in decision making is minimal. I see curriculum differently: children define the content they are studying with the
collaboration of the teachers. When this is the case, children's
energies, understandings, and actions determine various aspects
of the study, directly affecting how meaningful the material is
to them and how motivated they will be. Together, students
and teacher pursue directions that the study might take, and create the forms of knowledge. This framework renders sterile the
perennial debate over whether education should be child- or
curriculum-centered; curriculum is neither solely child-centered
nor teacher-directed. Curriculum is inherent *in* the relationship
among children, teacher, and content.

Education is a process, linking children's immediate interests with fully developed curricular content. This is how John Dewey defines the process in *The Child and the Curriculum*: there is, he argues, no "gap in kind . . . between the child's experience and the various forms of subject-matter that make up the course of study." [5] These two end points "define a single process." [6] I picture a teacher as literally a bridge, standing with one foot in what Dewey calls the "psychological reality" of children and the other foot planted in the "logical reality" of adult disciplines. The psychological reality encompasses the concrete world of children's day-to-day and highly personal associations, concerns, and sensations, their unique and specific responses to any given content. What do children see, what do they notice? Years ago, a girl in my class was drawing at a table. She exclaimed—to anyone listening—"I've never drawn purple eyes before!" Between her perception and mine, there was all the difference in the world. Her statement can stand for all the observations that children make of details that are relevant to them but may be hidden from our unseeing adult eyes.

The logical reality refers to what adults know about any field of understanding, something generally seen as a systematized ordering of reality. (This seems a more apt description when applied to the sciences, math, and social sciences, and less apparent in relation to the arts; also, we know all subject matters to be socially constructed to an extent, and continually evolving.) In Dewey's view, education is *rooted* in the child's psychological reality but *headed* toward the logical reality of adult knowledge; the seeds of disciplines are implicit in children's curiosity about and interactions with things in the world.

When teachers place children's conceptualizing at the center of the educational process, they must actively seek educational meanings in children's actions and products. Seeing teaching in this way doesn't minimize the teacher's role, either in planning or as children engage in work. It enlarges our role and makes it more complex. It is not enough for teachers to observe children's potential, to merely watch children and encourage them; that is a kind of passivity, an abdication of the responsibility teachers owe children. The teacher must know when and how to step in; the teacher must actively help children *see* their work. This implies that teachers must not only notice learning, but must also notice when learning is *not* occuring.

This task is a concern of Harvard educator Eleanor Duckworth. In her influential essay "The Having of Wonderful Ideas," she gives concrete examples of the work that can go on in this middle space—a space of trust, listening, and knowledge of both children *and* curriculum.[7] Duckworth's title essay takes a child's active learning as its starting point: the child jumps into a self-initiated task saying, " 'I know what I'm going to do.' " Duckworth goes on to conclude that "the essence of pedagogy" is giving children "the occasion to have . . . wonderful ideas."[8] In practice, this means that teachers "must find ways to structure subject matter so as to enable learners to get at their thoughts. . . . Then we must take those thoughts seriously, and set about helping students to pursue them in greater breadth and depth."[9] In another essay in this collection, Duckworth describes two aspects of teaching: "The first is to put students into contact with phenomena related to the area to be studied—the real thing, not books or lectures about it—and to help them notice what is interesting. . . . The second is to have the students try to explain the sense they are making, and, instead of explaining things to students, to try to understand their sense."[10]

This approach *doesn't* prohibit teachers from being, on occasion, pointed and specific; it prohibits only interventions that are not tied to the student's investigation. This is elaborated on by Tiziana Filippini, a Reggio educator: "The teacher has, for us, a role as dispenser of occasions . . . a provoker of occasions."[11] Teachers are responsible for that closeness, that tying of comments and questions to children's observed activities. When the teacher's goal is the opening up of the subject, the teacher's choices are infinite.

Moving Back and Forth

The group studying squirrels' homes produced a big collage—it was truly great, and it was David's idea. The kids—a somewhat feisty bunch, all boys—loved cutting the paper to make the tree and branches and grass... pink for the babies in the squirrels' nest. When I looked at it with David later, I saw that the long grass was at the top; it seemed as if the tree was upside down. I asked him, What's the story here? He said the grass was Michael's, for the squirrels' nest. I said, It's almost as big as the tree! You have to work with them, ask them, What's the size of the nest, how long should the grass be? You have to look at it with them. The next day, he worked on it with them again.

Our study of squirrels constituted this sort of opening up of a topic. We wanted to give the children opportunities to encounter new information, and to put information in the context of what they already knew, to "explain the sense" they were making. We moved back and forth between different kinds of experiences: actual observations, lengthy discussions in small groups and with the whole class, study of pictures and text in books, and production of drawings and charts that pulled together what the children were learning.

After the children's initial observations of the tooth marks on the acorns, I brought in books about squirrels, which I put in a book basket (labeled "skwls" by the children, with a drawing). The children began consulting these books at quiet reading time, poring over the pictures. When they found something interesting in a book, they marked the page with a Post-it so they could share the page at meeting. (Earlier in the year, I'd introduced the idea of using Post-its in this way, when children wanted me to show the rest of the class a picture or read a page; there was always a pile of marked books on a shelf near my chair.) When some point came up in a discussion, I would look for a relevant passage.

Next, we went outside the building to look for squirrels and for "things squirrels may have left behind, like acorns." The children drew their finds, and we made a wall display of these drawings. I set out the individual collections on shelves in the science area, so that they could consult these if they wanted to. The class environment began to reflect the squirrel study.

The next week, David worked with the class to make the first chart of things they knew and had observed about squirrels. The children contributed ideas at a meeting, and then four of them worked with David to illustrate their statements. This chart was put up in the classroom too. It was during that week that the squirrel appeared at our window. The children, beside themselves with excitement, were still able to quiet themselves and observe the squirrel's movements. They pointed out the way he scratched his ear with his back leg. Caroline asked about his balance. Brooke asked, "How does the squirrel jump onto the branches?" Hayley asked, "How does the squirrel get such a good grip on what he's holding?"

The following week, we took a second trip, to a stand of oak trees two blocks from the school. Here, we saw lots of squirrels. We'd taken clipboards and paper this time, and the children spent long periods observing the squirrels closely. Since we'd already been reading about squirrels, the children had ideas about what to look for. We saw the squirrels digging, and the children suggested they were burying their acorns. Back in the room, I'd found a page to read to the class about squirrels' burying of nuts. Squirrels, we found out, don't actually remember where nuts are hidden; they use their sense of smell to find buried nuts.

We organized small research groups. David began to meet with them, to read squirrel books and make drawings. I didn't want the children to simply collect random facts, so in organizing the groups, David and I kept in mind the questions we judged to be important, as well as the children's interests. We focused on questions connected to survival: how squirrels get around and protect themselves, how they get food, how they take care of their young. One group made a chart of the parts of squirrels' bodies. Another

Squirrel running down the tree (drawn by Joanna Berman)
Photo by David Vitale-Wolff

group compared humans and squirrels; several children were especially interested in comparing how people and squirrels care for their young.

The class also made a trip to the Museum of Natural History. The two docents with whom we met had a lecture-oriented approach, wanting to convey what they knew about squirrels. What was most valuable and exciting for the children, however, was being able to hold, examine, and draw stuffed squirrels. Despite the fact that the docents drew conclusions *for* the children, the trip enlarged the children's understanding of how squirrels' body structure aids them in escaping predators. The docents pointed out the position of the animals' eyes, on the sides of their heads, and explained how this helps them spot predators and escape quickly. The children could also see—and feel—the squirrels' curved claws (we'd already seen photographs of the claws in our books). Observing squirrels on our earlier trip, the children had noticed how they move down trees head first; they learned from the docents that the curved claws enable them to do this, allowing them to see danger ahead. The children made drawings of the stuffed squirrels.

Back in the classroom, we talked more about how squirrels survive. The children had clearly begun to appreciate the complexities of life for them. As I read a page from one of our books, we found out the answer to Caroline's question about how they balance: they use their tails. One of the children pointed out that their ability to balance meant that they could hold acorns in their front paws while looking around and listening for danger.

The squirrel groups continued to meet; each group produced a chart. There were other forms we could have used for reporting on what had been learned. The children could have made a mural, books, or models. David and I decided to make charts, because they would be big and would display information in a clear, organized way. Also, because some of the younger children were still struggling with representational drawing, we could adapt their contributions to the charts to their levels of skill. David had the idea of using collage as a technique, and this worked really well, for the children already had experience making collages, and they enjoyed cutting and gluing. The charts were shared at meetings and discussed before being displayed, first in the room, and later out in the hall. Eventually, all the charts were put up in the hall.

Every Friday morning, the class dictated a letter to parents about the week's events. I would photocopy the letters, and the children would illustrate them in the afternoon. As the children finished their illustrations, I'd write down their individual dictations. One Friday, I asked the class to say something about the dif-

Working on a squirrel chart
Photo by David Vitale-Wolff

ferences and similarities between squirrels and people. Here are
the comments that went home to parents that Friday:

> Squirrels are different from people. Humans walk on two
> legs, squirrels walk on four. Squirrel skeletons are different
> from people skeletons. People don't have tails, squirrels do.
> Squirrels have two big teeth in the front. People don't.
> Squirrels have their eyes on the side of their head and peo-
> ple have them in front. Squirrels have fur and humans don't
> have fur.
>
> Squirrels have claws and we don't. Squirrels have big
> claws and can climb on trees. Squirrels can climb down trees
> with their front paws first and we can't.
>
> People come out of their mommy's tummies and squir-
> rels come out of mommy's tummies. Squirrels drink milk
> and people drink milk. Squirrels run fast, and people don't.
> But sometimes people run fast.

A Last Trip to the Park

*As always, they ran with the sheer pleasure of running—in the
leaves, under the trees, on the packed earth—not on sidewalk or
playground rubber. It gives them a different sense of freedom, a
sense of more space, of more sky, the quality of freedom that children are offered in nature.*

For city children, there is no substitute for getting close to the
natural world: an open field in a park, a bunch of trees. Nature
provides rich material for the senses: the smells of earth, grass,
and trees; the sounds of crunching leaves and moving branches;
the feeling of the wind; the textures of leaves, bark, and stones;
the sensation of kicking a stone or dragging a stick through dusty
earth. The experience of being in nature touches children in a
way that man-made environments cannot, and adds to the identification between children and the living things they are learning
about.

I had a motive behind this trip: it was my new knowledge of squirrels that prompted its planning. From the books we'd looked at, we learned that squirrels' nests are called drays and that they can be spotted high in the trees. Another teacher told me that she'd seen drays in Riverside Park, so I scouted out the area after school one day. Once I knew what to look for, they were unmistakable, big bunches of old leaves high up among the top branches of oak trees. I've always considered myself good at noticing things, and I always look at trees when I walk in the park. But I'd never before noticed the squirrels' nests.

Our last squirrel trip was in early December. The drays were easily visible because the trees had lost most of their leaves, and the children happily spotted them. We'd brought along peanuts for the squirrels, but they were uninterested. I also wanted the children to draw trees on this trip. Before the trip, I talked to the class about really looking at the different *parts* of the trees.

In the park, the children sat and drew, working hard at their observations. One of them drew the trunk getting narrower higher up! Denay sat at the base of the tree, leaning against the trunk, gazing directly up in the branches, and drawing for a long time.

When the class returned to school, we looked at the tree drawings, and then I put them up for display in the hall, next to the squirrel charts. The drawings were wonderful in their variety: the different perspectives from which the children had drawn, close to the tree or far away; the different points of view. Some of the drawings showed the roots, others showed mostly trunk and bark; a few drawings showed the whole tree, with branches and twigs clearly articulated. Exhibited together, the drawings made a statement not only about children's ability to draw with close attention, but about the individuality of children's ways of seeing trees.

"What About Standards?"

*David wants some kind of answer to a question he's asked before.
What are your goals for the year? I pull off the shelf two or three of
the multitude of lists of learning objectives that I've been handed
over the years, and toss them to him: "Here!"*

There are real standards and phony standards. Phony standards abound, because boards of education feel they are only getting their money's worth if they put fat loose-leaf binders in the
hands of all the teachers in the school system. Teachers' guides,
lists of goals, mandated standards, scope and sequence: I have a
shelf full of them.

These lists of "goals and objectives" may serve a limited function. They may help us think about what we are seeing and
hearing. The better of them may form—in part—the "logical reality" that Dewey postulates. Teachers can use these lists to check
up on the range of what we are thinking about as we plan. If we
accept Dewey's formulation of the relationship between child
and curriculum, we ought to be able to locate children's interests
within the conceptual framework of adult disciplines and knowledge. For example, in studying squirrels, *did* the children learn
that animals' body structures are adapted to their environment,
that animals have evolved ways to find food and defend themselves? To put it differently, when curriculum content is age-
appropriate and multidisciplinary, the concepts listed in these
handouts are likely to be "covered."

For new teachers, guides and lists of goals may lessen the feeling of confusion that is a part of planning. But the danger is that
these will take the place of our actually seeing and hearing the
children in front of us. Rather than thinking about planning by
beginning with our real children in their actual environment,
teachers feel they must teach to the specified, listed goals. As
Karen Gallas puts it, "the curricula and the kits that the experts
present to teachers are heedless of children's questions, develop-

ment and potential as thinkers, and make assumptions about the kinds of experiences they have had before coming to school." [12]

The use of preplanned units of study can prevent teachers from considering whether a concept they have "taught" has been grasped in an *operative* way. This was brought home to me one long-ago fall, after the class had spent weeks studying apples. We'd bought varieties of apples, tasted apples, cooked apples. We'd visited an orchard and picked apples. We had read about how apples develop from seed to blossom to fruit. Yet when children drew pictures after the orchard trip, several of them drew those stereotypical circular green trees, adding red apples, each with a short stem. Their *idea* of an apple, that picture of a red circle topped by a black stem, took precedence over their memory of the apples we'd seen on the trees. These children were not ready to give up the idea. When I'd undertaken the "unit," I had started by looking at and thinking about what children knew or didn't know about apples—their *factual* knowledge. That is, when asked what they knew about apples, they would quickly say, "Apples grow on trees." But I hadn't thought about children's actual understandings, about what they *imagined* to be true, things that they might not explicitly say. I hadn't considered what it meant that the apples children drew on trees were always drawn with those short stems. I might have described children's knowledge this way: children *associate* apples with apple trees but don't know what it means that they *grow* on apple trees. If I'd said that to myself at the start of the study, the study might have proceeded differently, with an emphasis on students' development of understandings of the process of growth.

The standards that I set for myself are never included in the photocopied lists on my shelf. My commitment to attending to children's understanding of a subject is a *real* standard. Another standard: are the material, the theme, and the methods of inquiry meaningful and appropriate for these children? I ask myself all year, about one or another of the activities I've planned, Is this "real kindergarten work"? It's easy to get five- and six-year-old children to do what you ask: they (still) like to please adults. But when work is not appropriate, children get cranky, complain of boredom, quarrel with each other, and roll pencils off the table. These same children will work with concentration and intensity on tasks that they have chosen themselves, or assigned tasks that engage them.

Certain work is "authentic," by which I mean that it respects the child's style of learning and developmental stage; it respects children's intelligence and thinking. Authentic tasks—whether children have initiated them or they were suggested or assigned by the teacher—are congruent with children's intrinsic motivation, their intense desire to learn, explore, and make things. Much of kindergarten work does not have this character. Teachers and programs use cute pictures and artificial tasks to manipulate children, ignoring intrinsic motivations, as if children must be tricked into participation and education must be coercive.

One indication of whether or not a task or topic is authentic is the quality of children's involvement, the degree of energy invested. A child who may otherwise be labeled as having attention deficit disorder will spend a solid half hour or longer working on a puzzle or assembling a construction. A second sign that work is appropriate is children's use of a concept on their own initiative. I have often made a map of "rug spots"—to help children find their assigned spots when they sit on the rug for a story or discussion. The laminated map, with the children's names and photos, is in constant use, consulted when children come to the rug: "No! You sit *next* to Molly, not in front of her!" a child will say, pointing to the relevant spots on the map. The constant use they make of the map indicates to me that this particular symbolic representation makes sense and is an authentic tool for this age. In addition, the children often follow my lead and make their own rug maps, using drawings or names to represent people. They move on to other maps (including treasure maps, of course).

Of course, developmentally appropriate work is not a goal or objective mandated by local or state education authorities. In fact, were we to judge elementary-school kindergarten programs by the standards of authenticity and appropriateness for the age group, the majority of them would fall short. Not only that. The current emphasis on "standards" distracts teachers and educators from the job of looking at the valid educational questions: How do children learn? Where do we see learning occurring? How can we plan for learning?

I have found, in fact, that when children are genuinely engaged with content, when a study begins with their responses and concrete experiences and respects their thinking, the learning that results far exceeds the conceptual outcomes listed for the grade. Themes that arise in children's actual environments or their imaginations and that are pursued in open-ended ways will lead to far-ranging conclusions. The belief that high-quality work results when children's intentions and ways of thinking are respected has been articulated by various progressive educators, who have been warning for many years now of the current tendency to see children as, essentially, scores. I am thinking here of Vito Perrone, an educator associated with the North Dakota Study Group and with the Harvard School of Education; Patricia Carini, who documented children's work at the Prospect School and the Prospect Archive; and Deborah Meier, founder of Central Park East School. These educators have made the case that standards should be dynamic and evolving, and necessarily connected to children's ongoing efforts.[13]

"I *Love* Sea Horses!"

I always want to say something in my Friday letters that will help parents see learning as I do—see the role motivation plays, see the feelings that children bring to the things they care about. I want parents to see that you can't separate the social and emotional aspects of children's functioning. You can look at these aspects, describe them separately—but they occur mixed together.

Real learning is inspiring, particularly when it appears unexpectedly, as if out of nowhere. What does it tell us about the students or the content? In the fall, the class had studied patterns. Since the children were also studying and sorting leaves, we made up a "tree pattern": sycamore, sycamore, oak, oak, oak. This pattern was the class favorite; the children had generated more than a dozen patterns, and then had voted. The children then made a beautiful frieze of this pattern along the back wall, printing the sycamore and oak leaves with black paint on construction paper. In the spring, on our way to the Museum of Natural History one day to see the undersea-animal exhibit, children spontaneously broke into patterned chants as we walked: "octopus, octopus, squid, squid, squid." Others took up competing chants, exuberantly championing their favorite undersea animals, "sea horse, sea horse, sea horse, jellyfish!"

The exuberance that children bring to such moments is also not listed anywhere as an educational objective. To me, it's a vital mark of successful teaching: not something constantly present, but something that is visible from time to time. The real world matters to young children, something that's usually forgotten by the bureaucrats and educational planners, who look at them from afar.

Young children's ability to identify with almost anything is a striking characteristic. I watch my two-year-old grandchild pretend to feed her doll, and as she moves her hand to the doll's lips, her own lips move, *chomp chomp*. That readiness to identify is, I believe, one strand in what motivates children's learning.[14]

As teachers, our job is to see that children's feelings of intense and personal connection are maintained and extended. We can make space for their passionate involvements. We can allow the block builders to sign up for the blocks as often as possible; we can follow up children's desires to learn about those animals—sea horses or dolphins, sharks or giant squid—that particularly intrigue them. By ensuring that children's feelings about content are a central consideration, teachers integrate children's affective and cognitive selves, and curriculum is immeasurably richer. When teachers also ensure that a curriculum provides a multiplicity of approaches, children can make their own sense of a topic, and the topic is likely to appeal to more of them. Their discoveries and conclusions, their idiosyncratic juxtapositions, their eccentric observations and conclusions, and even their public challenges to what we know to be so add unplanned dimensions, layers, and extensions to a study.

More Questions

Eva is studying owls with her first-grade class, and came into my room with a question about how to organize the study. I was chatting with Theresa, who studies birds every year with her second-grade classes. Eva said, I don't want to do it the way I did it last year, where each group just produces a book on one kind of owl; how much does that really mean to the kids? Theresa and I agreed. We said, You don't want to just have a collection of facts, whether about all owls or about each kind. You need to have some way of organizing the information so you're helping the kids see what's important—the way animals survive in a specific setting, the way their body structure helps them survive, the way they rear their young. Theresa said that when her second-graders had discussed birds this year, the kids compared their own lives with those of the birds they were studying, and it added depth to the discussion.

My own list of goals for teachers includes something else that's not in the lists of standards: when children's thinking moves in unexpected directions, teachers must attempt to see the connections. This returns us, of course, to Karen Gallas's requirement that we see children as working to comprehend their world. Years ago, I looked at a piece of writing that a boy was working on, a mess of squiggles and dashes. I would have dismissed it, seen it really as a lot of scribbling, but he was proud. "A food fight!" he said, and I saw it. Mandated curricula don't prepare us to recognize ideas we haven't considered. The emphasis in mandated programs on teaching toward predetermined outcomes militates against unpredictability, as does the teacher's use of prescribed questions and artificial phrases.

How can teachers manage to remain open to possibilities that we can't even imagine? Where do we find the intellectual resources and the resilience to look and listen so intently? How do we go on weighing the intention behind children's confounding formulations, figuring out what question to ask next? My earlier example of missing Max's logic, when he insisted that newborn humans don't open their eyes, shows how easy it is to forget to ask the kinds of questions we need to ask.

In the early 1990s, I met weekly with colleagues with whom I'd initiated an alternative program within the public schools. We talked about *everything*: about individual children, management issues, curriculum. It was staff development at its purest, because no one was doing it *to* us. The meetings gave us a place to *speculate, together*; a place to *ask* questions rather than answer them. Unfortunately, reflective methods are uncommon. The dominant model of staff development is the "coach," whose role is to train new teachers in applying mandated programs.

Trust in children, trust in teachers: teachers must bring trust to their work with children, but teachers also require it from those who run schools. My school allows teachers initiative as to *how* objectives are met, *how* studies may be implemented. The science standard for grades K–2 asks that "students . . . gain the understanding that animals are adapted for survival in their environment" without specifying how the concept is to be taught.[15] However, in many school systems, teachers lack the opportunity to plan curriculum. Not only are the general learning objectives mandated, but so are the specific topics of study and the sequence of activities. In some cases, the guides that teachers are handed and expected to implement use scripted lessons that are to be followed word for word.

Yet teachers require something in addition to faith and encouragement. Just as the children in my class need to think out loud, so do I. This—talk that is public, recorded, and used toward further work—is where curriculum planning *begins*. Practice in this kind of talk—exploratory rather than goal-oriented—should begin in graduate school and continue as a standard practice in schools. If we want discussion of ideas to be a learning standard for children, it should also be a standard for teachers.

5

⌘

The Uses of Literacy:
Constructing Knowledge

Talk: What's the Point?

*Francie's question—Will a tree die if you pick a leaf?—has to be
seen as coming in part out of things we've been looking at and talking about. She wrote it with my help:* WL A TRE DI F U PK A LF? *We
put it on the wall, near the drawings of the rabbit.*

In my elementary school, in the 1950s, every inch of the playground rang with talk—conversation, questions, opinions, in-
sults, arguments—the topics as important as life itself: who liked
whom, what someone had said about you. And there was the organizing of games, and the formal language of play, the jump-
rope and ball-game rhymes and chants (A, my name is Alice . . .),
which were passed year after year from older kids to younger.
Classrooms were *not* for talk. You got in trouble for talking "too
much." You got in trouble for "answering back." You could and
should answer the teacher's questions—raising your hand, wav-
ing it, even whispering, "Ooh! Ooh!" You had to know the answer.
There always was an answer. What characterized talk then (and
in most schools in the world today) was the absolute line between
permissible talk—the responses that depended upon your knowing what the teacher wanted to hear—and the words that spilled
out when we were free.

If the *classroom* is to be a setting in which children's language
will be lively and robust—a central goal, I believe—teachers
must find a variety of occasions for talk that children see as pur-

poseful. One year, when my class had a pet snake, the children arrived one morning and discovered that the snake was dead. The
night before there had been a severe thunderstorm, and as we sat
and talked about the snake's death and the possible causes of it,
the children referred again and again to the storm. Perhaps the
window had been left open, and lightning had entered the room
and struck the snake? Perhaps the noise had killed the snake? The
connections seem absurd to an adult, but it mattered to the children to puzzle out a possible tie between these two natural phenomena. Both the loud nighttime thunderstorm and the snake's
sudden death were consequential events to the children, and both
were inexplicable. Because inexplicable, both events demanded
explanation and therefore, possibly, were connected. It's a general
rule that young children can't sit still for very long, but this
discussion—and others like it over the years—kept the class riv-
eted as the children explored their ideas.

The task for teachers, in addition to providing the forum for
these discussions, is to recognize when subjects command this degree of attention, for individual children or for a particular group
of children. Some talk catalyzes children's listening, hooks them,
perhaps because it is related to their experiences and to topics
they deem significant. One day, the class began to talk about
dreams:

Natasha said, I dreamt about Scooby after I saw the movie and it
was *the movie, and it made me really happy. They all said dreams*
seem real.

The topics that engage children most intently may emerge as
surprises to adults. Wonderful discussions often start as digres-
sions. One day, I'd been reading *Hey, Get Off Our Train*, a story in
which a child sleeps with a stuffed bear. The children began to
talk about the animals or things they took to bed to help them
sleep: *so many were patient about listening to each other—and gen-*
uinely interested. I decided to let the discussion go on because I
saw that the children were so involved in the topic. Was their involvement greater because the talk came about as a spontaneous

response to a storybook? Whether or not that was the case, a crucial element was my decision to stop reading the story to allow the children time to talk. When teachers decide to let the class pursue a topic, they don't always know if the digression will prove valuable. But an unexpected and intense interest may sidetrack a planned activity and end up making the curriculum richer. While teachers won't always know beforehand which topics will prove compelling, planning matters in other ways. When teachers plan for and provide multilayered and stimulating experiences, children will talk, compare, and question with unwavering attentiveness. It was, after all, the children's immersion in seasonal change—our collecting of leaves, nuts, pods—that led Francie to ask her question about leaves and the death of trees.

Talk, in this view, is work: it's what people do to make sense of things. It is both individual and social in nature, because we glean meanings from others' actions and words. As novelist Michael Chabon notes, "Every universe, our own included, begins in conversation."[1] Talk is the quintessential human exchange, beginning with babbles and ending with the mutterings of old age. If one of the primary functions of language is to make sense of experience, children's talk must be viewed as an essential aspect of their development: "The child communicates with himself in and through all his expressive activities. Through this he learns more about himself and the world. . . . He communicates his feelings and ideas both to children and adults through language and other media."[2] Teachers, then, should seek to multiply the possible uses of children's language in a classroom, to think about where and when it occurs and about their own role in expanding the significance of talk. They will take children's talk seriously, and *listen* conscientiously. To the extent that teachers see talk as having this central developmental role, they will aim to expand opportunities for this kind of talk throughout the curriculum and throughout the day.

I listened recently to children excitedly comparing their observations of the behavior of three different liquids: water, oil, and corn syrup. The science guide I was following, *Insights: Hands-On Inquiry Science Curriculum*, developed by the Educational Development Center, is one that is especially open to student exploration.[3] The children had first investigated the behavior of these liquids in closed plastic jars; they had described what they'd noticed by drawing and writing in their science journals and in lively conversations around the tables. When the class came together, many of the children were excited about the "tornado" that formed when they shook the jar of water. The phenomenon intrigued them, and as they talked about it, although I hadn't been prepared for the extent of their interest, I was able to connect the "tornado" with their knowledge of other properties of water.

What is worth mentioning here is not only that children gained information about water's specific properties, not only that they gained a strengthened sense of their own capacities for thinking about physical phenomena generally, but that students' construction of knowledge was furthered by the *unhindered* discussion that was part of the experience. Their talk was exploratory and speculative, it invited participation and associative thinking. This is talk that a teacher genuinely finds worth listening to—and that also allows teachers to know what children actually think: when we discuss the pregnancy of the assistant teacher, Arshea, Sam says a kind of bird comes and brings a baby in a bag. I don't correct him—in the first place, because I imagine he's been told this by someone in his family, which necessitates tact from me. But second, if children are *always* corrected, if discussion is always used to instruct, children will keep what they really think to themselves.

The Daddies Turn into a Mountain

I read the title, The Daddy Mountain, *and said, Hmm, what does that mean? They had lots of ideas:* "Maybe it means the daddies turn into a mountain. Maybe it means . . ." *Then someone said, "A*

*daddy as big as a mountain." The title was so rich because—
maybe—it functioned as a metaphor and as something real.*

Why do *we* care so much about the books we love? What are the
questions we ask ourselves as we read, and what do we talk about
when we talk with friends who've read the same book? Are the
reasons that children read essentially different from the reasons
adults read?

Children, like adults, bring their own experiences to the books
they read or listen to. When children listen to a book in which a
child sleeps with a stuffed dog, and jump in to talk about the objects they sleep with, it's because the content invites them in, and
they speak at length, with deep feeling. It also works the other
way around: something happens, and the discussion that follows
can lead the class to think about a book or poem.

*Denay started the day in tears. We'd begun the new routine of
lining the kids up outside, saying good-bye to parents outside. It is a
big change, and we began it the same day that the kids returned
after a week's vacation. It was a mistake to start a new procedure—
especially such an important one that is about the children's being
more "grown-up"—on the first day back after a week's holiday. In
any case, Denay cried for quite a while. I kept her near me and occasionally said, Denay, please be quieter, and I kept focusing on interesting things, other kids' reports of what they'd done over the
vacation, journal entries, things going on in the room. By meeting
time, she was better, and raised her hand to report on sledding. Then
we had this discussion. Not specifically centered on Denay, but
about times anyone felt "miserable." I'd said, well, we all feel miserable sometimes. Many contributions—about family fights and siblings being mean—led the children to recall the Gwendolyn Brooks
poem "Keziah," which we'd been learning:*

> I have a secret place to go.
> Not anyone may know.
> And sometimes when the wind is rough
> I cannot get there fast enough.

And sometimes when my mother
Is scolding my big brother,
My secret place, it seems to me,
Is quite the only place to be.[4]

In the afternoon, I made copies of the poem, and they illustrated it.

Teachers who are alive to the themes in books and poems can continually help make associations: "Isn't that like . . ." Teachers can notice when themes in certain books resonate; these books are likely to end up bent and worn with use.[5] When children are introduced to books in this way, through connections that are immediate and personal, they grow to become the kinds of readers who consistently bring to books their strong feelings about events in their own lives. They become readers for whom books are powerful sources of information and understanding.

While children love talking about things that have happened *to them*, they also are drawn to discussions of moral dilemmas, if the issues are put in terms that are relevant to them. Fairy tales, in particular, raise these problems, and certain questions take children to the heart of the story. In the fairy tale *Rumpelstiltskin*, the girl makes a deal with the little man: if he spins the straw into gold for her, she'll give him her firstborn baby. Afterward, she marries the king, has a baby, and forgets her promise. When the little man comes for the baby, she tries to get out of her promise. A question arises: if the little man did what he said he'd do, was it OK for her to break her promise? Is it sometimes OK to break a promise, to go back on your word?

Fairy tales teach children that moral decisions are not simple matters. When Little Red Riding Hood is going to her grandmother's house, the wolf encourages her to stop in the woods to gather flowers. The wolf exploits her innocence and goodness. (In a number of fairy tales, innocence and good intentions are punished.) Is the wolf completely to blame, or does Red Riding Hood share responsibility? Should she have known better and followed her mother's instructions to go directly to her grandmother's house? In *Lon Po Po,* a Chinese version of a Red Riding Hood story, the eldest of three sisters tricks the wolf and ends up killing him: the girls pull him in a basket to the top of a tree and then drop the basket. Was that cruel, or did the wolf deserve his fate? Or could both things be true?

In the book *Heckedy Peg* (a made-up fairy tale) as in *Lon Po Po,* children are left at home when the mother goes out (where's the father in these stories?). The children disobey their mother's injunctions, first playing with fire, then opening the door to a witch, who turns them into different foods. In *Heckedy Peg,* it's the mother who saves the children, pretending to cut off her legs, as the witch has insisted, and then recognizing her children in their disguised forms. The family returns home joyously, but did the children invite their fate because they'd been disobedient? What about the mother's having left them alone in the first place? Does her knowledge of her children, and the lengths to which she'll go to save them, make up for having left them? Children's answers are varied, individual, and refer to their own lives as well as what they know from the text itself. Their responses show that they can recognize and appreciate moral shadings, and these discussions give them the chance to weigh costs and options.

Many children's books contain elements of ambiguity. This is most obvious in books that end with the main character waking up, forcing the reader to wonder whether it was all a dream or it really happened: *Hey, Get Off Our Train; No Jumping on the Bed; George Shrinks; The Quilt.* At the end of these books, I ask the children: was it a dream, or real? Their reasoning pulls us back to details of text or illustrations. Ambiguity and ambivalence are, after all, characteristics of experience, and stories with elements of ambiguity allow children to better appreciate the complexities of their own lives.

Often discussions of books bring to mind other books: *Yesterday, I read* Hey, Get Off Our Train: *it was one of those lovely periods when the children are somehow able to muse, and to do it in a group. One response led to another. Oh, someone said, look, the ani-mals get larger, like in* Bark, George.

Allowing time for this kind of musing is crucial, I think. It im-plies the teacher's trust in the children to "get it." It recognizes the importance of letting talk go; it shows faith in their ability to consider, to take things seriously—to make their own experience something that can be at the center of school, of work.

Books open up a space in which children can consider a vast array of meanings—moral, aesthetic, emotional. By grappling with that content, by immersing themselves in the multiple worlds offered in books, children build powerful links between what they already know and think and some new and more com-plex thought or construction. As they talk about books, they at-tend to the plot, to each other, to spoken language, and to possible interpretations. They add to and qualify each other's remarks, and their insights accumulate. Reading books becomes a common endeavor; by the end of the year, it involves all the children, even those whose receptive and expressive language is poorer. Talk-ing about books in this way helps create a pool of knowledge and associations.

Our aim, in the course of the year, is to help children build up the ability to listen to each other. To accomplish this, teachers must perform an impossible task: balance relevance and account-ability with the openness that allows children to develop their thoughts. If teachers intervene too often or too persistently, chil-dren may be discouraged from pursuing their own thoughts or building on others' thinking. If we never ask questions, reframe statements, or ask for clarification or comments, we end up with self-referential and rambling talk, and children become bored and cease to listen. I want to give children space for personal expression and exploratory comments, while at the same time fostering their development of discussion skills and the ability to respect other speakers and add to discussions.

How do we help children participate in discussions as listeners and speakers? In pursuing this goal, teachers must be flexible, at times insisting on raised hands, at other times allowing children to jump in. We have to judge the quality of discussions. Are children interpreting? Are they responding to each other? Our long-term goal is for children to learn to attend to narrative in an active way, to choose what merits particular attention, and to ask, What did that mean? Perhaps children's development of the ability to interpret is fostered when they bring to conversations about books, and eventually to their own reading, a readiness for the unexpected.

Themes in Literature

I've been reading Leo Lionni books to them—today A Color of His Own, *yesterday* Fish Is Fish, *especially appropriate because of our tadpoles. I said, before beginning to read, I want you to think about the things that are the same in* A Color of His Own *and the other Leo Lionni books. Afterward, the comments were wonderful: there are two animals that get together; one animal wants to change, to be different from who he is (also true for* Alexander and the Wind-Up Mouse *and for the snail in* The Biggest House in the World*). I add that they want to change because they aren't happy being who they are, which is definitely a Lionni theme. Denay adds that the characters in* Little Blue and Little Yellow *also change—and are also together—and their being together is what makes them change. Denay produces this synthesis, yet it's built on what everyone had said before.*

One of the first books I read every fall is Lionni's *Little Blue and Little Yellow.* The two friends are torn paper circles. One day, Little Blue says good-bye to his family and goes off to find Little Yellow. When they find each other, they hug—and as they overlap, they turn green and become one circle. They return to their homes, going first to Little Blue's house, and then Little Yellow's, but both families reject them: "Where is our Little Blue?" "Where is our Little Yellow?"

At this point, the children are mesmerized, struck by the tragedy. Independence, so developmentally significant a goal, is not without risks. This short book with its cheery colors dramatically lays out the potential losses in life. Happily for the two friends, the solution comes—ironically, through their sadness. They cry, and their tears are torn yellow and blue scraps. They pull the pieces together to become once more Little Blue and Little Yellow, their old, separate, primary-color selves, whereupon their glad parents welcome them.

So many themes in this one book: friendship, identity, transformation, loss and abandonment, perseverance, recognition, home. What strikes me, too, is the unity between the themes and Lionni's collaged illustrations. The torn edge, Lionni wrote in his autobiography, "gave a certain vitality." [6] The illustrations are simple and uncluttered, in tune with the seriousness of the themes, and colorful and bouncy, in tune with the playfulness of the characters. Lionni made up the story for this, his first children's book, when he was taking care of his young grandchildren for the first time. Heading home with them on the train, he tore pages from a magazine to illustrate his story, and story and illustrations retain the immediacy of a grandfather's voice. This unity of spirit between illustration and theme is a hallmark of many of the finest children's books.

Lionni, in his autobiography, writes that as he continued to produce books for children, he "became ever more conscious of the problems children face and the importance of the messages we send to them." [7] At times, Lionni's books can be didactic. But children tune out the more explicit messages and take in his ability to speak to their concerns.

Other authors, too, write about transformations. The plots of many of William Steig's books hinge on magical changes (*Sylvester and the Magic Pebble* and *The Amazing Bone*). *Certain authors write books that lend themselves to analysis by children: Steig, with his magic pebbles and talking wishbones. Do children especially like transformation—is that why these writers take it*

*as a topic? Perhaps the subject has weight for children because
their lives are all the time transforming. Children certainly have
a transforming effect on us, parents and teachers, making us act
better or sometimes worse, pressing us always to do some magic to
make life be what they want it to be—utterly pleasurable, utterly
fair.*

Children's books present other significant themes—separation
and reconciliation, rejection and acceptance, independence and
connection, conflict, irreconcilable differences, power and vulnerability. Are these themes so different from those that form the
basis of books that adults love? If we care about children's reading, our concern has to be with two goals that trump other goals:
reading for pleasure and reading for the recognition of personal
meaning (and these are undoubtedly connected).

When we support these goals, we find children choosing a vast
range of books: books about princesses, books about dinosaurs,
books about cars and rocket ships. One year, each time we went to
the school library to borrow books, one boy chose books about war:
armies, soldiers, World War II bombers, tanks, and missiles. His
interest propelled other boys in the same direction, and as the
class returned from each library visit, several five-year-old boys
would be clutching books about war. This boy showed similar
concerns in the classroom: building with blocks or other construction materials, he never failed to include spots for weapons. Although I sought to understand *why* defense mattered so much to
him, and attempted, when we went to the library, to draw him toward other sorts of books, I didn't tell him no, no more army
books, no more books about guns. For this child, the theme of defense and protection was paramount, and he looked for books that
addressed it. Whatever it is that influences our choice of books, I
have come to see that a censoring interference with choice can
have the consequence of weakening the literary alliances we
want to build, alliances between teacher and children, between a
child and other children—alliances that, over time, may enlarge
a child's sense of what books offer.

We may influence children's choices, but we don't have the power to dictate what moves them. We do have other powers: to note which books they pick out, to consider carefully the books we decide to read to the class, to craft the questions we ask, and to listen carefully to the points children make during book discussions. Last, we can bring to these decisions and discussions our own openness to the topics children care about, which are, after all, recurrent *human* themes: the struggle against adversity in *Brave Irene*, the ambivalence about parental love in *The Runaway Bunny*. Certainly there are appropriate books that address children's concerns about defense and safety.

Just as adults have favorite books, a class may discover a book to which it responds passionately. At the beginning of this year, I'd read the class *Bark, George*, by Jules Feiffer. On the first page, the mother dog commands her puppy to bark. Instead, the puppy issues a variety of barnyard oinks, baas, and moos. The children howled with laughter at the comical incongruity of sounds; they roared when the mother, exasperated, covers her ears with her paws. Desperate, she brings her son to a vet, who reaches down the puppy's throat and pulls out animal after animal. I read the book several times, and each time, the children responded. Seeing their gleeful reaction, I looked for other books with elements of transgressive humor: *No Jumping on the Bed* and *No, David*. The children were delighted with these characters (who refused to obey or, in the case of the dog George, were unable to obey). The children's shared response helped define them as a class. Though I lent my conscious support, it was the books themselves, their themes and humor, that brought the children together.

Literacy Goals

We made bookmarks for Father's Day. I said they were to be for an "important male person in your life." Denay made hers for her three-year-old brother, writing—a perfect sample of authentic writing!—You always make a mess.

Each year, a number of children in my class begin to read and write. I'm honest with parents when I meet with them at the start of the school year: I don't *expect* children to start reading and writing in kindergarten. My ambitions are both smaller and larger. I want children to think about books and talk about books; I want them to know the difference between fiction and nonfiction, to care about the characters and their motives, to use books for research. I want them to develop, or build on, a love of books that will last a lifetime. I want my students to see writing as something that's natural to them, whether they are taping notes on classroom walls or labeling their buildings. I want children to learn alphabet letters and most of the sounds, and to gain a sight vocabulary of words they can recognize (the names of children in the class, and some of the words that appear in the morning message). But, I emphasize to parents, my aims in this area are integrated with larger intellectual goals: children's growth in confidence as learners, their growth in focus and a sense of resourcefulness; their development of a rich imaginative life; their growth in the ability to express what they believe and to integrate new information.

In defining my purposes, I look back to curriculum guides from the 1950s through the 1980s. These guides recognized that, for young children, communication of experience matters more than acquisition of specific "decoding" skills. These earlier materials used the term "language arts" rather than "literacy," with the implication that *reading* is not everything. Here is what *Early Childhood Education*, a pamphlet produced by the New York City Board of Education in 1958–1959, said:

> At the kindergarten level, oral rather than written communication is the foremost language need. During this period in a child's life he is making complex social and emotional adjustments. . . . This physical and emotional development . . . may be interfered with if pressure is put on the child for the mastery of the mechanics of reading at this

age. . . . The language program, therefore, emphasizes the development of concepts through experiences.[8]

Similarly, in 1970 in *The Teaching of Young Children: Some Applications of Piaget's Learning Theory*, teachers are advised against setting aside a period of the day for writing: "The opportunity to write when an interest and the desire to communicate is at its height will influence the quality of children's writing. If children are required to write at certain times during the day, or every day, they will tend to write the empty and trivial."[9]

In my classroom, children are engaged with language—with talk, books, writing—as one *part* of a program of active making and doing. Language-related activities should be a part of a rich curriculum, not just a means to acquisition of literacy skills.

Fish Juice: Talking, Reading, Writing, and Drawing About Real Things

Brooke found an interesting page in one of the whale/dolphin books, a picture of whales stranded on a beach, with people, including kids, helping by pouring salt water onto the whales' backs. She showed it to the class, and then I brought out a news clipping I'd saved about a dead whale on a Long Island beach. The article had been in my folder for over a month, but I kept forgetting to show them. This was the exact right moment. Caroline said, It's a baleen whale! I asked the job people, Lila and Philip, to cut the picture out neatly and put it up on the bulletin board (I'd torn it out of the newspaper). When I looked up later, Lila had glued it on construction paper, made holes in the top corners, and hung it up with yarn, like a framed picture. Later I read them Amos and Boris, Steig's story of a friendship between a mouse and a whale, a recycling of Aesop's story of the lion and the mouse: when the whale is beached, his friend the mouse rounds up animals to push him back into the water.

When children focus on real things, activities grow directly out of their desire to gain knowledge and to communicate. Reading

and writing are seamlessly connected, and both are related to children's talk and graphic representations. Children's explorations—
through their talk, reading, writing, drawing, construction—can
be the dynamic center of classroom life, a part of each day. The
teacher's job is to anticipate where these studies can take the class
(and as noted earlier, to put in place routines and structures that
allow children to explore).

By reading, I mean the *use* of books. In the spring, we began
our study of undersea life by adding to the class library nonfiction
books about undersea creatures. When we visited the school library, children searched for books on their subjects. Over several
days, I read the class *Baby Whale's Journey*, a book that is as suspenseful as any fiction book in its telling of the baby whale's birth
and survival. The story spilled over into drawings and writing.
Rosie wrote, "Baby whales are born alive." Other children drew
the mother whale pushing her baby up to the surface to breathe.
They wrote down their questions: Graham and Denay came up
with the question, Are whales and dolphins different? As we studied undersea animals, children used quiet reading time to go
back, again and again, to specific books. Once again, the shelf
next to my chair was piled high with books, the "saved" pages
marked with Post-its.

Children's writing, in this context, is an extension of their talk;
it is linked to drawing, and both are rooted in experiences that
matter. I brought in mackerels, and we dissected them. "Ugh!"
and "Yuck!" the children said, as blood and guts squished out.
Many of the children were eager to touch the dead fish, others
wouldn't do it: *Interesting, today, to watch how differently each
child approached the fish. Hayley didn't even want to look too
closely—her eyes kept zipping away, though she smiled. Mark and
Rosie plunged fingers in and poked at the eyes.*

Touching the eye, in particular, fascinated and disgusted them.
They learned anatomy viscerally: they saw the semicircle at the
back of the eye and apprehended firsthand the way eyes are set
into sockets and, as a consequence, the way the eye socket protects

the eye. They felt for themselves how principles of motion explain the overlapping of the fish's scales, so the water would flow smoothly over the fish's body as it swims forward. Teaching this way, I don't doubt for a second that learning takes place in an integrated way and that it is immediate and vital.

I had the children draw the dissected fish and asked them to label their drawings. Bits of fish juice ended up on the papers: the records took a very material form. Similarly, the juice of real experiences colors children's writing about real things. Their writing is informed by deep feelings, because the connections they have forged are unique and passionate: *As they write about real things—not* just *about themselves—their writing is taking off.* They are motivated to write whether or not these are positive experiences.

When children study real things, their own interests and passions dominate their approach to the subject. I let them choose which undersea animal they wished to learn about: several girls and one boy chose to study whales and dolphins; a group of boys

Records of the fish dissection
Photo by Julie Diamond

wanted to study squids and octopuses. The shark-and-ray group was co-ed, but different children had different interests. Some children were fascinated by the dried shark egg cases that I'd brought in, and attempted to trace them. Several children were intent on finding out which sharks are dangerous to people and which are not. The aggressive great white caught the attention of some children; others liked the odd hammerhead. A few children wanted me to read about the huge, peaceful basking shark, which swims along with its large mouth open. I brought some children outside to the hall, and we used rulers and masking tape to mark off the length of the basking shark. As each group met, the children looked through the books, finding photographs they wanted to know about and doing drawings. The finished drawings were shown to the class, and soon covered the blackboard.

My end goal was the production of a book that would be photocopied and sent home. I'd first made sure we had appropriate resource books, and I familiarized myself with them, to help children find relevant material. When I met with each group to look at books and read bits of text, I asked questions that focused on aspects of behavior and body structure related to survival, and encouraged children to make comparisons and draw conclusions. I asked them about their drawings: What does this show? What do you want it to say? I organized the numerous drawings and asked for some specific pages—we have to show whales' blowholes! Each research group would write one chapter; there would be four altogether. I made sure there was at least one page per child. I typed transcriptions of the children's writing. When the book was complete, I showed it to the class. The children suggested titles, and we voted: *Undersea Life*. Last, a parent volunteered to make photocopies. The book was terrific, combining detail ("Sharks and rays have 5 gill slits on each side") with appreciation of the diversity of ocean life. I played a crucial role in creating it, but the energy was theirs. The book was a product of their discoveries; it grew out of their innate desire to find out, and share what they'd found out. In the process of communicating

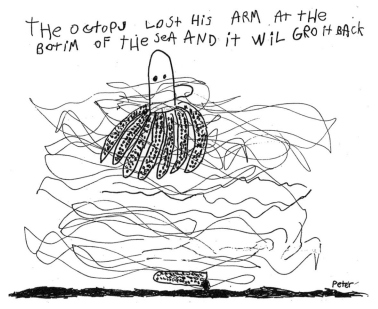

THe octopɕ Lost His ARM At tHe Botim oF tHe seA AND it WiL GRo H BAck

A page from the class book *Undersea Life*
Drawing by Peter Dinella

what they knew, the children learned the process of bookmaking and became co-authors.

When writing and drawing grow from children's real involvements, their work has a distinctive point of view; they begin to develop a unique voice and vision. Some children like to *know*, precisely and scientifically. These children are concerned with correct representation. They draw the orca's pattern of black and white with remarkable accuracy. For others, fantasy holds sway: their dolphins always have smiley faces. Their identification with animals has a magical, imaginative quality. They appreciate the eccentricity of sea horses and jellyfish, the drama of animal life, its beauty and danger. Whatever the source of their interest, the power of children's feelings keeps them focused; writing, they search for words to describe their thoughts; they stretch their knowledge to match their understandings, and come up with comparisons and metaphors. At the end of the year, the children observed caterpillars: *I staple extra pages to their caterpillar journals—What do you see? What do you notice? Use the magnifying glass! Nia wrote, last week, "He is like a line." And this week, "He is fat as a pumpkin!" She hadn't before been capable of that level of writing.* Authentic work: Rex, in a previous kindergarten class, was observing his caterpillar as it crawled in its vial. "What's the caterpillar doing?" I asked. "It is," he said, and later wrote, "thinking about its life as a butterfly." It is lived experience that gives writing energy and muscle, style and personality.

This level of work, I believe, is a result of a class environment that presents numerous opportunities for children to find out what they think. It is, I believe, children's *talk* that consistently knits the class together as it highlights their developing ideas. With a different class, some years ago, after the children had been observing the metamorphosis of caterpillars for some time, one girl asked me, "Why do caterpillars change into butterflies?" I brought the question to the class. I transcribed the discussion for our weekly letter to families (just about everyone in the class had something to say):

Because everybody grows up.

But furniture doesn't grow up.

Food doesn't grow up.

Yes, it does.

Food grows 'cause it's a living thing, and plants grow because they are living things just like humans except they can't walk.

Or touch stuff or talk.

Caterpillars change because they have to do it.

When they're like babies, the caterpillars are like babies, and the butterflies are like grown-ups.

Caterpillars change because that's what they look like when they are grown up.

Because the caterpillar could get more beautiful to fly.

Other kinds of animals grow too.

People change when they grow up.

Only animals have to grow up.

Books don't grow. Fish grow up.

Snacks or your clothing can't grow.

Paper, buildings, or instruments don't grow.

Caterpillars change into butterflies because they need a change.

It's like in their bodies, they have the wings, and when they grow up, the wings come out.

Caterpillars need to change 'cause like a creature that's hungry could get it and eat it, so they need to fly so they could find a place to hide, so the creature won't eat it.

If a caterpillar didn't turn into a butterfly, the caterpillar would be too slow and a bird would eat it.

Caterpillars, if they don't turn into butterflies, if a bee is trying to sting them, a caterpillar could stick its feet because its feet have points, so it could stick its feet in the bee, so the bee can't sting.

Butterflies need to fly because when a creature or a bird is trying to eat it, it could fly away.

The transcription illuminates what children do in discussions. The second statement, "But furniture doesn't grow up," was one child's facetious rejoinder, but its meaning was taken up as children went on to distinguish different categories and explore what features distinguish the categories. The class is considering, in effect, the characteristics of living things, the notion of growth and change, and later in the discussion, how animals' body structures help them survive. While the children work together to piece out their thoughts, individual contributions constitute leaps of thought. "Because the caterpillar could get more beautiful to fly," while grammatically confusing, introduces the notion that butterflies' ability to fly is what the change is all about. The children return to the general topic of growth and change but then explore the significance of flight. The child who made the comment about the caterpillar getting "more beautiful to fly" was a child who spoke English poorly and was often impulsive and inattentive during discussions. Here, he was absorbed, contributing a valuable insight that moved the discussion forward. Without the transcription, I don't think I would have noticed his comment.

The children used journals to write about themselves. I introduced journal writing in October, explaining that journal entries are about themselves and their lives. They wrote in journals in an organized ongoing way, making two entries a week, one on Thursday morning and one at home, over the weekend. I told them that an entry was to be about something that really happened or was going to happen, about something real. "Real" was not always so apparent:

There's Sam, doing a drawing of a monster zapping him. I say, No, something real, do another journal entry—and he draws a monster. I say, Draw something that really happened! He draws a rain forest and writes a string of random letters. I accept that, and say, Rrrrrain, like in Ricky—and he writes an R.

Children's journal writing reveals things that surprise me:

Alyssa is grabby and critical. The other children don't like her. But she writes in her journal about going to Mark's birthday party, and that's the page she chooses to share. It's clear she likes him and likes having been invited. I wouldn't have predicted it—her admiration for Mark, who is one of the nicest, kindest children in the class. I think about it in the afternoon, when she snubs Sam and is once again unable to find a partner.

We keep the journals in a bin and have "journal share" in the morning or last thing in the day. I try to have every child share at least once a month. To keep track of who's shared, I keep a class list on a clipboard; the children stamp the date next to their names when they've had their turn. A child talks about an entry, shows the drawing, and calls on two children for "questions or comments." The children draw themselves walking to school with parents, celebrating special events, eating in restaurants. Reading the entries or talking to the children, I learn what they notice and what they care about. Graham says, "I was in an airplane and I saw a forest or a rain forest or a jungle when I was in the air looking out the window." Someone asks, "Where were you going?" He answers, "Nebraska or Cape May." I listen carefully to the questions; in the course of the year, the children grow in their ability to ask pertinent questions. Rosie describes building an igloo, and one child asks, "What happened to the igloo?" When we write in journals on Thursday mornings, some children do all the writing themselves. Others write one or two words, ME and MOM, and turn to the adults to take dictation for the rest. Some dictate, going on and on, until I say, "OK, that's all I have time for." Toward the end of the year, we're very lucky—another teacher, Phil Firsenbaum, who's been supporting teachers' use of technology, has volunteered to work with the class. He documents journal entries and children's comments, and produces a book with one page of photographs and text from each child. A parent photocopies the book, and every child takes a copy home. They not only have their own journals, but a record of the journal keeping of everyone in the class.

Thinking about Language Acquisition

I am struck by the talk of children whose English is poor. How do they explain to themselves what's going on? We were talking about a book yesterday, and I asked, Sam, can you tell us. . . . His answer showed his lack of comprehension—of what we call comprehension—because he had obviously made up some story of what the book said. For several days, he has been drawing people, cutting them out, gluing them on construction paper. Yesterday I sat with him, and we used heavy paper to make the men stand, to guard the bridge Sam had made. For the bridge, Sam had cut paper into strips, and he'd placed the little men alongside; the bridge went from one table to the next. So I folded and glued pieces of heavy paper to make triangular stands for his men.

There are children whose language use puzzles us. Is something wrong? How wrong? What are our options, and what are our responsibilities? If I describe children's talk as one way of making sense of the world, what do I do when I can't *find* a child's sense?

Sam was a small, slight child whose expression was often blank. By late October, he knew the names of only a few of his classmates. He played alone for the most part. When he attempted to make friends, asking others to be his partner on line, he was often rebuffed. During discussions, Sam played with the Velcro on his shoes. I wondered, could he not decipher, not process, public talk? Yet if I focused only on his deficits, was aware only of what he *couldn't* do, I couldn't teach him. To be fair, and to be helpful, I had to *observe* his talk and his listening, describe it without judging it. What did he actually say? What did he do? I had to see his language behavior as a mystery, something I didn't yet comprehend, to which I can't immediately assign a name:

I call kids to go to snack, saying, "People with four letters in their names may go." Sam looks at the sole of his shoe and says, Me!— because he has a number on the sole of his shoe. That's part of the puzzle of Sam: he heard that one piece "four" and took that in, filling in the rest; as he heard it, I was calling people who had numbers somewhere on their clothing. His ability to express himself, however inadequately, masks his inability to process spoken language when the environment gives him no clues about what to do.

I met Sam's mother and big brothers (he is a much younger sibling, with a brother in high school and a brother in college), all of whom spoke English fluently. His mother worked, and he was cared for by his Spanish-speaking grandmother. A language picture emerged: conversation in Spanish with his grandmother; Spanish-language television; some English conversation with others in his family, and his presence during English-language conversations he probably didn't understand; attendance at a daycare center the previous spring, where English was spoken—but where, I found out when I spoke to the center's director, he was frequently absent. He had relatively little experience playing with peers. How did that affect his language development?

Children with Hispanic surnames are mandated for testing as "English language learners." Sam tested out; his score was above the cutoff for services. But in the classroom, when we talked at meeting or I read a story, Sam concentrated on other things, like the Velcro on his sneakers. Words passed him by; he would catch occasional words, but the meanings would escape him. By mid-December, he knew the other kids' names, but I noticed something else: *Yesterday he had a complaint about Lila. He came up to me, "She . . ." I said, "Who?" He pointed to her. I asked him, "What's her name?" Sam: "Lila." So, that pointing, is it partly that recalling words requires effort? Is it partly that he's not used to making an effort?*

I talked more to his mother, who complained that his grandmother "spoiled" him. I speculated: did he *learn* to be passive in connecting to his social surroundings, and therefore passive in drawing inferences from the environment? Had he taught himself to tune out? I asked his mother if she would agree to have him tested for a learning disability. Did he have an impairment that affected his ability to recall words? Was his solitary play a *result* of a problem with language acquisition, not the other way around? Or could both things be true?

I'd waited until December to set in motion the process of getting Sam evaluated. For another child in the class, I'd recommended evaluation immediately, in September. This child spoke English without hesitation or accent, but had been exposed to two other languages and spoke in a confused and repetitive syntax, as if he'd memorized phrases. His discussion comments were widely off topic and he didn't follow directions. I spoke to his mother, who agreed to refer him. The decision is always hard: which children will benefit from a supportive, language-rich environment, and which need special help? If English is a child's second language, does difficulty with English cloak a language processing disability, or does the child simply need time? In general, I'm slow to refer children. I see language growth as part of overall growth during the kindergarten year. Perhaps, too, I'm reluctant to cede

part of what I see as my role, unless I'm convinced that intervention is required; children who receive services normally spend
some time out of the classroom. Some teachers are critical of the
special-education system. They feel that children, particularly
boys from low-income or non-English-speaking homes, end up as
"special ed" students not because they are unable to learn but because classrooms don't accommodate a range of learning needs.
Once in a special-education track, these children are likely to remain in special education for their school careers. Many educators
believe it's wrong to describe children by their failures rather
than their strengths. The problem for me is figuring out whether
a particular child might benefit from services.

Sam's evaluation process was not complete until the spring. The
question remained: how could the classroom environment be better adapted to his language needs? I thought about what his
mother had told me about his previous language experiences.
Language growth is spurred by the intensity of children's desire
to communicate. Children who are energetically engaged with
others use language constantly to mediate play. I listen to children in the playground as I babysit for my four-year-old granddaughter: "You mean *ev-ry-thing* to me!" one child shouts, and
another, "*You* can't catch me!" The language is ritualized and
repetitive, but because play is innately variable, involving constantly shifting situations and a shifting cast of other children,
language develops alongside play. Perhaps Sam missed out on this
daily use of language as a social *tool*.

Viewing Sam's language as part of the way he *is* in the world,
my aim was to enlarge his classroom role. In the words of Lillian
Weber, I wanted him to expand his "use [of] language in the
school, working at different things, explaining [his] work, being
listened to." [10] Weber, a New York City educator, was pivotal in the
1960s and 1970s in bringing to Americans' attention the reforms
in British schools. In "Comments on Language by a Silent Child,"
she analyzes the home and school environment in relation to lan-

guage acquisition. Her picture of language use is colored by her memories of her own childhood language use—and by her sympathy for children as they take in, and later wield, the words that are, as Weber puts it, a feature of the "human context we share." Language, she writes, "occurs around an object": "speech clots out like cream in clumps around a context." [11] Weber sees young children's language as an inseparable part of their ongoing lives. In learning language, she writes, a child brings "all the drama of his existence." [12]

Weber advises teachers to work in ways consistent with children's existing language uses, consistent with what the child has already achieved: otherwise, "we may actually be *cutting across* the path of their development, instead of using it." [13] When differences exist between school language uses and the language used in the family, it is especially necessary for teachers to help children develop an inclusive framework, a framework of common meanings, and also to help them build "diversified" language, which includes "higher level language, lower level language, street language, love language, this kind of language, that kind of language." [14]

To help Sam, I needed to see purpose in his behavior and enlarge my definition of "language"—to *read* meaning in his actions and insert myself in those actions, so that we could add spoken language as a functional accompaniment. It's the role I played in the description earlier: I sat with him as he worked and asked him what he was doing. I extended his play by suggesting we use heavy paper to make the guards stand. Through our work *together*, language "clots out." Just as Sam built a paper bridge, I made a bridge to more explicit, expanded language use. What was initially implicit for him became public, first between the two of us, and later, between him and others. In January, when we were talking about babies, Sam jumped into the discussion: *Today, Sam talked about Vanessa's little brother and said, When he's five, you'll be ten! I said, Yes, and when he's ten. . . . He added something else about getting bigger and growing.*

Sam's evaluation was complete in the spring: he did just well enough *not* to qualify for services. By the end of the year, he made relevant comments more frequently. He could read the names of the other children in the class. He was a master cleaner-upper, highly organized, expert in his knowledge of the room and of where everything went. Yet he continued to seem out of it at times, and to have difficulty processing talk addressed to the class as a whole. Although he knew the alphabet, he wrote only with adult help in sounding out words. In first grade, Sam was in an adjacent classroom, and I informally followed his progress. The greater demands placed on him in first grade to process verbal directions made his weakness in this area stand out. His first-grade teacher referred him again. This second evaluation indicated a language processing disability, and Sam received services.

However, whether or not children have shown evidence of a language disability, teachers must plan for children whose language use is of concern, and must ensure that the classroom environment fosters language growth. We listen actively to what a child *seems* to be saying. Our responsibility—to gain children's trust in our listening—remains even when their language facility is excellent. When Adam asked me, "Are there really powers?" he trusted me to listen to his question and take it seriously. When Raquel whispered, before she shared her journal, "Will you help me read the words?" she knew I'd whisper my reply. In teaching young children, we should keep in mind two central uses of literacy: helping them to know the world and to make themselves known.

6

❦

The Uses of Literacy: Reading and Writing

Names and Other Words

The words they choose come out of months of building castles in the block area, drawing princess after princess. The words are appropriated by individuals from the culture of the class. You have to create the culture, as we have begun to do, through experience, and descriptions of experience. This is knowledge about a way of living, showing children that they can name anything, that there's nothing they can't look at and think about.

Teacher, the best-known book by New Zealand teacher and writer Sylvia Ashton-Warner, describes the use of a "key" or "organic vocabulary" to teach reading and writing. Every morning, the children asked for words, from *jet* to *house* to *bomb!* The words, which Ashton-Warner wrote on heavy paper, became the first words children learned to read and write. Ashton-Warner denies she was doing anything new, citing Egyptian hieroglyphics, which she calls one-word sentences, and Helen Keller's first word, *water*, which she says was a one-word book.[1] (The educator Paolo Freire utilized a similar technique to teach reading to adults. In Chile, he had peasants write words with their tools "on the dirt roads where they were working.")[2] "First words," Ashton-Warner writes, "must have an intense meaning."[3]

Children can collect words, just as they collect other things. Some children, of course, come to school knowing how to read and write a few words, but in my classroom, the first written words children officially meet are names—their own and each others'. This begins on the first day of school, as I hold up the name cards. Reading these cards becomes a morning routine. When we take attendance in the fall, the name cards provide countless reading lessons: *We read the name cards, which they are becoming adept at. They find similarities—visual and auditory: Mark and Marcus, Rosie and Francie and Jamie. It is a way of playing with names, with sounds, just as the art work is a way of playing with shapes.*

Their interest in each other moves naturally into informal study of these words. As we talk about the names, I introduce or reinforce knowledge of letters and sounds. The children comment on names with the same letter ("I have an *a* in my name, too"); they compare long and short names. We look at the placement of letters ("Marcus's *m* is the first letter of his name, Adam's *m* is the last letter"). Soon, they begin to read and write each other's names. Their friends' names are the first that they read and write; the work of reading and writing occurs in the context of these new relationships.

The children write list after list of names, for all sorts of reasons, taking the plastic can of name cards and copying the names with great care. They stick magnetic letters on a board to match the letters on the cards; they print names using letter stamps. I initiate some of these activities, but others are invented by the children: Denay makes her list of children in the Click Club, and ambitious Lila makes her own set of name cards. In the late fall, as children begin to wear winter coats and need help zipping, two children survey everyone, using a class list on a clipboard, and then make a chart, Who Can Zip? They write the names and add the children's xeroxed photographs; as more children learn to zip, their names and photos are added. The chart is consulted at the end of the day when children need help zipping. Other surveys and graphs inevitably follow: Who can tie shoes? Who lost a tooth? How many letters in your name? What is your favorite letter?

Writing children's names
Photo by Julie Diamond

Word cards are used to label class collections of leaves, seeds, and nuts. When we study the family, we need family words. One small basket holds blank index cards. Some other years, in the spring, I followed Ashton-Warner's example by giving out word cards, which the children kept in shoe boxes. Once a week, children could get new words if they could read their old words. They would practice, reading their words to each other. One year, we stuck the words up on the closet doors; each child had one section of a door. The children liked it, but the cards kept ending up on the floor, like snow. Still, I liked the idea of all these words up and visible: *castle, dragon, robot, princess, tiger, mom, love.* They borrowed words from each other when they wanted to spell something; the words were a cross-section of the class culture.

These are *their* words; the children chose them, and I made no judgments. In the first-grade classrooms, "word wall" words come from the literacy materials that the school uses; thus the words are the same from room to room, except for the names of the children in the class. Visiting a first-grade classroom, I notice that the word *mom* is included, but not *dad*, and I ask about it. The teacher replies that she was concerned about the feelings of children in her class who lived with single mothers. But what is the message about children's ability to acknowledge experience? What if a child wanted to write "I miss my dad"? And what's the point of word lists if words aren't generated by children in the class, if the words don't reflect their lives? For Ashton-Warner, word cards were a sign of her faith in children's wish to represent things and feelings that had meaning.

When reading begins with real things, children are more likely to remember the words, because of their associations with what the words represent. I engineer different contexts in which children can see and hear these words. Once a week, we do a secret code word. Children use a "secret code" sheet, on which each alphabet letter is next to a corresponding number (A—1, B—2, etc.). They copy that week's secret code numbers and figure out the word. Here, too, I start with children's names, because these are so familiar, and then move on to other words: *Today our secret code words were* shark *and* dolphin. *Vanessa brought up her paper with* shark *on it but said* dolphin. *I said, Well, does it begin with a D? Certain words—now, for this group, not only* love, mom, me, *but* shark, dolphin—*are part of the environment; they've been given a context. These are words they hear and see, that are needed for something they are doing, words in a favorite song or poem, or words connected with an activity or trip. Each different context adds a layer of meaning, adds hooks to memory, until a child says, "I know that word."*

Writing on the message board
Photo by Julie Diamond

My job is to introduce children to reading, not to teach it. I encourage the acquisition of reading and writing, but I don't push; I've seen too many children who weren't ready to read, pushed by parents or academically oriented preschools, who've ended up bored with books. But I use a variety of written texts to help children move toward reading. On the morning message, children see the same words daily (*today, school, is*), and after reading the message, children take turns locating and circling specific words. By the spring, I expect children to read a number of these words, and I begin to omit some letters or words for children to fill in. They may add sentences to the message about birthdays or wiggly teeth. Some mornings, if I haven't written the message, children volunteer to write the entire message. Other written material—charts, signs, poems, chants, songs, labels, messages for holiday cards, books—help children gain confidence in their ability to recognize certain important words.

In the spring, I provide baskets of beginning readers, at various levels of difficulty. (Teachers can also write, as Ashton-Warner did, simple readers about the children in the class.) At quiet reading time, I sit with an individual or two or three children, and we read these books, working together to figure out new words. I note the strategies of individuals: Do they look at the pictures when they're stuck? Do their guesses make sense? Do their guesses reflect sounds associated with the letters in the text?

My central goal in all these activities is for children to gain confidence. I want them to feel confident in their ability to read some words and in their ability to guess thoughtfully at unknown words. Above all, I want them to feel that in the classroom world, written text is meaningful.

Beginning Where They Are

Yesterday, when they were writing, Mark suggested to Adam that he copy a word he needed from the morning message. Adam: No, I want to sound it out.

In the fall, children begin to write immediately. I give them writing folders, and I tell them writing is *about* something. Children's writing, especially in the fall, may consist of drawings, plus random letters that convey spoken words or sentences. As they begin to label their drawings, they utilize letters that correspond to sounds in the words: *m* for *me*. Children who enter school with little free-drawing experience need time to explore their own ability to be inventive, to make decisions about topics, and to concentrate on the act of writing—that is, making marks. They may—to a teacher's dismay—draw house after house after house, or make designs. But children see each others' drawings—of themselves, dogs, cats, and spiders—and after a while get the idea. When teachers value children's efforts at these initial levels, and children don't feel rushed through this period, subsequent efforts will be significantly richer.

The teacher's role is crucial and complex. Through conversations, teachers help children define topics. They ensure that work is regularly shared, so that children are exposed to different writing possibilities. As noted earlier, they see that classroom organization and routines provide the infrastructure to support writing (e.g., easy access to materials for writing, baskets or files to save ongoing work, routines for talking about work, display space for work).

Yet teachers should not impose writing. When writing is imposed, when it occurs outside of authentic contexts, disconnected from children's real experiences and purposes, when it is a product of pressure on teachers to follow units of instruction and of pressure on children to write during daily writing periods, children's long-term interest in and commitment to writing may be sapped.

I believe that teachers should not be dogmatic about young children's writing, and should feel free to judge whether writing down children's statements from dictation would help them develop their ideas. When rigid instructional methods preclude dictation and children are expected to depend solely on their own skills, their ability to expand on thoughts and tell long, complicated stories may be shortchanged. At times, dictation *should be* the primary method of recording communication. For example, when children engage in dramatic play, the teacher's recording of the story can lead to numerous other activities: the story can be read to the class, subsequently acted out, or used for a book that children illustrate. (Whenever I read one of Vivian Paley's books, I'm reminded of how powerful a tool dictation can be.) Because children are at different levels of competence in writing, and approach it in individual ways, we must encourage a variety of approaches to recording.

Teachers should be deliberate in their teaching of skills and conventions *as these are appropriate*, not according to the time-table of a commercial guide; teachers should always judge the level of children's existing understanding and experience. Explicit instruction in writing is meaningful for young children when the piece of instruction matches what a child actively needs to know. The task for teachers is to figure out what children will find useful at a particular moment and find ways to provide it. Courtney Cazden, a Harvard educator who has focused on class-room language use, describes the "instructional detour" that aids the learning of specific features of language use.[4] She warns that, without instruction, children's progress may be stymied, but she also argues that the primary context for language learning must remain the child's desire to "talk and read and write about the world."[5] One example of this sort of instructional detour: when Peter—who likes sounding out words—wants to write a word with an *er* sound, I point to his name: "There's the *er* sound!"

Young children who come to kindergarten without knowledge of letters or sounds benefit from exposure to the alphabet and from involvement in activities that aid acquisition of letter names and reinforce letter-sound association. But while I believe instruction should be focused and explicit, it also should not replace children's experiential learning (building with blocks, painting, dramatic play). It should utilize what children already know and should maximize *active* rather than mechanical learning processes. Children can use plastic or rubber alphabet letters and put them in sequence. They can make their own alphabet cards, alphabet book, or wall alphabet in a variety of ways; they can print their own alphabets using letter stamps or write individual letters that they glue in order onto strips of paper. They can form alphabet letters with their hands or bodies, which the teacher photographs. They can identify alphabet letters in the environment. As noted earlier, name cards provide endless ways to reinforce knowledge of alphabet letters. For example, children can organize the name cards to make columns of the names that begin with or include a given letter, and then write those names (creating, in effect, a simple graph). There are wonderful alphabet books that should be a part of every early-childhood classroom library, e.g., with photographs of letters found on city streets. As children's knowledge of letter names increases, letter-sound activities become more meaningful. Classes can make alphabet books or wall exhibits of things that begin with each letter, drawing objects (using commercial alphabet books and picture dictionaries) or bringing objects from home, which the teacher then photographs or which they themselves draw.

These activities are very different from activities in which children color in or circle pictures on photocopied sheets. When alphabet-related tasks are active and occur in small groups, children make choices and decisions. And because there is more action and more talk, teachers are better able to assess what individual children know.

As writing grows more sophisticated, teachers should highlight conventions of writing and teach techniques or skills to children who are ready to utilize these (e.g., spacing between words, use of exclamation points). But, again, instruction (in reading *and* writing strategies) should be tied to actual purposes. When children are writing letters or cards to someone, the direction to space words makes more sense. Once children begin to build up a bank of words that they know they need to write frequently (*this, the, is*), teachers can work with them to generate a high-frequency word list. Teachers can ask the class, "What words do you write again and again?" These lists can be photocopied and laminated. What remains central is that instruction be viewed, by teachers and students, as providing *tools* for writing about experience. Instruction should *support* writing, not take the place of meaningful activity; writing should develop out of children's genuine wish to communicate something that matters to them.

In first and second grades, when reading and writing receives more instructional attention, most children will benefit from explicit instruction in auditory and visual discrimination, decoding strategies, rhymes, blends, word families, and syllabification. However, returning to Courtney Cazden's criteria, what remains crucial is whether a particular piece of instruction matches what a child can actually make use of. Children's *purposes* in writing should remain of central concern to teachers. This is a natural outcome when teachers remember that children genuinely value the power they gain from the ability to write down their thoughts. (Vivid pictures of first- and second-grade literacy learning driven by children's purposes are in Karen Gallas's *Imagination and Literacy: A Teacher's Search for the Heart of Learning*, and Anne Dyson's *Social Worlds of Children Learning to Write in an Urban Public School*.)[6]

Programmed Instruction

The faith that is called for by progressive educators is the faith that education need not be something that is done *to children.*

In classroom after classroom, children as young as four years old sit at tables, working at paper-and-pencil—or crayon—tasks. In many kindergarten, first-grade, and second-grade rooms, the "literacy block" is *two hours* long. Classrooms dominated by literacy activities have little time for the *experiences* that give children things to write about. Academically oriented (and essentially barren and boring) assignments are supplanting richer multidisciplinary curriculum. By mandating these programs, schools also ignore what is known about *how* children learn. The National Association for the Education of Young Children called "hands-on activity and experimentation . . . more appropriate for [six-, seven-, and eight-year-olds] than fatiguing mechanical seatwork."[7]

The program in use at P.S. 87, where I taught (and in many other city schools), was *Accelerated Literacy Learning* (ALL).[8] ALL divides instruction into preplanned units that are the same for all children, beginning with "Unit One: Living Life Like a Writer." (This title, of course, is grammatically incorrect. And what does such a highly abstract phrase mean to young children?) Although teachers using the program are permitted to vary the pacing, lessons are sequenced and essentially scripted, guided by the logic of instruction, not the inner logic of growth. Because each unit has a predetermined outcome, there is less scope for individuality and variety of style than would be the case with an open-ended program, one committed to the broadest possible definition of writing. A critical viewpoint on the approach is provided by Lillian Weber in her discussion of children's language styles. One child, she says, has a "visual focus" and continually sees things as looking like other things. Another child "is a storyteller." Another child "with great deliberation savors the sounds, the syllables . . . another child speculates." [9] Teaching based on programmed literacy materials cannot take into account this range of styles. In addition, by narrowing the possible outcomes, teachers are less able to assess individual needs.

The prescriptive nature of the materials is revealed in the teacher's guide, which is written in a strange, stilted, artificial language. The teacher is asked to describe her own "noticings," to talk about her "life as a writer" or "life as a reader." Teachers are to say, "The more reading we do, the easier it is for us to make connections between the books we read. For example, you can compare different books by different authors with a theme like 'friendship,' and notice how the characters are alike or different." [10] When teachers talk in this stiff and programmed way, students tune out.

The approach often substitutes abstractions for reality. In one kindergarten classroom, a chart reads, "In Writing Workshop, we're doing Purposeful Writing." The chart is a perfect example of *purposeless* writing; it bears no relationship to anything children see themselves doing. (Of course, in the kindergarten classroom where it hangs, children can't read it anyway.) Purposeful writing occurs when children *have real purposes.* Indeed, a phrase like "purposeful writing" exposes the poverty of this approach, its failure of empathy with children's minds, its disrespect for children's real abilities and distinctive ways of thinking. A similar model, the Teachers College Reading and Writing Project, prompts teachers to address children with fake enthusiasm: "Wow, you guys! You look so ready to talk about your books! How great!"[11] The self-conscious terminology results from the belief, stated in the materials, that teachers should highlight metacognitive processes, so that children learn to be *explicitly aware of the strategies* they use in order to become "good writers" and "good readers."

It is certainly the case that making knowledge explicit—"enabling children to know what they know," in Karen Gallas's words—helps children draw on their knowledge. But the *terms* in which explicit knowledge is formulated should remain close to children's experience. For Gallas, this happens when children use an "expressive" medium—"drawing, painting, music, movement, dramatic enactment, poetry, and storytelling" to "synthesize and apply their ideas to new and different contexts."[12] In contrast, literacy materials dictate the terms in which ideas are to be formulated: "Today I want us to practice this strategy and pay particular attention to why we have chosen to use certain tools when we are not understanding what we are reading."[13] Whether or not children learn any strategies this way, it undoubtedly kills the joy of reading particular books and makes it harder for children to respond to literature in heartfelt and thoughtful ways.

Overall, the approach restricts the meanings that children may encounter. This is even more likely to be the case when the approach is used by new, inexperienced teachers who become adept in rigid, by-the-book teaching but don't learn to listen and watch children, and to adapt instructional methods to the needs of a particular group.

Reading Workshop, a feature of the literacy approach, occurs daily and is predicated on children's choice of "just-right" books. Teachers "level" classroom libraries, organizing book baskets according to reading difficulty. Once a week, children "shop" for books from the baskets; these provide reading material for the week. Although teachers are expected to include additional baskets—books by specific authors, books on specific topics—in actual practice, because of the pressure to keep children "on track," children may have few opportunities to peruse a variety of books, including books that are too hard or too easy. Given the daily pressure of literacy-related activities (Reading Workshop, Writing Workshop, Shared Reading, Guided Reading, Read-Aloud, and Independent Reading), there may be no time during the school week when children may simply *browse*—look at books for pleasure,—and forge personal ties to reading. While practice in reading is very important in order for children to become fluent readers, that goal should not be met at the expense of *pleasure* in reading.

Rather than prescriptive guides with timetables and scripts, teachers need *resources* that suggest "instructional detours" and tools: children can work with partners, write "how to" books, label shelves and bins. Teachers can introduce genres, literary forms, and writing conventions as these become relevant to a classroom's ongoing work; teachers should be asked to find the right time to teach them. Children's work should be the source of lessons, not the other way around.

"Let's Write That Down"

As the children dictated the Friday Letter to Families, someone said, Our caterpillars got bigger. Michael immediately said, Not all of them. Then Mark said, Well. . . . And so on—that back and forth . . .

This discussion, with its additions and qualifications, occurred toward the end of the year. It resulted from months of judging, on my part, when to intervene in discussions, when to comment on someone's comment or pose a question, months of deciding when to end a discussion, or call on a child who hasn't said anything. Now, they added to each other's remarks, disagreed, jumped in to qualify a statement.

Children's writing should have the same energy, verve, and vivacity as children's speech. This is the result when we teach writing in ways that let children explore the widest range of meanings. How broadly is writing defined, how various are the uses it serves? How authentic is it, how much is it their own? Where do we see it? "Its guuowey!" writes Catherine after mixing water and cornstarch. How much personality there is in that spelling! When writing is generated by lived experience, it is exploratory, broadly constituted, rich in variety—even overwhelmingly plentiful. Thoughtful teachers make it happen through the search for connections between children's purposes and writing. Writing resulted when Francie asked her question about leaves and trees, and I said, "Let's write that down, and we can ask the other children what they think, later." Writing was the result when I added a mix of writing materials to the pretend area: notebooks, pads, Post-its, pencils and pens, little calendars, tape, envelopes; the pretend area was soon papered with notes. Writing happens when teachers find the places in the room and in the day to make it happen, and *trust* children to write.

The teacher's job, then, is to consider what children are striving to say—and to aid them in their efforts. Guiding children is what teachers do best, through their knowledge of what these particular children might be seeking to communicate, and their respect for the richness of children's thinking. This is the source of teachers' authority: their reserves of intuition about children's thinking and concerns, about the topics and forms that matter to them.

Just as teachers must trust children to write inventively and meaningfully, teachers have to trust themselves. Teachers need faith in their own ability to judge, develop standards, ask the right questions—a faith that develops inevitably and ironically as a result of doubts, mistakes, and corrections. I keep in mind times I'd lacked faith—the time I'd looked askance at Harry's drawing, which seemed a mess of lines, only to have him inform me it was a food fight; the times I'd doubted children's insatiable appetite for meaning.

We want children to produce writing that is honest and compelling, direct and thoughtful. Does the language—written *and* oral—of teachers and educators meet the criteria that we have for children?

There are several educator languages: that of official school documents and policy directives, of teaching guides, and of professors of education and academic texts. Reading any of these, I'm struck, again and again, by how the writers cloak straightforward statements in murky prose, which almost pushes the readers' eyeballs away. Over the years, I've found it harder and harder to read official documents: I scan them and can them, often to my peril. Every field, of course, produces a specialized language whose obscurity separates practitioners from laymen, but educational writing seems to set a standard for lack of clarity.

Much educational writing is abstract, clichéd, full of generalities, weighted with mystifying words and phrases; clear and precise prose is the exception. Phrases like "at risk" generalize the problems specific children face and absolve the society, and the schools themselves, from responsibility for children's failures. Vito Perrone, former director of the North Dakota Study Group, wrote of the "distancing, uninspiring, heavily technological language . . . beginning to capture so much of the public discourse of education." [14] Here is a sentence from Accelerated Literacy Learning: "Teaching students to intentionally activate their background knowledge before, during and after reading may help them: 1) selectively look for information most relevant to their purposes for reading, 2) retain and recall what they've learned and 3) modify their schema about fiction and nonfiction text structures, formats, author style, craft and content area topics." [15] In other words, students should connect reading material with their own prior experiences, in regard to both content and form. By using jargon and obfuscating language, the authors claim a more objective, "research-based" point of view. They also transmit a lack of respect for the daily experience of teachers.

A contrast is provided by teacher-writers. Reading Karen Gallas's *Languages of Learning*, for example, I find sentences that are accessible, grounded in her experience of classroom life.[16] In style and substance, her writing confirms teachers' sense of their own importance in relation to children's development. Teachers, then, must be critical readers, recognizing when material obscures their knowledge of children, or when it honors children's efforts and their own efforts, when it adds to their ability to see and hear children, and challenges them to think more deeply.

The language that teachers use in classrooms also transmits attitudes. Their speech can be fake or genuine, manipulative or direct, encouraging or punitive. Teachers sometimes refer to themselves in the third person, perhaps to hide the authority of their role. There are teachers who habitually use fake, cutesy phrases. Before a lesson, they say to children, "Put on your listening ears." These kinds of phrases are condescending to children and don't take seriously their intelligence and their struggle to communicate and to know.

Only if we speak to and listen to children with respect and integrity can we define literacy activities in broad ways and tie them to children's desire to communicate. The classroom can then tap the raucous intelligence and the comparing, arguing, and questioning that are normally heard outside school walls.

7

చౕ

Midwinter Doldrums and Quarrels

Starting Over

A hard week: I was out on Monday, and Thursday and Friday of last week, with a viral infection—and weak all the rest of this week. Children very quarrelsome when I'd returned—Well, she did it first! Emily and Francie the worst. Emily—there's a thing she does with her elbow, pushing someone else's arm or hand out of the way of something she wants.

In December, the class had seemed cohesive, stable, and familiar: *we're way beyond the fall; the introductory stuff is over.* I knew the children well, had already spent so much time with them that I seemed to hear them at night: *I'll hear a hum of a voice, the tone, rhythm, recognizable—but won't know right away who it is. Sometimes I'll figure it out. It's often just there, a kind of auditory wallpaper.* Their strengths, weaknesses, choices of activities and companions: *I feel as if I know them—am not likely to be very surprised. Vanessa's friendships—the way she floats from friend to friend.*

December marked off the first part of the year: *it is winter next week, the shortest, darkest day—it has gotten significantly colder. It seems a point of balance. But between what and what? We are at the end of K-104, Part I. What strikes me is how happy they are—at least, a good enough amount of time. The kids who were more watchful and wary for a long time—now, they say, "Can I . . ." and when I nod, they skip off.* In the weeks before the Christmas vacation, the children had worked with a fury, and I had too, putting together the gifts they'd made to take home. They'd made photo books of their lives in school, chosen three photos of themselves at work from the photos that David had taken, and dictated text for each page, which I printed up. They'd decorated the pages with watercolors or Cray-Pas. For the cover, we used self-portraits they'd made earlier in the year. David had bound the pages, and the children made wrapping paper by printing on tissue paper. But after the Christmas break, everything changed. David, a sturdy, caring presence, was gone, his internship over. The study of squirrels that had absorbed us for months—finished: *I have taken down the squirrel charts*—told the kids, OK, *our study of squirrels is over. We learned a lot, but . . . enough squirrels.* It was January, the weather was cold, I got sick, the children got sick. Worse, Arshea, the assistant teacher, had to stop working because of her pregnancy. We had a new assistant and new student teacher. Everyone would eventually adjust, but at the moment, it felt as if nothing was the same.

Yet if time and change played roles in the drama of classroom life, at times they seemed invisible. Perhaps I was too close: *I'm at the center of this whirlwind—"Julie! Julie!"—I can't see because everything is moving so fast around me.* All I noticed were the consequences: *Things feel too loose. What's nagging at me? Is it the time of year? Midwinter doldrums? The blank walls? I have the feeling the central theme of our class isn't there, that we're pursuing activity in a mindless, unfocused way . . . it's not clear what's central.* I experienced this time as a frayedness, the feeling that the routines that had organized our days and weeks were coming undone: *I've been forgetting this and that, forgetting to have kids read the story on Wednesdays. The end of the day is when everything catches up with me. We start running late, and I have no energy to stop and set things right. It's a judgment on the rest of the day. I see things being done wrong, routines I think I've taught, and I feel at a loss—mad at the kid who made me feel at a loss, mad at myself for getting mad at the kid.*

Books with photo portraits
Photo by David Vitale-Wolff

How quick I am to blame myself! I kept thinking there was something I should have been doing: *I say to myself—what's wrong, why aren't you leading here?* My job *was* to ask what was wrong, and when I stepped back, I gained some perspective. I saw where we were in the year, and remembered other years: *The history of my teaching is always a low at this time of year, a formlessness, as we lose one student teacher and slowly integrate another. This year there's a double loss, of the student teacher and of Arshea. Simply getting to know these two new people—what are they good at doing? In the afternoon, the new assistant—who will, I know, be wonderful, and just needs time—leaves after setting up snack, but I haven't made sure she knows exactly what to do, so we end up without the juice pitchers set out.* It's inevitable; the sense of things being "off" is a necessary consequence of change. We've outgrown our old clothes, but the new clothes don't feel right. Mid-January, and I had to start over, as if it were September again; I had to look at everything differently.

In most classrooms, one study follows another without gaps. The teacher has it all planned out in advance and knows precisely what will happen every week and month. Everything must fit in—and teachers get upset when they can't keep to their plans. Yet just as a day has a rhythm, a year has a rhythm, of attention and inattention, purpose and purposelessness. Why should we suppose that children operate at peak capacity all the time? Or that *we* do. The spaces that are between involvements have a function, difficult as it may be for the teacher, who—at that moment—doesn't have much of a plan. Yet in the spaces, children can rest, consolidate, and put out feelers. The attentive teacher can gain some knowledge, despite the disquiet of being *between*: *It's been a slide-y time, before whatever is coming next. I get impatient with myself, yet there always have been these between times, when it's as if I have to* not *be focused somehow. Do the kids need it too?*

The ebb and flow of interests is particularly characteristic of classrooms in which teachers aim for intrinsic motivation, for gaining true involvement in classroom activities, for enlisting children's wholehearted commitment. If I expected children to bring energy and passion to their learning, I had to find topics that mattered to them and find ways to engage them. I had to tolerate this time of year.

One day in January, Emily came to school with a photo of herself as a baby. The fact that the walls were blank suddenly seemed perfect, ordained. We would study babies. The class had already been talking about Arshea's pregnancy, and about the baby, due in March. Some of them had information about newborn babies, how tiny they are, their black belly buttons. Victor, a triplet, volunteered a story from when he was first born—about being hungry for his bottle—and we talked about his being inside with two others.

I'd studied babies with other classes. I usually start by asking the children to bring in baby photos, with their names and ages on the back. It's always funny seeing these photos, presages of the children to come, baby versions of the personalities we've come to know. This year, I made two color photocopies and sent the originals home. One copy would be for a wall display: the children glued the pictures on construction paper and decorated around the photos to make a frame, leaving space at the bottom for dictated text. The children shared their photos with the class and put them up on the conveniently blank walls; eventually I moved the photos to the classroom door, adding, next to each, a small current photo portrait. The other photocopy was used to make a timeline of development. I put brown paper up on the wall outside, in the hall, and a small group of children marked off months and years to make a timeline. I added a new basket for the class library, books about babies and babies' growth. We looked at the books and talked about what babies can do. The children learned about developmental milestones: when babies start to focus their eyes, hold their heads up, clap, sit up, crawl, walk. The children glued their photos on the timeline, and wrote down or dictated something that they noticed about their baby selves: "I could feed myself!" On index cards, they wrote their names and how old they were. They added drawings. Children from other classes, walking down the hall, stopped to look at our timeline.

We had baby visits, too, younger siblings who came in with their mothers. These visits were chaotic: the babies lurched around, the children cracked up, trying to get the babies' attention. We'd talked beforehand about what we wanted to know and prepared interview questions for the mothers. It was always unpredictable. But the children observed, and when we wrote up the visits, they had plenty to say. We made short books: *Baby Lili's Visit*, illustrated with drawings and photos. I added baby stuff to the pretend area—bottles, flannel blankets. Soon we began to talk about babies in families, and from there, shifted to talking about families. The children with siblings, younger and older, talked about the things they liked and disliked about being big or little siblings; children who didn't have siblings talked about the things they liked and didn't like about *not* having them. We invited the fifth-grade twins, Ariel and Tara, to come in to talk to us about being twins; we'd already read a photo book about twins, in which these two appeared as cute three-year-olds. *The kids now report sightings of either twin.* We talked about big families, small families, parents and grandparents, uncles and aunts, cousins, relatives who live close by and relatives who live far away. Another book basket: books about families. More photos from home—of the children and their families; this time, we made a book with photocopies of the original photos and dictated text.

Some years, a family study would come first. Some years, I've asked parents for their own memories, a story from when the children were babies. I asked the children for their earliest memories. One year, the class produced a book, illustrated by the children, with all these stories. The baby study has evolved over many years, and each year, the structure of the study has become clearer: it is about growth and development. The study places the children at this moment on a timeline that implicitly moves toward further growth. When the baby study is part of a bigger look at children's families, children also gain explicit understandings about the requirements of growth, and about how families function to fulfill these needs.

There were also changes, during the post-Christmas period, in the structure of activities and in children's work modes. I began to let them leave block buildings up for the whole week, so they could work on them over several days. The rules were: loose blocks get put away, and buildings must be labeled with what the building is, and who made it. I noticed more self-initiated projects by children who had previously been followers: *Jamie, at the table, working on a book—a project I just discovered, looking through the workbasket. For days and days she's been taping pages together, after writing on each page. A signal to me of the need to take time to walk around, see what everyone is doing, and write it down.* There were more group projects, two to five children working together with table blocks, inch cubes, teddy bears, producing incredibly complex constructions.

New activities, new projects seemed to arise without warm-up; certain moments stood out because in one way or another they went against the grain of something I thought I knew about the child. These bits—encounters, choices of someone to work with, something that was made—moved away from what had come before, what was already known, and perhaps because of that, they tended to add some new element to the class culture. Sam, always a wild card, began to use the pattern blocks. His designs—wilder, more original than the others' hexagon and triangle flowers— brought him, at last, some admiration. Looking back, it seemed not entirely unpredictable, but I couldn't have planned it. It was *his* accomplishment.

Short-term projects filled in at moments when we lacked longer, larger goals. We did a lot of measuring. We used yarn to measure things in the room: the children cut a length of yarn to make it "as long as" something else. I wanted them to focus on the idea of "equal to" in length. Then the children used Unifix cubes (plastic cubes that fit together). First, they measured the length of their sneakers or shoes: each child, working with a partner, removed one shoe, traced it, and measured it. Another day, they measured parts of their bodies. They chose what they wished to measure— e.g., neck, arm, head, hand—again working with partners. Another day, they measured objects in the room—a book, the rabbit cage, table, chair. Later on, they used different units of measurement—paper clips, crayons, pencils—to measure one thing. These activities and projects led to more surprises. On their own, during one work time, Amina and Henry, unlikely partners, measured the rug with Unifix cubes. Other children had been making long trains of the multicolored cubes on the rug, but on this day, Henry and Amina got to a new level of understanding first making short trains of ten single-color cubes, red, yellow, and so on, and then attaching these to make one long train: *perhaps because of Amina's mathematical sense of the importance of making groups of ten? Her knowledge that it would be mathematically*

Using crayons to measure
Photo by Julie Diamond

useful to do it that way, rather than to simply join cubes randomly?
I helped them count the cubes by tens—the rug was 183 cubes
long, and they announced the fact to the rest of the class.

In February, the children used doilies, silver and gold paper,
and ribbons to make collaged cards for Valentine's Day. Since we'd
been talking about relatives—aunts and uncles, grandparents,
and cousins—I asked the children to make the valentines with a
family member in mind, someone in their family with whom
they *didn't* live. They wrote messages inside the cards. I sent
home a request for the names and addresses of relatives, and for
stamps; I purchased manila envelopes and ruled off lines for the
address. Addressing the envelopes took a serious amount of time;
copying the addresses correctly and legibly was a challenge for
most of the children. We stuck the postage stamps on, borrowed
the return address stamp from the office, and when everything

was complete—the valentines made, the messages written, and the envelopes addressed, return-addressed, stamped, and sealed—we traipsed out, in the rain, to drop the envelopes in the corner mailbox, and the valentines made their way to the Bronx, New Jersey, Michigan, Eritrea.

Around this same time, we celebrated the one-hundredth day of school. Children brought from home one hundred objects, in labeled plastic bags: one hundred barrettes, one hundred paper clips. They counted out one hundred Unifix cubes, or crayons; they filled in photocopied ten-by-ten squares, making one hundred fingerprints, or Xs, or flowers. The class worked together to make a hundred-heart paper quilt. I ruled off a big ten-by-ten grid on brown paper and cut small squares of white paper on which the children drew hearts using Cray-Pas. The whole process took days: after the children drew the hearts, they cut them out and glued them in the grid squares. Other children filled in around the hearts with contrasting colors, and used watercolors for empty spaces and for the border. When the quilt was finally finished, it was remarkably beautiful. I painted it with gloss medium and hung it up. We handed it over to the parents, who framed it to sell at the Parents Association auction. (Ultimately, the class parents decided to purchase the quilt, as a present for Arshea's baby.)

Despite all this, I continued to feel the class lacked focus. I felt ideas weren't accumulating, that there was no center, no source of energy pulling the class forward together. The children looked at the books about babies and families and looked at each other's photos, but the topics seemed more mine than theirs; it was *my* interest propelling us. I found scribbling on a table, and small objects were disappearing, like the little rubber people that were used with the table blocks. What was missing was a deeper commitment to what they were doing: *What's their real physical and intellectual involvement? I feel as if I am waiting, looking for some hint of what's ahead, what I will learn from this year. Maybe that's the point.* I consoled myself, telling myself that they had been

Working on the heart quilt
Photo by Julie Diamond

busy. But busyness wasn't my goal. The truth is that I remain uneasy with the invisibility of change; I'm not tolerant of the unknown. It's hard for me to be *between*, waiting for the class to gain purpose and momentum.

"She Did It First!"

Tears twice from Hayley, fight between Mark and Jonathan, Max laughing at everyone . . . I'm cranky too.

Teachers hate fights. There are different kinds of fights: one kind is between two children who continually pick on each other; the teacher learns to put them at opposite ends of the line, and never puts them in the same group for activities. There are fights between friends, when one of them makes a new friend and the other feels left out—that child, usually good-natured, all of a sudden turns possessive and mean. There are fights that are sparked so quickly, both sides drawn in so instantaneously, that the teacher can barely figure out what happened. There are fights that originate during recess and are brought back into the classroom; fights when children have to share some new material; fights when children come to the rug for story or meeting.

At cleanup, one child ignores the teacher, wanting to complete the house he's building with little blocks. Another child comes up, forgets to ask (purposely neglects to ask?), "Can I help you clean up?" He reaches down to take some blocks, and his move causes one side of the building to collapse. The builder is instantly furious: the building he'd worked on with such care, which was almost finished, is knocked down, ruined. "Hey!" he exclaims— and he shoves the helping hand. The other child, indignant, shoves back, justified in his countermove: two claims, two injured parties. This is how each child sees it; the teacher sees only a fight that diverts everyone's attention from cleaning up, a situation that must be dealt with—a situation requiring that the teacher produce, on the spot, a solution everyone will accept. Which is, of course, impossible: one child wins, smirks; the other departs in tears.

Teachers often fail to *think* about quarrels. We react, seeing fights as irritants, boulders in the road. We don't, perhaps we can't, ask the questions we should: what issues spark confrontations, what are the moments when fights occur? We tend to see quarrels as separate from what's happening around them, as self-contained episodes rather than events occurring in specific settings.

In one classroom, fights often occurred as children sat and drew. It turned out that each long table had only one plastic marker box, which of course was always being pulled toward one end of the table or the other, hands grabbing or holding on. Little time was left for drawing; the important issue was gaining control of the box. It was a game, marker soccer. Easy solution— more boxes. Busy, distracted, pulled in opposing directions ourselves, teachers often miss the underlying problems. What we need to do, and to do repeatedly, is to examine the details of the environment—including the physical organization of the classroom, and the schedule—and ask what changes of routine or setup would prevent conflicts from arising. Preparation and fore-thought count, often crucially: if a group sits at a table while a teacher busily gathers supplies for the group's activities, trouble ensues. Asking children to sit or stand and wait leads inevitably to problems. Instead, whenever possible, I assign some children to gather supplies and, as far as possible, set up the table for an activity.

The social as well as the physical environment can create conditions that lead to fights. Teachers may unintentionally create dissension. When teachers pit children against each other, when they seek to motivate through competition, they appeal, essentially, to selfishness rather than cooperation. Teachers who hold out material rewards—stickers, candy, or pizza parties for the table that wins the most points during the week—exploit children's motives of acquisition and competitiveness for their own purposes.

Whatever short-term gains in control such systems produce, they breed a resentment-filled atmosphere: twenty children go off to the cafeteria for lunch, while eight children remain in the classroom to share the pizza their table has "earned." Food, with all its associations, is particularly potent in creating resentment, a feeling that then draws together all previous experiences of life's unfairness and withholdings. I have seen children sobbing because, while their friends left the music teacher's classroom with stickers, *their* behavior didn't merit one. Difficult, defiant, uncooperative as that child may have been during that period, all that he considers as he walks down the hall is that he is once again a victim. Will this aid him in controlling his behavior in the music room next week? And when children do behave "better" in these settings because of bribes or threats, it is with an added quotient of bad feeling—shame, resentment, envy, or fear.

This is not to say there's no place for material rewards or competition in classrooms. My argument is against these as a way of motivating "good" behavior. Many kinds of material rewards are appropriate in classrooms: these include all kinds of celebrations, ice cream parties, small gifts (from stickers to pencils and note-books, to books). What matters is that these are gifts to the class, and bring the class together, rather than exclude *anyone*. Such gifts, in fact, are motivating, because they indicate the adult's good feelings toward the children as individuals and build up a bank of trust and identification. Competition may have a role in the classroom, in spelling bees, and similar activities. However, teachers have to consider the age and experience of the particular children when deciding on the role of these kinds of competi-tions. It's important for children to feel successful at something, and competitions can, at times, allow children to feel success in the effort they've made. Judgment about the place of competi-tions must be made on the basis of the teacher's knowledge of children's experiences.

In general, systems of management that rely on competition and material rewards don't help children develop their own un-derstandings of right and wrong, their own notions of justice and fairness, cooperation and conscience. Approaches to classroom management that rely *primarily* on external motivation, on re-wards and punishment, are centered on adult power and control; they cannot effectively teach children to think about and regulate their own behavior, nor are they intended to. The threat is what carries weight: if this class doesn't behave nicely, we won't go to the play! In a sense, when children in this kind of classroom fight, they are merely replicating, in a more direct and violent form, the governing assumption of social interactions, the tit for tat, the lack of faith in cooperation as a motive, the absence of a thought-ful, open, questioning response to problems.

Last, no method of managing children's quarrels works all the time for all children. Too often, we generalize about children ("Denay always cries when things go wrong"). When we do, we assume an unchanging child and an unchanging adult: "we" manage "them." This point of view permits a stereotyping bias in relation to that child; it doesn't allow us the distance to help. We don't see the specific child *in* the specific conflict: what is it that set her off? If we see children in generalized ways, we're less likely to ask questions, to look back at exactly what happened, and at everything we know about this child, to dig for full explanations that will add to what we know about the child. Children are not inorganic, stable elements. We need to manage particular moments, to see each child with greater specificity, to take as much as we can into account. We can inform that difficult moment with details that are obscured when we react in a more immediate and unthinking way:

Denay cannot catch her breath. I send her with Hayley to wash her face, but still she sobs every time she tries to talk. It was what she was like the first day of school; I'd forgotten. It's a sort of zone of discomfort, of nonfunctioning. What triggers it? There is still, sometimes, a fragility to her—even though at other times she seems easy, even though she is generally so competent. I remember the way she held onto Graham as a partner, in the beginning, someone she knew, someone she could completely depend on.

When we see children with more detail, we look differently at the two children who continually squabble, who seem to rub each other the wrong way. Although we might still separate them, we also ask ourselves questions. What is it about the two of them that brings them into these perpetual conflicts? What are the traits that draw them into battle again and again? Two children with short fuses? Two children who tease? Two would-be leaders? There are as many answers as there are sparring children. What draws them to each other—is there anything *positive* in their relationship that the teacher can work with? The teacher's response has to be built from knowledge of these two and their unique antagonism. It's over weekends, away from the two and their barbed encounters, that the teacher can plan a long-term strategy that might help them replace hostility with a measure of civility. When this is possible, even for short periods, the tone of the entire class is affected.

We must use weekends, too, to look at our own reactions to a particular child who gets our goat, because *we* can find ourselves taking things personally, or disliking one child—it is a topic not often discussed. A teacher friend had a telling story: one day she heard the blocks crash, and without thinking, called out one child's name—the boy she'd assumed had knocked a building over. Then she remembered he was absent that day. Those kinds of automatic responses should make us think. For each of us, one attribute may be especially annoying or disturbing. I'm challenged by defiant behavior, I overreact; for another teacher, it's whining or tattling. Some teachers can't stand bullying. We like to think teachers are above such personal weaknesses; not true. Self-knowledge may be uncomfortable, and gaining it may entail doubt and unpleasant truths. But when a teacher catches herself quarreling with a child, she must begin by examining her own preferences and antipathies.

What Do We Mean by Managing a Class?

That is what teaching is, our continual looking at and asking questions about a child or children, and about ourselves, about something we did or didn't do. It is how we continually become professional—rather, become who we are in this profession.

Just as children are not set, stable elements, neither are we. We manage things better or worse on different days, at different times. Thus, when we think about "managing" a class, we have to take into account many elements. Ultimately, when we think about managing a class, we're describing how motivated, energized, responsible, and *together* a class is, but we're also talking about ourselves. What's the teacher's role in achieving this? We have to search for elements we *can* control, understanding that just as children change, we do too.

These matters are not, most deeply, matters of management; they are not, most deeply, technical. There are techniques involved: we can train ourselves to put our directions in a positive frame whenever possible: to say *walk* rather than *don't run*. I have found it works to give a child a direction, then walk away, busy myself, and check back. When I talk to the whole class, I make sure I can see all of their faces—and that the faces are turned toward me. If two children are still talking, I say, "I'm waiting for you!" I make certain, as noted earlier, that supplies are prepared; make sure that if I am brimming with anger because of what a child just did, I *wait* to talk to the child, saying only, "I'm too upset right now to speak to you!" There are effective methods, effective tones of voice, effective looks, and effective actions: we seek them as beginning teachers; we test, fail, test again, and refine. These must become our own. My colleague Hollee Freeman used to say, "You are plucking my last nerve!" I say, "What did I *just* ask you to do?" and "Can you hear how irritated my voice is sounding right now?" We learn to count to ten; we learn to hold children's attention; we learn to use humor and a light touch. That quality of touch: present, not grabby.

We learn when to ignore something, when that's the better part of wisdom. We learn when *not* to ignore; we learn when to call an "emergency meeting" or make the time to have a conference with a child whose behavior we're concerned about, to ask, "What's going on?" We learn to recognize the circumstances that set off a particular child, to help the child recognize those circumstances before something occurs, and to praise the child for changed behavior afterwards. We learn when to *yet again* practice getting on line, and when to give it a break, let it go. We learn what kinds of compromises to suggest, what kinds of negotiation will work with individual children. We learn to *see* the progress being made by a difficult child, and to give that child credit; we learn to take into account the occasional steps backwards. Teachers can, with perseverance, find what works.

But the job of teaching is a human job: techniques rest on the spirit with which they're applied. Our feelings matter, and are communicated; when adults' intentions or tone are at odds with their words, children aren't fooled.

In the conclusion of *Teaching Children to Care*, Ruth Charney takes up the notion of the connection between our "deepest selves" and our work; she refers to the "authentic teaching" that is possible when teachers draw on personal resources.[1] Authentic teaching reflects both our "unique strengths and passions" and our willingness to "reveal our vulnerabilities."[2] Charney outlines the difficulty of our dual task. "Care for children," she writes, "is both a burden and a gift of the spirit."[3] We must take responsibility for our own growth, as well as our students'. As Charney aptly comments, "Authenticity is knowing oneself well enough to allow others to know themselves."[4] Knowledge of children and knowledge of ourselves develop in tandem; respect for ourselves parallels respect for our students.

The teacher's genuine authority resides in the ability to *repeatedly* inhabit and communicate a self that is just, fair, open-minded, responsible; not someone perfect, but someone accountable—accountable most crucially for building relationships with students. To the extent that that's who we are—who we can be *for our students*—we make it more likely that our students, through their identification with us, will find and nourish those qualities in themselves. To the extent, too, that we see those qualities in them, we not only encourage their development, we gain strength for ourselves.

To this end, when we reflect on our mistakes, it should be with a generosity of spirit. At the end of the school year, adding up pluses and minuses, I can't wipe out the memory of my reaction when Emily and Francie bickered over the possession of something or other for the tenth time that morning—and wrote on each other with markers. I snapped at them. In that moment, I took the quarrel as a judgment on myself and my teaching: *it doesn't happen, after all, when they are immersed in activity.* With distance, I can think about the quarrel and about my own feelings. I can find a viewpoint that is critical but not judgmental.

Authentic teaching is, I think, a product of our ability to learn—to learn about ourselves, to learn about the children in our care, to examine the possibilities that a teaching setting can provide. This openness is, in turn, a product of our empathy with children and with our own struggles for growth.

Our authority as teachers, I believe, rests squarely on the continuing commitment to knowing our children and ourselves: *Right now, I'm learning how to not let Sam disappear, how to not let him not know what we are doing. I pull him out. Or, to put it differently, I try to find out, when he disappears into himself, what that "himself" consists of. The learning I have to do is endless and infinite.* The authority we gain as *knowers* of children gives us the strength to stand up for what we believe is best for them; it makes it incumbent on us to do so. Our commitment to this goal also legitimizes a continual search for forms of authentic learning, a continual questioning of what authentic work is.

Student teachers sometimes confuse my teaching style— my concern that children take responsibility, my preference for curriculum based on children's interests, my repudiation of dependence on external rewards and punishments, my informal manner—with adult passivity. Nothing could be more disastrous. *The student teacher, Valerie, was lining them up, but they were a mess, all over the place. She stood there and made no attempt to get them in line and quiet. I didn't want to take over. We'd just talked about her being less "formal" in how she speaks to them—or rather, finding a way to be herself-as-a-teacher. Does she think that means to simply allow them to be unruly? When we got back to the room, I was short-tempered with the children. It wasn't their fault—I was annoyed with her for not taking charge.* We take responsibility—as adults—by insisting that children take responsibility for themselves. In this way, we promote the development of social attitudes; we work *with* their better impulses: *I say to the class,* Look at this! *Who left the table like this. Another time, Hayley comes to me and says,* I don't know what to write about. *I say,* I don't know! *Later, I check back, and if she still hasn't begun, offer an idea.*

It's ironic that this role should be taken as a passive one; it's anything but passive. It requires activity and engagement, although those may take the form of looking, listening, and looking again. We gain authority and legitimacy to the extent that we manage this balancing act: knowing when to watch, knowing when to step in.

Valuing Childhood

So many management skills are physical. I've learned a way of talking, looking at the child and then away, communicating an absolute belief that they will do the thing asked. A faith ... a confidence in what's expected from each of us. It's how a relationship is made real—that, and the commitment I have to only asking of them things I have a right to be asking as a teacher. Which means knowing what a particular child or group is capable of.

The underpinning of this sort of teaching is faith—faith in children's ability to learn, to grow and change; faith in my instincts as a teacher, a knower of children. This faith is so ingrained that it expresses itself through tone, through touch, and through the slow building of relationships. Faith in children's learning is part of a system of values. It is built, Charney writes, on "a strong foundation of what we believe and value most ... [our] ideals and principles." [5]

Seeing teaching as a value-laden enterprise is especially important at this time, when we are repeatedly told that *research* should drive instruction, as if research were objective and value-free. That assumption is false: What questions are studied? How does the preference for quantitative data affect the questions we're able or likely to ask?

Values are embedded in all we do and say, in all our decisions. To put it differently, they are given meaning through what we do; as John Dewey declared, "There is no such thing as educational value in the abstract." [6] When I call the class to the rug because children are cleaning up in a disorganized and distracted way, I'm likely to question them: "Why did I ask everyone to come to the rug?" The question implies the existence of a social contract, applied to the class as a whole.

Values are inherent in such practices as my frequent sharing of children's work, the space I make for children's individual solutions, my insistence that children pay attention to each other, my encouragement of rituals that children invent, and my use of management techniques that emphasize the needs of the class as a whole. Values are inherent when I give children the space to develop individual passions and allegiances, for example, when I allow them to choose which undersea animal they wish to study.

Children's passions add to the richness of the classroom's common life, but in valuing individual feelings and the common good, I'm making a choice of values. My purposes are social and moral, and refer, as Dewey put it, to the quality of "human experience."[7] For Dewey, educational values inhere in actions that give meaning to human lives. He makes this point beautifully in concluding his discussion of values in *Democracy and Education*: Education "is not a mere means to . . . [a conscious, moral] life. Education is such a life."[8]

Our values may be invisible, but they affect our functioning. The parent of a child I taught once told me how much she appreciated the fact that the children who were articulate and responsive, who were easy to teach, weren't favored in my class. I hadn't thought about it consciously. My behavior grew from the conviction that every life has value and weight, that, as Patricia Carini writes, "the person . . . has intrinsic value, and his or her being and experience have both coherence and durability—that is, integrity."[9]

This point of view gives us each responsibility in relation to others' lives. It defines teaching for me as the work of seeing each child, knowing each child. It helps us find a position from which to respond when faced with conflicting demands.[10] Our moral responsibility in relation to children is, as Charney puts it, "not a simple imposition"—it is *allied* with children's developmental requirements, their "desire to be included and attached." [11]

We also ally ourselves in a consistent way with children's urge to *know*. When children choose which animal to study, their feelings fuel investigation: "What we feel deeply about . . . evokes our thought." [12] These spheres are not separate: children's social and moral development and their intellectual development can be viewed together. In Reggio schools, children "are active and competent *protagonists* [emphasis in text] who seek completion through dialogue and interaction with others, in a collective life of the classroom, community, and culture, with teachers serving as guides." [13]

These moral and social imperatives inform my understanding of educational purposes. Day to day, they translate for me as a sense of what *childhood* demands from adults: *What do we know/ believe about the nature of childhood? I think about what childhood is for, what it "wants to be." It is an art, perhaps, the art of being a child, and not all children are equally good at it, or rather, equally allowed to become good, given the conditions of becoming good— not "good children," but good at* being *children, which implies, allows for, the normal difficulties of reconciling one's will with the realities of the world. What do children need from us, from adults? Consideration, kindness, concern/understanding for their essential weakness and vulnerability; a love of their love of play, of beauty and movement, and of their love of action; appreciation of their physical need to act upon, to gain mastery, to look into, to squirm.*

Our job, I believe, is to take into account the qualities specific to children: their openness to experience, their plasticity, their ability to identify with things, their almost compulsive interest in exploring, examining, seeing what will happen. These qualities take different forms in different places and times. Yet if we carefully observe children at play, listen to them as they converse, we can learn more of who they are: *I just thought about "Doughnut Girl," my granddaughter's imaginary friend. I'm struck, again and again, by how quickly children come up with imaginative explana-tions that exactly suit their needs.* How did she come up with this perfect name—food in the form of a friend, or vice versa? What is central for me is faith in children's ability to tell us who they are. In an interview, Carlina Rinaldi, former director of the Reggio preschools, put it this way: "The cornerstone of our experience, based on practice, theory, and research, is the image of the children as rich, strong, and powerful." [14] My task as a teacher is to dis-cover the unique capacities and aptitudes of the children I teach, and then to create conditions that make it possible for them to work with others to extend these capacities. To set up conditions for them to be children—curious, inquiring, socially involved. In short, our job is to *see*, and to give importance to what we've seen.

Much bad teaching—well-intentioned bad teaching—stems from distrust of children, bad faith, and inattention to the details. Here, David, the student teacher, grapples with the gap between his ideals and reality:

David said, I think the squirrel study is boring them—and as he's proceeding, it's true. He'd insisted on beginning with the old chart of what they knew, asking them, What did we say, right here? The only child who might confidently answer that question was the one who'd drawn that picture. Then he asked, Is there anything you wonder about? No one answered. They didn't know what to say. That formulation is too abstract; it gives the kids no concrete con-text. Later, I suggested that he try focusing on one picture or one piece of information, e.g., that squirrels build nests, and then ask, Is there something about squirrel nests you want to know? He tried it, but the children kept making statements, perhaps thinking he again wanted to know what they knew. He turned each of these into a ques-tion: Oh, so you want to know . . . He wasn't honest with them, he didn't say, No, that's something you already know, that's not a ques-tion. He doesn't yet have enough faith in them, in the process through which they become engaged; he doesn't yet get what it means to actively look at what they are offering, what they are thinking. Afterward, I said, You can't pretend a comment is a ques-

tion. You can't simply rephrase it. He said, I was *trying to trick them.*

David's idealism, combined with his inexperience, made the children in front of him less visible: *It is possible to see last term as a map of David's growth, as someone learning to learn about children, learning how much he didn't know, how much humbler he had to be.* He had to learn to be less concerned about his own performance, about being a good teacher. Ideals—in this case, a new teacher's notions of what he might accomplish—can sometimes distract us and make it harder to be attentive to children's actual functioning.

Wasting Paper

It's impossible to capture the flow of the classroom; it is hard enough to see and think about it as it's happening. This morning, I used Emily's name for the secret code word; someone informs me we did her name already, and I apologize and say we'll check the names off on a class list, on a clipboard, to keep track, so I don't repeat anyone's name. I ask, Whose names did we already do? Meanwhile, someone—it's often Vanessa, which says something about her wish to know what's going on and to be job person—comes up and asks, Who are the job persons? (This is her usual locution.) I say, Get me the job clipboard. Someone else, passing by, says, I know what letter "job" begins with. Was that Victor? Graham asks, How many days until I'm job person? So we look at the clipboard, and I say, It's complicated, two or three, because it depends on when Ariel comes back. Then I remind them to cross off the day on their calendars, which they're supposed to do every morning.

There are moments, even days, like this: so full of content I don't know what to do with all of it; ideas and emotions spill over. While these moments require faith, they also require *time* and a certain kind of tolerance. The challenge of providing these without *indulging* children is summed up for me in the issue of wasting paper, a perennial problem. I pass the garbage can and notice many pieces of drawing paper tossed in, each with one mark. I stop the class and hold these papers up: "Look at this!" Once again, I'm asking them to take responsibility; yet I can't do this without being silently aware of the contradictions. Sometimes it's necessary to waste paper. I think about Amina's book about caves, which appeared after a long period during which she produced piles of uninspired drawings: *Yesterday, on her own, she made this marvelous book, A Book About Caves. She'd cut the pages in the shape of a rock. "Caves have darkness. Caves have spookiness. Caves have water. Caves have moss. Caves have buckets." It was probably modeled on Denay's fish book of last week ("Fish have scales," etc.). It's a lesson to me: trust their ability to use what's around them.* And another lesson, too: allow them those in-between periods when not much seems to be going on.

Vito Perrone speaks of the need for children to have time, "time to complete work they can truly honor." [15] Providing time depends on our recognizing the role of *effort* as children learn; recognizing the necessity of confusion, meanderings, mistakes— the role of wasted paper. We need time for wrong turns, for paths that double back, for change that may be invisible.

Yet the taking of time is one more casualty of the quest for "accountability" in education. Pressed for time, teachers are unable to allow children time for anything: time to sustain and develop ideas, time to go further, time for unexpected insight or innovative thought. Everything is sacrificed in pursuit of scores.

There are other bad consequences of making schools more narrowly academic. Teachers are less and less encouraged to incorporate children's diverse strengths into planning. There is less and less time for legitimate pursuits, for the actual work of childhood. As academic pressures have mounted, behavioral expectations have become increasingly inappropriate and unrealistic. Work that is formally more advanced is valued above work that is less advanced, although the latter may in fact have more meaning to an individual child, or more curricular significance. Children at younger and younger ages sit for longer periods, take in information orally, are pushed to write and produce representational drawings. I was told of a kindergarten teacher who made a student sit out because he didn't want to write.

Behavioral problems are manufactured when classrooms set overly academic demands. Teachers constantly have to suppress children's energy, which is seen as an impediment to their plans rather than as a resource, something vital to educational purposes. As teachers strive to keep children's normal liveliness at bay, extrinsic rewards predominate. Teachers issue warnings, they move children's names to the "sad face" side of a behavior-management chart. Children—boys, particularly—face days in school as failures, by age four and five. At some point in the future, they won't care any more. Even successful children suffer, becoming increasingly concerned with pleasing adults, and all students are in danger of burning out academically as they move toward the middle years of childhood.

I think of my management style, sometimes, as "harness and harangue." I take a stance in relation to their growth; the engine is theirs. Meanwhile, I harangue: "Who left the table like this?" These poles frame what I do, whether I am exasperated with Vanessa for playing with her myriad bracelets, hair decorations, and sunglasses; or suggest Emily look in the dictionary for the picture of an airplane for her journal page; or take the student teacher to task when he dithers leading the class out at 3:00, and we're late. The students accept my occasionally rough tongue, a mother-of-puppies rough: "Sam! Look at what *everyone else* is doing!" It's a question of tone—it's rare that my roughness is really rough—because I genuinely like them, and they know that. I set the rules and enforce them but seek words that reverberate for children. If they flick the math materials, I tell them, "No pinging!" My concern is that they have confidence as learners: I want to increase what they *think* they can do. Just as I have faith in them, they have faith in me, and in each other, as they operate in this classroom, a world they have helped create, *the world of K-104: loyalty—though not all the time; caring and concern—*

ditto. Above all, shared knowledge, and knowledge of each other. Maybe I make myself so available to them, within the structures of what is fair and just (waiting their turns), and they, in return, don't hold back.

That was written on a good day. There were plenty of days when I concluded my tone was too rough, or my roughness wasn't justified; or when the children's roughness just seemed too much for me. There were days that the class lacked energy or focus or equilibrium, days I felt cranky or distracted. I reach, sometimes painfully, for the experimental attitude that I want my students to take. On the bad days—an inevitable part of *every* teacher's year—what carries me through is faith, faith in the qualities I value in childhood, faith in my own ability to recognize those qualities and make a place for them in the classroom.

8

∾

Welcome to the Aquarium: Knowing One Child

Teacher Talk

What is the story of Henry—the child who is difficult for the teacher?

Teachers' knowledge of children occurs as narrative. "Teachers tell stories," Karen Gallas says, "about what [they] know about children, learning, and teaching." [1] Unlike "objective" standardized assessments, narrative accounts represent a process, something ongoing. They are accurate in a way that tests aren't, because they include the unexpected and allow room for the elements of live, fluid action that we experience as teachers. Our goal, after all, is to describe something that is alive and continually changing. Teachers talk to other teachers or to themselves. They tell stories as a way of looking for meanings, of comparing and drawing conclusions, of figuring out what they know and what they want to know.

Harriet Cuffaro, another teacher-writer long associated with Bank Street College of Education, notes that teachers' "anecdotes . . . describe children's accomplishments, their struggles, and their discoveries." [2] Their stories also give form to their own struggles: the puzzlement, confusion, distress, even anger. Their most telling anecdotes are about children who seem to frustrate their intentions, the ones with whom they feel locked in battle.

At the beginning of each new school year, my mother—a teacher herself—would ask me, "Any pests?" I would pretend not to understand her question. I refused to divide the class that way, to label children "good" or "bad" (or "smart" or "slow"). I think part of my job is to *like* my students—to find something likeable in each of them. Yet for each teacher, some children are harder: harder to like, harder to work with. Out of a classroom of individuals, each with requirements, these children can absorb a teacher's thoughts and energy. The paradox is that it's these children who force us to learn something new.

The stories we tell about these children are also about ourselves, as we come to figure out what to ask of a child, how to ask it, and what to ask of ourselves. We may hope to recast the story, so it is not simply a list of the child's incapacities, so it is not dictated by the need to protect the image of ourselves as good teachers. The struggle to teach these difficult children not only tests our limits and resources, it exposes the truth of our beliefs, of what we can actually accomplish. The story may have a subplot: the teacher's engagement with other adults, the child's parents. This relationship may be difficult, too. Whether or not we were successful with a child, whether we were conciliatory or wrong-headed with parents, we will undoubtedly go over and over events in our own minds and with colleagues.

As teachers work to form relationships, to figure out what went wrong on any given afternoon, what we let ourselves know depends on what we can tolerate knowing about ourselves. The teacher is both narrator and character in classroom stories. Narrators in novels may be unreliable; in real life, *I'm* a semi-reliable narrator. When teachers talk, they tell *their* version, filtered through a lens that's not transparent, that has flaws.

But by telling and retelling this or that incident, by remembering these difficult events months or even years afterward, we're offered again and again the possibility of gaining a more balanced understanding—of who the children were, and who we are as teachers. Long ago, when I was beginning to teach, I had a very hard time bringing a group of children in from the yard one afternoon. As I saw it at the time, they just wouldn't listen. I was furious, and yelled and threatened—they finally came in. One girl railed back, in full five-year-old disdain, "Julie, you know about teaching, but you don't know about children!" It stung, and stayed with me, stating exactly what I needed to learn.

First Impressions of Henry

The only one who challenges my ability to like him is Henry, although he is intellectually capable, imaginative, "smart." But he is "sneaky"—aware when an adult is around and watching. He knocks down others' buildings—two complaints about this today. He makes himself an outsider, then resents being an outsider. Doesn't talk or explain . . . doesn't look at the person he's talking to, adult or child.

What did I notice about Henry in the beginning of the year? He was tall, slightly heavy. He moved as if not quite knit together, a marionette with no puppeteer, as if he were putting no muscles into play. Things near him got knocked over. Was it intentional? Working at a table, he would sit with his body draped over a chair, one leg stretched out, foot half out of an untied sneaker. Writing or drawing, he held marker or pencil in a loose idiosyncratic grip, and his drawings and letters were poorly formed.

But he worked with terrific concentration. It was clear what activities he liked: building with large Legos, construction materials, blocks. He always worked alone. He signed up frequently for the table near the sink, working with markers, paper, scissors, glue, and whatever other materials were offered; as the weeks went by, the collage activities appealed to him more and more. He volunteered to make signs for the room, illustrating "meeting" by drawing a lone child on the blue rug. He did not like *assigned* activities, especially those involving paper-and-pencil tasks. This could partly be explained by his weakness in this area. When he copied numbers and letters, the lines were shaky; when he wrote his name, the letters marched uphill. Things he didn't want to do, he just didn't do: when we went out on the street to collect squirrel-related stuff, he was one of two children who came back empty-handed, and when children drew their finds, he had to borrow an acorn. I'd found scribbling on the tables and floor, and wondered if it was Henry's doing: *I want to know who's doing it. To me, it's antisocial, antigroup. Maybe it's someone more marginal, who's unable to make the kind of contribution that I make space for—so this becomes a way of being public without having to be public through me, the teacher. So the first question should be not who, but why.*

His physical stance in relation to other people seemed to emphasize his isolation. When others spoke to him, child or adult, he turned his face away, and his eyes cut away, his face blank except for a wisp of a frown. This looking away was not, it's important to note, something that could be explained as a cultural norm. Henry's parents were from Europe but spoke English fluently; they looked directly at me when we spoke. Every morning, when he came to the rug for meeting, he would sit next to the bookcase, his body turned 180 degrees away from the others. Every morning, I would say, "Henry, please turn around." He would comply, but seemed to make a mute point: he would turn his head away, with a tiny, tiny smile. At other times, emotion would just flit over his face—a quicksilver smile, a quicksilver pout—and disappear. His physical separateness paralleled an emotional distance: he didn't initiate conversations with the teachers or with other children; he came to me only to complain because of something someone had done to him—knocked a building over, or taken something from him; he would talk to me with his head turned away. In October, I noted that, working at a table with others, he seemed "peripheral." He didn't show interest in anyone else's work, as the other children did, never said to someone sitting next to him, "That's cool!" He never showed his work to other children, asking, "You like this?" He never showed his work to me. But he wasn't exactly unaware of others. When he thought he wasn't observed, he would give a little shove to someone else's building, or make marks on others' drawings. One day, I caught him scribbling on the floor. He ignored adults' requests, or would comply *very* slowly—he would be the last to clean up, the last to get his stuff, the last on line.

Had I considered whether this description might fit a child with Asperger's syndrome? This question arises when children are significantly lacking in social skills, because the spectrum is broad and includes a range of behavior. Children with Asperger's typically are unaware of—don't observe and internalize—common social protocols that other children pick up without thinking. I remember one child who, when crossing the classroom, would walk smack through the middle of a group of children who were sitting on the floor playing a game—much to their extreme consternation; to this child, it made sense as a direct route. He hadn't learned to walk around a group of people. Henry, while most at ease working alone, showed social awareness: his antisocial behavior—observable when he was carefully watched—was proof that he knew norms but preferred not to follow them.

In those first weeks of school, Henry's sneakiness and resistance got to me, brought out an oppositional streak in me. He challenged my authority—a passive resister, a classroom Gandhi—as I was attempting to teach routines and help children get to know each other. So here I was, frustrated, accusing, labeling him sneaky, a word that substituted for thinking on my part. It was not how I wanted to see him. It wasn't how I wanted to see myself; I didn't want to take that accusing tone.

Henry's behavior puzzled me. It might not have posed a big problem for another teacher, who might have labeled him a loner and moved on to children whose behavior was more disruptive. Henry was not out-and-out defiant, wasn't aggressive; he didn't get into fights with others, didn't interrupt others during discussions. (In fact, in the fall, he didn't contribute at all during discussions.) But I was concerned about the gaps in behavior, his avoidance of direct emotional engagement with others. His isolation worried me more than it would have if he'd been younger, if this were a nursery-school class. I have a framework of expectations for this age group: five- and six-year-olds normally display some degree of sociability and positive connection to others; *most* children are engaged with their peers *and* with adults. When children tune out adults to focus exclusively on their peers, or focus only on adults, seeking approval and attention, ignoring peers, I will wonder about it, and help, if I can, extend their ties to include adults *and* peers. Henry did not involve himself in an on-going way with either children or adults. Although he was physically present in the class, he was not *socially* present, except in the negative ways implied by his small antisocial actions. What troubled me was not so much what he *was* doing, as what he wasn't.

One day, I noticed him—when he thought no one was looking—under the easel, loosening the nuts and bolts that held the easel together. I'd found them loosened on other days too. This was different from the scribbling; it required more effort. I was impressed by the effort, intrigued by how purposeful his actions were. But what was the purpose? What was the meaning of his behavior *to him*, what could this indirect, nonconfrontational behavior tell me about him? *How does it in some way function for him?* My assumption is that behavior is caused; if this had been the only thing of this sort he'd done, I might have taken it as evidence of strong curiosity and persistence, which it certainly was, but there was also the scribbling on the floor, which couldn't have been motivated by curiosity. The defiance of social norms in indirect ways, when adults aren't looking, makes sense in classrooms where adult controls are continually imposed, where children lack legitimate means of expression. How did it make sense in a classroom that devoted time and space to expressive activities?

My observation that day reframed what I had termed his sneakiness: he liked doing things in secret. That way of putting it helped me fashion a strategy: moving him away from secrecy by focusing on his work; building a relationship with him and helping him form ties to others in the class *through* the work he was doing, the products he was making. It was a strategy I arrived at intuitively: at the time, I didn't put it in words in this way. But when I found him working so intently that day, I was able to see his behavior from his point of view; I found something I could identify with. It made it possible for me to take into account the force of his desire to make an impact upon the world.

Teacher and Parents, I

From the parent information form: Henry is "shy"—no mention of defiance, resistance, though I've seen him, often, ignore his father's requests. His parents appear to set no limits for either him or his sister; both children do whatever they want.

There are teachers for whom the classroom is a separate world: as far as they're concerned, children leave their home selves behind when they step through the classroom door. These teachers may intend, in this way, to avoid the trap of accepting lower expectations for children whose lives may be especially difficult or impoverished. Other teachers are motivated by the wish to protect children whose home circumstances are unhappy. These are valid motives, but I believe that children invariably bring the rest of their lives, and their feelings, with them into the classroom. I find that knowing something about a child's life at home may help me see who the child is in school, may help me perceive motivation I hadn't considered, and give me insights about how to work with that child. Yet a danger exists that on the basis of information about children's lives, teachers may draw oversimplified conclusions about the causes of children's behavior. This, I believe, is what I did with Henry. It is all too easy for teachers to blame parents—just as it is for parents to blame teachers—and this is especially the case when parents and teachers don't start out with the same goals and values.

I send home a parent information form at the beginning of the year. I ask about the names and ages of the children's siblings, about their previous school experiences, about any health problems. I ask parents what they wish to see children accomplish during their kindergarten year. I also ask, "What do you see as your child's strengths? Do you have any concerns about your child? What are your child's interests? Is there anything else you think I should know about?" Answers to these questions vary enormously. One parent's analysis of her child's interests fills a page; another parent answers the question in four words: "Sam likes to draw." In addition to my careful reading of the information forms, when a child is especially challenging, I will usually seek other reliable sources of information. With the parents' permission, I'll speak to teachers at the child's previous school. I also observe children and parents as they separate in the mornings.

When Henry began school, I already knew him and family. His older sister, Lisette, had been in my class two years previously. She, too, had been a silent, watchful child, isolated and uncommunicative; she, too, had been quick to complain about other children. In the notes I made for her spring parent conference, I wrote: "pattern of her not wanting to play with other children." But while I'd been concerned, there were many children that year whose social and educational needs were more pressing. I had discussed my concerns with her parents, who seemed to me to dismiss the matter. However, at the end of the year, they told me they felt Lisette had gained confidence. A year later, they requested that Henry be placed in my class. For the most part, I enjoy teaching the siblings of children I've already taught, seeing similarities and differences. I know I can depend on these parents, on the basis of trust that's already established. With Henry's parents, the opposite was true. They began the year—without knowing it—with a history: I had already characterized them as hard to reach.

When I taught Lisette, her mother would drop her off, and Henry, then three years old, would be with them. He would wander unsupervised around the room, grabbing and scattering whatever he could reach. His mother made no attempt to run interference, and I would have to ask her to stop him from knocking over tubs of construction materials. When they entered the classroom in the mornings, a frowning, pouting Lisette would often ignore everything going on around her—other children, the room's activities, the teachers—as she sought to gain her mother's attention, usually complaining about something Henry had done. There seemed to be another side to this sibling relationship: I was told by Lisette's after-school teacher of Lisette's daily meanness toward her little brother when their father and Henry came to pick her up. Again, the parent did not intervene. While this information came to me informally, I paid attention. Teachers are professionally obligated to respect parents' privacy. However, over the years, I've occasionally discovered pertinent information that parents had deliberately withheld, and so I've learned to listen—warily—to reports that come in a roundabout way. I try to balance caution and responsibility. I'd wondered at the time if Lisette's parents had chosen to let the two children work things out on their own. I wondered about the connection between Lisette's school behavior and what I saw as her parents' failure to protect the two, and to set limits.

When Henry started school, it was his father who dropped him off. Like Lisette, Henry would often start the morning complaining to his father. But for the most part, he would ignore his father. He would stand at a shelf and play with some material, paying no attention when his father would ask him to put away his coat and backpack. There was sometimes a little dance between them, of his father's requests, and Henry's mute defiance. When his father said good-bye, Henry would never look up or reply, and his father would make no effort to gain Henry's compliance in acknowledging his departure. I remembered how Henry's mother didn't stop him when, as a three-year-old, he'd moved rambunctiously around the room; I remembered the earlier reports that their father had not gotten involved when Lisette teased or was rough with Henry. As I observed Henry's disengagement from others, his reluctance to participate in the give-and-take of group life, I quickly drew a conclusion: I blamed his parents for not stepping in to protect both children from impulsive behavior, for failing to set limits. Now, looking back, without negating what I'd noticed—the siblings' competition to get their parents on their side, Henry's defiance of his father, his isolation from classmates—I believe I would have done better to have left open the question of the connection between his behavior in school and his home life.

Making a snap judgment, I focused on what I saw as his parents' shortcomings. The conclusion I drew about the causes of his behavior was simplistic and highly speculative, and didn't help me work with his family. Just as I'd initially seen him as a difficult child, I saw them as difficult parents. What also strikes me is the gap between my reading of Henry—as passively defiant and isolated—and his parents' description of him as shy. It was essential that I work with them; at the same time, the judgment I made, and the gap between our readings of him, would make it harder to find a basis for agreement. Just as it was a stretch for me to find a path to work with him, it would prove to be a stretch for me to find common cause with them.

Departments of education, principals, and education-school professors all speak of the value of teachers "making parents their partners." I agree that teachers should try to involve parents in a variety of ways, all year. My experience is that when teachers and parents have values and goals in common and make the effort to work together and share information, they can support each other even when a child's problems are severe. What matters is the tone of the exchange. When children know teachers and parents agree, things are (relatively) easy. I taught one child who, on his worst days, threatened to kill other children and had to be watched around the class pets. His parents had asked to meet with me before school began; they were forthright and hid no information. Their trust in me—and mine in them, because of their honesty—was rewarded: the child had a good year, despite his serious difficulties. The tone his parents set with him—they were not judgmental, punitive, or permissive—helped me take similar responsibility in the classroom, and we worked together all year.

But when there isn't a match between parents' and teachers' goals, views of children, or values, partnership remains an elusive ideal.

In November, I met with Henry's father for the fall parent conference. I described Henry's behavior in school and asked about his behavior at home. I started with what was positive: I talked about his great ability to concentrate, to focus on his drawings and construction. Then I talked about his struggle to write letters and numbers, and his isolation from other children. Since this was our first conference, and his father seemed ill at ease, I made the decision not to bring up Henry's small antisocial acts. I may have been wrong to do so, but I tailored what I said to what I felt his father was prepared to hear. His father listened attentively; he said he hoped he would make friends. I suggested they encourage playdates, but he said this was difficult, because Henry was in the school's after-school program every weekday afternoon. I described the way he turned away from people when he talked to them. His father acknowledged that he did this at home, too, and said he would talk to Henry about it.

Our conference was friendly but formal. It confirmed for me what I had imagined to be true, that we looked at Henry very differently. I could say that we wanted the same thing for Henry—a successful kindergarten year—but it meant different things to each of us. I wanted us to develop a more complex understanding of Henry, to develop a common ground for thinking about him, to agree that we *didn't* understand him, that we had questions. In my eyes, the change that his father hoped to effect in his behavior was a surface change: he would talk to him about not turning away from people when he spoke with them. He didn't seem to be asking what impelled Henry to turn away.

When I look back on the conference and my feelings about it, something else seems evident that I didn't recognize at the time. I defined the gap between us as a failure on his father's part: he wasn't acknowledging—not perceiving—Henry's social and emotional difficulties. I should have tried to take his father's point of view, but I just couldn't do it. I was too committed to my own point of view. In fact, his father *was* aware of a problem, but in his own terms. If I'd cared more about teacher-parent partnership, would I have focused on the goal as he stated it, of helping Henry make friends? My one suggestion, planning playdates, was turned down. Couldn't I have come up with other ideas? Within the classroom, I might have frequently paired Henry with a socially engaged child, and occasionally invited the two to stay in from recess with me to work on projects. Whether or not that would have worked, we would have had a plan connected with his father's stated concern. But focused as I was on *my* goal, I didn't see that it was an important step for his father to ask Henry to look at people when he talked to them. Imperfect as the conference was, because we put Henry's social development at the center of the discussion, it had served a valuable function. Yet I may have been mistaken in not speaking more frankly. I concluded that his father and I saw his behavior differently. I ended the conference feeling I was on my own to find a way to engage him with others in the class.

Henry at Work

Henry was working on another stick collage in A.M., which he talked about to me. The "snow" was two balled up bits of paper doily. He wanted to use watercolor on them, as I suggested—but no time. He used the sticks to make "monsters"—popsicle sticks and coffee stirrers, pointed out aggressively . . . but for all that, he seemed more open, more communicative.

The afternoon when I'd observed Henry taking off the easel's bolts, I felt that the pieces were beginning to fit together. I was beginning to grasp who he was, and this would make it possible for me to teach him. As I wrote earlier, I see teaching as mediated by relationships. The better I knew Henry, the better I could take into account his individual capacities, strengths and weaknesses, preferences and interests. But my purpose wasn't only to make possible better planning. By *knowing* him, apprehending and appreciating his uniqueness, insisting on his individuality, attending to what distinguished him from everyone else, I would forge a relationship, through which teaching and learning could occur. Overall, my goal was not to make him conform, but to find openings in the classroom for his pursuit of knowledge, ways for him to be himself and also a member of the group.

Not all teachers see this as a goal; for many, teaching means finding what's the same, not what's different. At some point every fall, I check in with the first-grade teachers, to see how "my" children are doing. As we talk about these children, one of the newer, younger teachers will invariably say, "Oh, he's a Brian," referring to a child she'd taught in a previous year, who displayed similar traits. This view of children—as if they come in generic brands—can have negative consequences. It restricts the resources that we imagine in children and limits the meanings we can help them make. When teachers see children in categories rather than as individuals, we are more likely to make snap judgments and label behavior. I did this with Henry, in the early fall, and I know I am likely to do it when a child's behavior seems to be preventing me from getting things done. Most of the time, as was true with Henry, I become aware of my frustration and can step back, but for many teachers, the labels—"sneaky" or "lazy" or "defiant"—stick, and explain behavior. Then, because "bad" behavior is expected, it's more likely to be noticed. A cycle sets in, precluding teachers from seeking causes for behavior and obstructing a view of children's positive traits. As teachers find themselves increasingly frustrated, they may compound the problem by speaking to these children in demeaning ways, or speaking about them to other adults, in their presence, as if they weren't there. Fortunately, watching Henry work away at the easel's nuts and bolts sparked my interest. With a different child, it might have been something else—a joke, a thoughtful act—something that, however small, would allow me to see the child in a positive way, and would permit the building of a relationship based on some identification and interest, rather than on disapproval and annoyance. Just as different teachers find different behaviors off-putting—one teacher's expressive child is another teacher's fresh child—teachers find different connections. What is necessary is that teachers pay attention so that they are prepared to notice when a child's action offers the possibility of a changed relationship.

The work of seeing children as unique individuals requires from teachers an attitude of inquiry and openness, as well as techniques of observation, recording, and reflection. When I was a student at Bank Street College, the core course Assessing and Interpreting Child Behavior, taught by Dorothy Cohen, trained us to observe children. Cohen pushed us to develop the capacity to observe precisely and objectively, to place behavior in a context, to be aware of our biases, to avoid moral judgments. She asked us to look and listen and record, to catch the quality of children's actions and interactions. We had to attend not only to what children did, but to how they did it, the emotive quality of movement and voice. The belief that we can best understand children's learning by observing them *in action* was integrally tied to the belief that children *learn* through active engagement with the world. Teachers also have to be able to see what children are doing when they seem to be doing nothing. In *Encouraging Children to Learn*, Don Dinkmeyer and Rudolf Dreikurs recount a teacher's story of reading poetry aloud to the class and noticing a look of concentration and pleasure on the face of a difficult child.[3] The observation helped the teacher find a way to work with the child.[4]

To the proposition that observation should be a central task for teachers, I would add a corollary, that the degree to which children can be known depends on the curricular richness of the classroom. The more scope that classrooms allow for children's individual choice and involvement—the more active children are, the greater their freedom in pursuing activities—the more we can learn about who they are. In the spring, I wrote: *as the months*

have passed, I can see the way certain themes recur with each child,
because I have allowed them space in the classroom, public space.
Dewey commented on this relationship: a teacher gains "knowledge of the individuals with whom he is concerned" when he
moves away from methods that stress "passivity and receptivity"
and broadens the range of activities viewed as educational—that
is, when schools give children "outward freedom." [5] The classroom gave Henry creative freedom to work on his own projects
and represent real things in his own way. In the course of the year,
it became the context for his remarkable drawings and constructions: in the fall, when he worked on a group collage showing
squirrels' nests, and in the spring, when the class studied undersea
life.

In recent years, educators have carefully examined children's
work in order to illuminate their thinking and learning styles. In
the 1990s, when the "whole language" approach to literacy was
more popular, teachers were encouraged to collect student work
in portfolios and to record children's reading strategies. I'd always
saved work, but I began in those years to save work in a more systematic way. I saved work that reflected children's beginning
writing efforts, and also work that displayed some aspect of how
a student looked at the world: drawings that incorporated pattern or symmetry, or, for example, a representation by one child
of herself, her mother, and stepfather—labeled "Kate, Mom,
Ken"—which captured the meaning to her of her family.

The educator Patricia Carini, co-founder of the Prospect
School, devised specific protocols for looking at children and their
work.[6] For her, the study of children's work is more than a means
of gaining information about children. By describing children's
work and children themselves in concrete detail, teachers educate
themselves as reflective thinkers and place individual children at
the center of educational practice. Thus, teachers' study of children affects how they teach, a process that assumes some reciproc-
ity of relationship between teachers and children.

The educational philosophy governing the Reggio Emilia mu-

nicipal preschools takes educational processes to be inherently re-
ciprocal. Learning is defined as occurring *through dialogue*
(among children, as well as between teacher and child). In Reggio, documentation of children's work and of teachers' thinking
is the visible form of that dialogue, and is viewed as essential to
the process.[7] In this formulation of the educational process, children take "paths" that teachers both facilitate and monitor; the
teacher's documentation of these paths creates a context[8] that
permits children's "search for meaning" as well as teachers'
search for "the meaning of school."[9] One way to sum up the
approach is to say that in traditional classrooms, teaching is believed to lead to learning while in the classrooms in Reggio
Emilia, learning—as teachers document and analyze it—leads to
teaching.

In the schools in Reggio, documentation of work is a *necessary*
part of study itself. When I was first introduced to the approach, I
saw documentation as a powerful tool, and one that fit my earlier
training in observational techniques, although my documentation of work and my use of documentation for planning is limited
compared with the work done in Reggio schools. In my classroom,
children talk about their work; I take photographs and dictation.
Work becomes the content of wall displays, with dictated or written text, and photographs. I make notes and use them to plan. In
these ways, children's work is the center of the classroom.

With Henry, the loop began with his work and continued as I
looked at his work, aware of its density and mix of materials. *I
have been focusing on him, concentrating on him. Thinking about
him and spending time looking at what he is doing.* It was clear I
could only connect with him through his work, would only be
given a role in his life to the extent that I allied myself with his
creative endeavors. As a result of this insight, I concentrated on
playing an especially active role in relation to his productions; I
would stop by at intervals as he was working.

In the winter and early spring, Henry's love of making things
continued to dominate his school life, despite his poor coordina-

tion and weak grip. The area where he worked would become littered with paper scraps, scissors, markers, open glue sticks. Soon, he needed more than one day to finish a project, and I found a place on the back counter for him to leave unfinished work. I would remind him to write his name on his work. To save materials he was using, he would dutifully write his name on them, too: a scrap of paper or a lone popsicle stick would have his name. At some point, I gave him a little plastic box in which to save scraps. As he used more materials, his projects became thicker, more and more three-dimensional: he built up and out, rolling and taping paper, using cardboard, pen tops, popsicle sticks; the levels multiplied as he used everything that would add density and height.

Throughout this period, besides taking the time to look at his work and talk to him about it, and making space for him to save it, I ensured that his work was shared at meetings. I wrote down his words, photographed his work, and displayed the photos. As he saw teacher and kids valuing him and his work, his secretiveness became, to an extent, transformed. He still didn't talk much to others at the table, but he seemed to pay more attention to others as they worked alongside him, cutting, gluing, taping. His works in progress were saved next to those of others; the photos of his work went up on the wall next to photos of others' work. He became—again, to a limited extent—what he hadn't been before, a member of a group.

Certain group activities appealed to him. Despite having refused to pick anything up when we'd gone on our first squirrel trip, he worked enthusiastically with the student teacher and other children on the squirrel collage. The activity suited him perfectly; it utilized his strengths, his preference for working with paper and his interest in representing things in forms he could physically manage. He also liked David, the student teacher. One day, after working with David, Henry went off on his own, cutting up big pieces of construction paper, then taping the cut shapes together to make a huge squirrel. "Could we put it up on the wall?" I asked—and he agreed, if somewhat reluctantly.

As the year progressed, although Henry's work had become a link in his relationship with me, and to a lesser extent, with the other children, he continued to pursue activities in a solitary way (one exception was his pairing up with Amina to measure the rug); he still seemed not fully present in the room, not quite to belong. He continued to dislike assigned activities, did not yet participate in meetings, and disliked being *required* to produce a piece of work. When we made self-portraits in a session of Studio in the Schools, Henry was frustrated and threw away each drawing he began. At one of our last Studio in the Schools sessions, Andrea, our resident artist, asked everyone to say what they had especially liked doing. When it was his turn, Henry shouted out (which was unusual for him), "Nothing!" There were still things he did behind the backs of adults. One day, at lunch, unprovoked, he'd spit on the food of the child sitting next to him. For me, it wasn't a question of "bad behavior" but of wondering what to do next. Was it possible for him to become more actively involved with the other children? How could I help make it happen?

One morning late in the fall term, Betsy Grob, David's supervisor from Bank Street, had noticed Henry at the turtle tank, peering at the fish that we'd put into the tank. She went over and talked to him. He'd seen that when he put his finger on the tank wall, the fish swam over; when he moved his finger, the fish followed. He led them around the tank, creating a path for them with his moving finger. He hadn't told anyone. It was Betsy's interest in *his* interest that led him to reveal the phenomenon, to bring it to the attention of the rest of the class. That he'd discovered this trick said something about Henry—his ability to observe and concentrate, to experiment; but the fact that he hadn't communicated his discovery until an adult asked him what he was doing revealed something else about him. Few five-year-olds would have kept such exciting news to themselves. I can picture him at the turtle tank, standing alone, intrigued by the game he'd invented. A few months later, by early spring, his world seemed to have opened up a bit, yet he didn't seem decisively different. Parent conferences were coming up in March, the last official conference of the year. I decided to recommend to his parents that they seek an evaluation by a psychologist.

Teacher and Parents, II

A danger of speaking of my concerns to children's parents is that they may only hear there's a problem, may focus solely on behavior, may not see causes, and may then merely issue a command: "Behave yourself in school! Listen to the teacher!"

In March, before my conference with Henry's parents, I asked myself if I was overreacting. Looking over my notes, I concluded that Henry's social isolation was different enough from the *range* of behavior of fives and sixes for my concern to be justified. I don't want to decree that development follow one "normal" path; I don't want to stigmatize children for whom solitary activity is essential—the passionate builders or painters who prefer working alone, who don't want to compromise their clear ideas about what they are constructing, the children who sit and study books intently, well before they can actually read. Many children this age have the capacity to work on their own with intensity and commitment. However, most of these children also team up with others at other times of the day. It was this urge for companionship that I failed to see in Henry.

By this point in the year, I would have expected to see Henry beginning to develop friendships, to join groups. There was also the incident in the cafeteria, his spitting on another child's food. He continued to look away when talking to people. What worried me was the *degree* of separation that characterized him *throughout* the school day. I see children's emotional well-being, their comfort and ease with others, as very much part of my legitimate interest as their teacher. Yet these are difficult issues to take up with parents.

With few exceptions, the parents of the children I teach are caring, involved, thoughtful. Conferences are taken up with children's progress, examination of their work, and discussions of their social relationships and ability to manage the ups and downs of group life. Often parents use conferences as an opportunity to think aloud about who they are as parents: *Sandra, Nia's mother, has struggled to know exactly what being a mother is all about.* My role is to listen, acknowledge, reassure, returning again and again to the child's strengths and their strengths as parents. I share a mantra learned from my own experience as a parent as well as from teaching: Children teach us to be the kind of parents they need us to be. I do my best to listen: to concentrate on what's being said, to find ways to make my points relevant, and to be prepared if something completely unexpected comes up, as it often does.

In some conferences, I have to bring up difficulties a child is having, problems whose origins are connected to parental actions or assumptions. When this is the case, I seek an alliance with parents' interests, an alliance based on genuine respect for the challenges parents face. Emily, one of the oldest children in the class, is socially immature and lacks confidence; and I've noticed, when I see them together, how critical her mother is—a layer of anxious carping and nagging sits on top of a layer of love and affection. The issue comes up in the course of the conference: *When her mother comes for the conference, Emily comes too, in tears, but her mother says she must sit on the chair outside, and can't play or draw. Her mother explains: Emily is "on punishment." What had she done? Wet her pants. Her mother and I talked about getting children's compliance. I said, You have to be her ally, she wants to be grown up, you can use that. Her mother looked skeptical. It's clear to me that it's Emily's body, and I said that, but it's equally obvious to me that, when I talk to her mother, I can't just be on* Emily's *side.*

In these conferences, I depend on parents' goodwill and the trust I've established with them. The challenge for me is to talk in a way that isn't judgmental. To develop goals *with* parents, rather than impose my own. It's often the main issue: *How to help people empathize with their children—as someone like Billy's mother does, automatically, as a matter of course—when it isn't something they do naturally?* I want to extend their understanding, so parents see they have options beyond simply telling their child, "Listen to the teacher!"

I know I am judgmental at times, without consciously intending to be. I want more influence than I actually have; with some parents, I do want to impose my values. I can be rash, a missionary. There are parents who've thought me interfering, accused me of stepping beyond my legitimate role. It's ultimately counterproductive, because when parents—who are, rightly, highly invested in who they are as parents—perceive themselves under attack, they inevitably become defensive and close up. This judging on my part is more likely to happen with children I am more worried about, whose parents, not surprisingly, seem to me most unaware of the profound impact they have on their children's lives.

In the vast majority of families whose children I've taught, the parents recognize and take into account their children's feelings, much of the time, either consciously or instinctively. However, even in otherwise loving and caring families, these connections can break down. One fall, John had trouble separating from his mother. Every morning, there were not simply tears, but clinging sobs, and his mother and I had to pry him loose so she could leave. He could not be comforted, and would have to sit for a while, shaken; the rest of the day, however, he was competent, involved. When the pattern persisted for two weeks, with no lessening of his terror when his mother left, I met with her. I asked about any changes in his life in the recent past. She mentioned—in passing—that her father had moved in with them the previous spring because he'd been very ill. I asked what happened, and she told me her father had died that summer, in their living room. But, she assured me, John had been fine, he wasn't affected by it. Did John's parents assume that because he was a child (and additionally, because he was a boy?) he was insulated from feelings about this death? That he didn't *feel* sadness or fear if he didn't *express* his feelings in words, and if they didn't talk about the death? Since they didn't see him as affected by the death, they were unable to help him feel better. When he entered school, his anguish at separation from his mother spoke loudly, but his parents hadn't connected the loss of life he'd just witnessed in his living room with his response to the temporary loss of his mother every morning. Had I known about his experience of death, I might have worked with his parents to ease the morning separation and to make his transition to a new school smoother.

This child's distress was temporary, but it points to problems that, for some children, are not short-term. Children's feelings—of loss and pain, fear and suspicion, love and shame and hate—are intense and real, even when the causes seem trivial to adults, or irrational and unfounded, or when children lack the words for them. When parents are insensitive to children's feelings or lack a vocabulary for them, they are unable to help them make sense of difficult experiences. These parents may be unable to manage their own emotions and therefore unable to discipline children in ways that support the children's development of inner controls and self-knowledge. Their emotional blindness may have been inherited from *their* parents, and they pass on to the next generation a limited capacity for self-awareness and empathy. I'm not concerned here with adults who act decisively and strictly in situations that call for that. Nor am I concerned about the variety of faults for which every parent could be held accountable if everything were recorded somewhere: reasonably good parents are still guilty of short tempers, unjust decisions, and ill-considered rebukes. Parents, like teachers, learn on the job as children develop, and they cope with their own feelings and lives.

Nor am I describing here children who have been physically abused, although child abuse and neglect are terribly serious problems. My concern here is with family problems that are less recognized. In some families, the problem is adult permissiveness: the parents who lack a sense of their authority as parents, who find it impossible to set limits, don't protect children from siblings, or give in to children's every expressed need. In these households, parents and children may continually jockey for power; faced with a child's intransigence, these parents may respond at the child's level. The children in these families are often anxious, because they have no ally against the power of their own emotions. Anxiety at having the upper hand may make them especially demanding, and they may come to feel entitled to dominate social situations.

With some parents, I've become aware of repeated verbal abuse, as damaging in the long run to a child's development of inner resources and trust as physical abuse. The mother of one child I taught was unfailingly sarcastic toward her child. Noticing one morning that other children were arriving with homework papers, she publicly disparaged her daughter for not having told her about the homework, then turned and walked out of the room. The child sat on the rug, slouched forward, face hidden by her hair, as if hoping to disappear entirely. When parents are consistently controlling and harsh, when they routinely threaten and punish or criticize, they engender in children either fear or an intense desire to please. Parents who belittle or humiliate may sabotage children's belief in themselves. Parents who tease may excuse it as "only a joke," but these "jokes," by taking advantage of children's weakness, emphasize to them their vulnerability.

The children who, in the daily give-and-take of classroom life, demonstrate little emotional resilience and few inner controls are those who have been routinely treated in arbitrary and hostile ways, those whose development was shaped by the adults' misuse of power and their own weakness. One parent, incensed when his child had talked back to him in a "fresh" way, locked the child out of their apartment. The mere threat of such punishment is destructive of a child's sense of safety and ability to trust adults. Without a sense of safety, and trust in adults, children are more likely to misbehave in exactly the ways that parents so strongly wish to prevent. I sometimes face a difficult choice. In the nonpunitive atmosphere of my classroom, children who have been treated harshly at home, who obey their parents out of fear, are *more* likely than other children to be physically aggressive or testing. With these acting-out children, a partnership with parents is problematic: I am reluctant to keep parents fully informed if I believe they will physically punish children. I am slow to turn for help to parents who I know depend entirely on threats and material bribes ("No visit from Santa unless the teacher says you're behaving!").

For a few parents, children's powerlessness and vulnerability do not lead to protection and thoughtfulness; rather, these qualities of childhood encourage the abuse of power. These are the parents who are most unable, for whatever reasons, to offer children guidance. Children's classroom behavior and sense of well-being—their ability to manage their emotions, sense of resilience, ability to learn—are directly affected by family life, by how they are treated and how they are expected to treat others, and by particular circumstances like separation and loss. As a result, parent-child relationships are within the realm of our concern as teachers. But while we can express concern about what we see as the impact on a child of parents' actions, can suggest alternatives to harsh discipline methods, and can recommend books on parenting, our ability to affect parent attitudes may be limited.

Still, it's important for us to remember that our knowledge of children's circumstances is always incomplete. Our understanding of their lives remains informed speculation. This is also true because people contain contradictions. In our desire for simple, direct explanations for behavior, we may not perceive and take into account parents' strengths. Teachers' perceptions may also be distorted because of differences between their culture and expectations and those of parents.[10]

Adults' knowledge of children depends, too, on what we—parents *and* teachers—bring to thinking about them. At any particular moment, our ability to see, question, and reflect varies. Just as circumstances affect children's responses, circumstances affect our ability to perceive; circumstances affect what we are able to see and hear. Often, it is a matter of facing something more than once, hearing it more than once. For parents—for any of us—being able to take in what's said may be a question of trust and of how something is said.

Knowing how difficult it would be for Henry's parents to hear what I was prepared to say to them about him—that it would be heard as a judgment on his behavior, and on them—and knowing too how difficult it would be for me to say what I wanted to say, I was apprehensive about the conference. Both his parents showed up. We started out in agreement: his academic performance was excellent. Henry was reading and writing by this time, even though the lines he produced when he wrote and drew were shaky. But, I said, I remained deeply concerned about his relationships with other children, and his behavior. I brought up his spitting on the other child's lunch (which I'd let them know about at the time). Immediately, his father countered: boys will be boys. I should have been prepared for this response, but I wasn't.

I went on to describe another incident, something very small. Sitting next to Amina one day, Henry had rolled her pencil off the table when she was looking the other way. I'd happened to catch his deliberate action, and had thought it a curious thing to do. It came out of nowhere: there was no existing antagonism between the two of them that would have explained it. It seemed to me to be something a boy might do to another boy, not something a boy would do to a girl. It was not the sort of teasing that's commonly observed in this age group, which is not sophisticated, not hidden: the teaser picks openly on someone with whom he has a relationship. So if Henry wasn't challenging Amina, what was he doing? It was provocative, but at the same time secretive. The act fit the pattern of other things he'd done, but what was the point, what was his motivation? I don't know how well I said any of this, if I did a good job of explaining why this small act concerned me. In any case, Henry's father immediately said it was a normal thing to do. I responded that well, no, from my years of experience teaching kindergarten, young children don't usually provoke other children for no reason. With that statement, both sides were set in hardened opposition.

To his parents, as I found out afterward, the stories were proof I didn't like Henry. To me, the stories were news his parents didn't want to hear, and his father's rejoinders were as effective in their way as Henry's behavior when *he* ignored others in the class. I made the recommendation that they consult a psychologist, but it was obvious it would be rejected. I saw it as their failure; I wanted Henry's parents to see him as I did. But looking back, I see that I failed to find a way to make my concern about his emotional well-being relevant to *them*, failed to enlist them.

During the March conference, as Henry's father and I sparred, his mother had sat silently. That silence was expressive; her unwillingness to participate seemed to send a message, even though I couldn't read its meaning. Some days after the conference, when I saw her after school one day, I asked her if we could talk. My intuition was that there might be some opening if I met with her separately. I said, I didn't know what *you* thought about Henry's behavior. I'd managed to find the right way to put it. Sitting with her, I was able to make the case for my genuine concern for Henry. I talked about my values as a teacher, saying that I care about children's emotional well-being as well as their academic progress. I was worried, I told her, by Henry's indirect defiance, though it was something many teachers might not care about since he was doing well academically. Was that very different from what I'd already said? Whatever the causes—the different circumstances? the implicit message that I valued her role and her opinion? a difference in my tone? speaking about my own values?—unlike the earlier conference, this meeting produced a feeling of shared involvement rather than judgment. Late in our talk, she told me she'd earlier felt that I didn't like Henry. She'd felt I was picking on him. She said she saw that wasn't the case and agreed to have a psychologist do an evaluation.

Late in the spring, the psychologist observed Henry in the

classroom, and I spoke with him briefly. I never learned the results of the evaluation, never saw a write-up, and received no official word. But events in the spring—the March conference, with his father's quick defense of Henry's behavior, my subsequent meeting with Henry's mother, where I'd learned that his parents had seen me as picking on Henry, and his parents' decision to have him evaluated—somehow changed the picture I'd formed of Henry *in* his family. I reconsidered the notion that I'd begun the year with, that the cause of Henry's behavior was his parents' failure to set limits. Instead, I saw Henry fitting into a family that was characterized by distance on his parents' part from the emotional world that he and his sister inhabited. In this family, perhaps, a certain disengagement was the norm. My assumptions about the central place of social interactions in childhood were simply not shared by his parents. In drawing this (possible) conclusion, Henry's scribblings and acts of defiance somehow made sense as reactions to a pattern in which his emotional life perhaps received less direct attention from adults than he needed. Yet whatever the psychologist concluded and recommended, in making the decision to consult a psychologist, Henry's parents altered the pattern to a degree. I'd played a role in that decision, partly because, in my second meeting with his mother, I'd managed to override my habit of being judgmental when I felt stymied with parents. Whether or not Henry was aware of it, and whatever the impact on his world, the fact was that his parents and I had acted in concert.

Henry at the End of the Year

Henry came up to me and said, Do you want to marry the BFG? I said, What do you mean? He said, You said you love the BFG, so that means you want to marry the BFG.

One afternoon, when the class was getting ready to listen to a chapter of Roald Dahl's *The BFG*, which I'd been reading to them, Henry teased me because I'd said to the class, "I *love* the

BFG." His comment showed off the changes in his behavior as the year moved toward its end: *He now comes up and offers comments to me, spontaneously, just as the others do—for him it is a huge step.* He had begun, more and more, to talk to me, to show me his drawings. One day when two other boys were drawing, continually coming up to ask me to write about their drawings (these were actually like sketchily illustrated stories they were *telling*, about monsters), Henry did it too.

It was true that he continued to resist certain imposed group projects, but now he said what he felt. When we made plasticene models of undersea creatures, Henry complained, "I don't know how." Arshea, the assistant teacher, who had by this time returned to the classroom after giving birth, sat with him and talked him through the problems of representation. *Where Henry has progressed—and this is where I feel most pleased and proud—is his willingness to take risks in communicating his thoughts and feelings.* Yet the changes had limits. He still didn't look at me when he talked to me, which set him apart from everyone else in the class; he didn't have any steady friends, although he now often asked Max to be his partner when the class lined up. He was still not fully engaged with others. What seemed different was his knowledge that he could rely on me. I was careful about not letting him get away with things. I insisted he pay attention to me, to the adult; I didn't ignore things. I wasn't neutral or blank. I forced him to take me into account, providing a kind of ballast for him, keeping him grounded against whatever emotional winds moved him. I didn't pry, I wasn't intrusive; I didn't ask him about his feelings. But I watched, and I was ready to listen when he had something to say. I steadily ensured that his work was valued, by me and by the other children. All the tiny steps he made—his comments, drawings—were placed in some public context.

When we undertook our study of undersea life, Henry, in his own off-center way, played a leadership role. It was a public role. This wasn't the Henry who liked *hiding* what he was doing. He was clearly attached to the subject, and he drew many careful detailed illustrations of the fish he was studying.

Because his strength was in making things, Henry's contributions to the class were things he made. After the class had made mobiles of undersea creatures with Andrea, our Studio in the Schools artist, Henry independently made his own hanging paper jellyfish. He cut a semicircle from construction paper, punched holes along the flat side, and came to me for help in tying on ribbons for tentacles. He even made a paper fish that was caught in the tentacles. It was his idea to hang the jellyfish overhead: we tied a string on it, and I attached the string to the light fixture so that the jellyfish floated above our heads. Henry produced this jellyfish by working in his solitary way, but the solitary nature of his pursuits had been profoundly altered by the group's activities. Soon, everyone was making paper undersea creatures—sharks, rays, dolphins, giant squid, more jellyfish. One by one, as these went up overhead, the classroom took on an undersea ambience. In the block area, children had begun building an aquarium, others were labeling the displays of plasticene animals; the class aquarium was to be the setting for our last family-invited event of the year, in late June. Henry, again working on his own, made a sign for the classroom door, a page full of sea creatures. On the top he had written, WELCOME TO THE AQUARIUM. While Henry worked alone on these products, they showed his involvement with what was going on around him; they demonstrated how much he had become part of the class.

Henry's participation in the making of the aquarium, his visible stamp on this environment, summed up his growth. It was material proof of how far he'd come. "Welcome to the Aquarium," he'd written; the words had a deeper meaning for me. His message is a metaphor for the world of the classroom, which like the sea provides a home for very individual creatures, a space of both cohesion *and* immense variety. The steps Henry made, the particular place he made for himself, came about over many

months as a consequence of his own strengths *and* of what was offered in the environment. What contributed to his development
was his love of making things, his interest in the animals we'd
studied, and the opportunity, within this classroom, for him to
pursue his interests, day after day—in the company of others.

His story is, in large part, the story of the class. It was the class
that provided lessons for Henry about a possible role he could play.
He began to make things that had meaning for the others; it was
a significant development. It was the class that didn't allow him
to stay alone, that valued and copied his creations, giving him reason to create more. The social environment of the class supported
his growth and changed the nature of his ties to others. The impact of the other children *as a group*, in affecting Henry's growth,
is a lesson for me when I look back and draw conclusions from this
story.

Henry's social environment included, also, the adults: David,
our fall-term student teacher, and the assistant teacher, Arshea,
whose kindness Henry could count on. I don't want to underesti-
mate my role: the story of Henry is also the story of one teacher
and one child; this account illuminates one teacher's positive *and*
negative qualities. All year, I sought to steer him toward friendships, toward work and play with others. I struggled to understand
him, was persistently interested in him, and engineered a relationship with him that I hoped would help break through his
isolation.

Yet I couldn't dictate his path: this was another lesson for me
from my year with this "difficult" child. The progress he made
was *his* sort of progress: he wrote the script. Although he moved
toward engagement, he was engaged with others primarily
through the work he did. I would have written a different role for
him, one that gave him more lines, more dialogue. The lesson—
which I seem to learn over and over—is that children's stories
are their own. Teachers conspire with them, aid and abet, but the
plot is theirs. However, while my goal wasn't realized in the way
I'd envisioned—he continued to pursue activities in a solitary

way—I believe that the shift in his connectedness to others came about partly as a consequence of conscious effort and commitment on my part and partly as a result of his physical and social environment.

Henry's story illustrates one child's growth over the course of a year. It is only that: one year. What came next in Henry's life? How have his subsequent teachers seen him? How have they seen their role in relation to him and to his emotional and social development? Seeing Henry's first-grade teacher from time to time, I'd ask how he was doing. She saw that he needed support in making connections to others, yet I am not certain that she sees children's social and emotional development as a goal equal to their academic progress.

My school's focus is children's development as *students*. A conflict resolution program is funded by the Parents Association, and a guidance counselor is available to work with individual students, but as is true for public schools generally, there isn't a consistent commitment to children's social and emotional development. The teachers share some values and beliefs but have different management styles and help children handle conflicts in a variety of ways. Children are exposed, in each class, to different expectations, routines, conversations, consequences.

When schools define their role in a broader way, they put in place a variety of institutional arrangements in relation to children's emotional and social well-being. When this is the case, teachers' stories about encounters with children move to the center of school life, rather than being peripheral. They take place at planned meetings, rather than during lunch break. They generate more complex knowledge about the children we teach, and help us plan for them. Most especially, by telling these stories in professional settings, teachers can come to see children differently; the work of describing transforms our understanding of them. Then, our stories are not just things that happened to us; they are critical sources of information about our work with children.

9

⚬

June: Meanings and Metaphors
at the End of the Year

Paper Casts: Classroom Metaphors

The last week: they are making casts out of paper. It started on Monday—they wrap paper around their arms, and tape the papers, making casts for a "broken arm." They write their names on one another's casts.

Toward the end of June, as we were counting down to the last day of school, Caroline made a paper cast for her arm. She said, "I broke my arm!" Soon lots of them were taping paper around their arms, wearing a paper cast or two, asking for autographs. Children are often dramatic about their injuries, knowing they'll get attention and sympathy. But watching the activity, I decided more was going on. The broken arm was a metaphor: *the class* was breaking up. It wasn't a conscious metaphor, and I wasn't about to use the occasion to teach about metaphors. The casts were *casts*, and the children were very happy making them.

Looking back at those last days, it made sense to me that the idea had been Caroline's. She was young—a fall birthday—and her transition to kindergarten hadn't been smooth: in the fall, she cried easily when things went wrong or when I left the class at lunch; by the winter, she'd begun to show more resilience. Now, her playfulness reigned, and through it, she'd found a way to manage this next change, the end of the year, the end of kinder-garten. She was in a sense a conceptual artist, a performance artist. She'd turned her body into an art object, and when she introduced this form of art to the others, they took it up with gusto. It was Caroline's gift to the class, a product of her imagination, her high spirits, her sense of joy. Perhaps the interpretation says something about me, Caroline's teacher. In any case, I couldn't separate the activity from the point in the year when it occurred, a point full of meaning for the class and for me.

When do we come up with metaphors? Are there circumstances when metaphors are more likely to pop into our minds? I'm not asking about the metaphors that occur to poets or writers of advertising copy, but about the metaphors that occur naturally, spontaneously, to children or adults as part of our lives.

I had begun talking to the children about the end of the school year in late May. I'd told them they'd be going to different first-grade classes, and that Brooke was going to go to a different school. They'd have different teachers, and I'd have a new class of kindergarten students. In early June, I brought the class to visit Eva's first-grade class. They wrote their questions beforehand on index cards. "Will we study animals?" "Am me and my friends going to be in the same class?" When we visited, they asked their questions, and Eva's students answered.

The class *was* breaking up; things would change. The year was almost over, and the friendships formed this year might not continue. But whatever changes lay ahead, the names signed on the casts were records of the children's year together. The year was ending as it had begun, with children reading and writing each other's names.

Metaphors arise when people have need of them. They are creative constructions, manufactured by imagination and emotion, and often connected to important events. The meanings they convey may be hard to put into words, or may be things that we don't want to talk or think about directly, something we wish to escape. Or the meaning may be too beautiful or wonderful, something that would be flattened by plain talk. Thus, metaphors perform a job for us; when they work, they work for us. They can weave different—even opposed—meanings into one dynamic perfect image. Coming up with a metaphor constitutes play; just as the children's work with shapes was a kind of play, this is play with the meanings of things. Just as the best play—the most purposeful play—is exploratory, and occurs when there is some internal challenge, perhaps metaphors follow a need to explain to ourselves new facts and feelings. Metaphors then, whether or not we're consciously aware of their role, help by creating a public truth out of private disturbances, out of *breaks* in continuity.

Metaphors are clues. They are in plain sight, but we don't necessarily see them for what they are. Jamie was an especially quiet child. In the fall and winter, she wouldn't respond verbally. When I called on her, she would simply shake her head, although she was otherwise cooperative and highly responsible. She made books, one after another, page after page, always about her family. I saw her numerous books as a metaphor for the volubility that she didn't allow herself. It was not only that they communicated the specific thoughts that Jamie might have said aloud, if she'd felt like it. In addition, they were, in their numbers, in the passion with which she worked on them, a stand-in for the loud, communicative Jamie who wasn't just then present in the classroom but who—as her parents assured me, and as I found out for myself later in the year—did really exist.

Metaphors are everywhere. Certain everyday classroom activities have a co-existence as metaphors. Lining children up, I'm sometimes aware of the demands that school, as an institution, makes on young children. I feel my role as socializing authority: like a sheepdog, I herd these recalcitrant, straying individuals into a cohesive *line*. No clumps, no gaps, all heads turned the same way; it's unnatural. Toward the end of summer vacations, I dream about lining up large numbers of children.

There is also metaphorical content in the small things that sum up for me aspects of the personalities of specific children. Vanessa's variety of clothing accoutrements, her barrettes, jewelry, bows and ties, mirrored her bouncy self and the intensity of attachment she brought to her shifting loves and hates. Denay's

"Click Club," which was the first survey the class produced, was a metaphor for her delight in cataloging and in patrolling the border of right and wrong. Sam's paper men, who guarded his paper bridges, reminded me of the space around him, the moat of white noise that separated him from his environment and made it hard for him to know what was going on. I saw a metaphor in the collage that Brooke and Hayley had made together, an object they'd created jointly, which perhaps would glue them together as friends.

The fascination of many of the children with the animals we'd studied seemed to me in part metaphorical. All the drawings of playful and happy dolphins, the drawings by the boys in the octopus-and-squid group of battles between squids and whales: these animals seemed to me to personify the children's own passions and wild feelings. Thus their drawings gave me information about the topics and themes that mattered to them.

The children's relationship to the class pets had elements of metaphor. Years ago, I'd find one boy, for whom controlling impulses was generally a losing battle, following the rabbit around the room; it was frequently impossible for him to focus on anything other than the rabbit, its free movements, twitching ears and nose. Other children loved the imperturbable guinea pig, and would sit for long periods patting it, combing its hair. The different animals represented qualities that, for whatever reasons, had special meaning for particular children.

Day to day, it's easy to miss metaphors in the constant motion. What drives certain children to always be the mother or big sister, the kitten or bad dog or robber, in dramatic play? Why do some children always draw dinosaurs or racing cars or rainbows? The point for teachers emphatically is not to search for *literal* one-to-one meanings in children's work and play; there is a danger that teachers will oversimplify, attributing meanings that misrepresent children's actions. We have to know the children if we want to know the meanings *to them* of their involvements. Our responsibility is to notice, to be open to meanings that may be part of the objects children draw and make, part of dramatic play, part of the attachments they form. Our observations may lead to interesting or important conversations, but the information that teachers may derive is secondary; the primary purpose of these metaphors is their usefulness to the children themselves, in giving form to something inchoate. Teachers need to understand that these activities, for whatever reasons, have special importance and deserve a place in the classroom.

Teachers can also make use of metaphors in planning, as long as metaphorical meanings are not artificially imposed. In May, the six kindergarten teachers had gotten together to order caterpillars from a biological supply company. The cardboard boxes came in the mail in late May: the caterpillars had arrived. There were enough for all the children to have one. With my help, each child took one caterpillar out of the plastic container they were in, and using a small paintbrush, gingerly placed it in a small plastic vial, with some green mush that was its food. The children wrote their names on the lids, and a few of them named their caterpillars. For the next two weeks, the first thing the children did every morning when they came into the room was to check out the vials as, day by day, the caterpillars got fatter. The children kept caterpillar journals, using magnifying glasses to observe activity and growth, drawing pictures and writing simple descriptions. I read books on caterpillars and butterflies to the class, and the children learned about the stages of the insect's metamorphosis. By the end of the second week, each caterpillar had crawled to the top of its vial, attached itself to the lid, and pushed off its skin to reveal a shiny opalescent chrysalis, inside of which a fantastic shape change would occur over the next several days. Waiting, the children drew countless caterpillars, chrysalids, and butterflies. They made models of caterpillars and chrysalids, rolling and cutting paper, using pipe cleaners and sticks. They drew many beautiful, symmetrical-winged butterflies.

As each chrysalis was formed, I attached the lid to the top of a big net bag that I'd hung in the room. There was great excitement

one morning when the children came in to find that some butterflies had emerged. They clung to the sides, trying out new wings;
they fluttered around the net cage. I'd left a sponge with sugar
water on the cardboard bottom of the cage, and had also brought
some flowers. The butterflies ate, unrolling their long proboscises
like very flexible straws. It took several days for all the butterflies
to come out. A couple of the butterflies had badly crumpled wings
and died. By the time all the shell-like chrysalids were empty,
only a few days of school were left. The children loved their butterflies and wanted to keep them, but knew we had to set them
free. We took the net bag to the school garden. One by one, the
butterflies took off as the children watched, cheered, and yelled,
"Good-bye, butterflies!" While this event would have been mem-
orable for the children at any time in the school year, it was loaded
with meaning because it occurred in June, as the children themselves were going out the door, leaving behind their lives as
kindergarten students.

In fact, the theme of change and transformation ran through
much of what the children did all year. They'd learned about
seeds and plants, nuts and trees, babies, families, caterpillar metamorphosis; they'd learned how baby squirrels and whales are
cared for; they'd let snow and ice melt, and let water evaporate;
they'd watched tadpoles develop. They'd talked about how these
changes make a circle.

The children, too, had changed. With some, progress was limited: *Alyssa cried, feeling she has no friends; it is progress of a sort.
She had pushed Victor when he tried to get back in line. She came to
complain to me because he'd pulled her backpack. I said, Did you let
him back in line, or did you push him out of the way? After a while,
she admitted she'd pushed him. In general, she ignores others' requests. I said, If you're nicer to the other kids, they'll like you more.
She has moments of friendliness, but she can't sustain it.* With others
I looked for, and found, significant progress: *Victor, first to see the
tadpole's back legs. Harry, struggling to use language to explain
himself. Max's effort to think about someone else's feelings. Sam, en-*

thusiastic in his knowledge of how fish tails move. Nia's greater con-
fidence as a writer. Jamie's ebullience, whereas once she didn't talk.
Caroline's faith in herself; yesterday she cried about something, and
it was the first time in months that she'd cried. I remembered the
fall, when she cried all the time.

Throughout June, I was aware of the children's competence and confidence. In the middle of the month, a group had worked on the block aquarium. *They finally made walls, and separate areas. Denay made a beach where the animals got stranded, then she parked a row of trucks, ready to pick the animals up and bring them to the aquarium tanks. There was a "deep dark" water area. Caroline raised the issue, Can the sharks and the rays go together? I brought a group in at recess to make labels. Caroline and Denay worked together, with lots of discussion of spelling, to write "Welcome Fish!!!"* I thought about Caroline and Michael: this year, again and again, they had opportunities to extend themselves, their thinking and abilities. They have built on their existing strengths, developed a greater sense of themselves as competent, interesting, rich people.

This was my primary goal for them; this was what I wanted them to achieve. I have practical goals for them too: becoming comfortable in this new school, versed in the rituals of school—lining up, cleaning up, raising their hands, balancing impulses with the demands of group life. And I have academic goals for them. But their accomplishments must, for me, encompass a central goal, for them to be more consciously, recognizably themselves. The hope implies that children's selves count, a moral belief, one that more than anything else anchors my understanding of what this year is for and what teaching is for. It's the goal of progressive education: to not merely add to a child's accumulation of knowledge, but add to a child's ability to be a full human being. More than traditional teachers, progressive teachers concern themselves not only with the mastery of tools, but with the spirit in which children come to gain mastery.

On some of those last hot June days, everyone seemed out of

sorts. The classroom was not air-conditioned, and everyone was sticky and ill tempered: *I was snappish—and the children, too. Lots of arguing. The room was messy in the morning—the after-school sewing class had left bits of stuffing all over the rug, needles and pins on the floor.* Brooke, who would be changing schools in the fall, was getting into fights. *We'd just read the questions we'd be bringing when we visit the first-grade classroom. I said to her, You are having an especially hard time getting along. Could it be that you're sad about leaving, because you're going to a different school?*

In addition, there is a concentration of June events and necessities: rehearsals for the dance festival, planning for the end-of-year celebration, projects to finish. I have my reports to write. In my Friday Letter to Parents, I gave the wrong date for an event, and phoned one of the class parents to ask for help in letting the other parents know. She thanked me, and said she was glad someone else had "event overload" and forgot things. *I love phrases like "event overload" that help me put things in a frame—give a name to something that I would have blamed myself for.*

In late May, I'd begun reading to the class *The BFG*, Roald Dahl's chapter book. The language is hard, but despite not understanding all of it, they listened: *As I read, they are attentive—quieter than when I read a picture book, mesmerized by the words. It is a language-rich book, a lot of it over their heads ("Hold your horsefeathers," says the giant to Sophie), or rather, built on expressions they're not familiar with, but the content—Sophie's peril, the growing friendship between the giant and Sophie—is not over their heads, and the images are full of action, the giant galloping along with his great strides, with Sophie in his pocket.* The problem was that as mid-June approached, I saw I'd been overambitious: we'd get to the end of the school year before we'd get to the end of the book. Better planning would have helped; in fact, I'd done it once before, years ago, reading *Stuart Little*. When I told the children that we wouldn't be able to finish *The BFG*, no one seemed to mind terribly, perhaps because so much was going on. I sent home a note to the parents, in case they wanted to get the book from the library. But my poor planning bothered me; I asked myself whether it was a result of my wanting to deny the reality of the year's end.

In June, this is the subtext for me, reconciling myself to the year being over. Caroline's cast-making activity said something to me about the double meaning of the end, the loss and gain: gain of vacation, certainly, and of whatever would come next; loss of the shared experience of being a class, a loss for me as well as them. While growth is undeniable and physical for the children, as they try on outgrown summer clothes, the breaks that occur for teachers as classes move on don't quite heal. These losses remain losses and leave some sadness, a professional hazard that's rarely discussed. The degree of sadness felt by teachers may have to do with their own experience of losses and separations, their adult knowledge of mortality, their feelings about growth and change.

Ambivalent Feelings

Everyone says children grow up so quickly. But really, it's a comment people make as they look back, when their own children are grown. I've always thought that what people are really commenting on is that their children—the children they remember—are irrevocably gone, not recoverable. When Amina was about to turn six, I said to her, You'll never be five again!

As children in the class turn six, I teach them the A.A. Milne poem "The End," and we recite it at each six-year birthday. Part of what I love about the poem is the way that it turns against all the earlier ages ("When I was Three, / I was hardly Me. / When I was Four, / I was not much more.") and enshrines six: "But now I am Six, I'm as clever as clever. / So I think I'll be six now for ever and ever." [1] The poem stops time—for that moment, that year of being six. (And the poem, in unwritten extension, allows the child's parent to forever enjoy being parent of that six-year-old.)

Year after year, as each class breaks up, what teachers deal with—after the intensity of a year together—is that cliché, the forward march of time. I see the children's growth and feel great pride, but in some irrational part of my mind, I want to prevent it, I want to keep these children five years old. I know that they're ready to move on: *they are so much more independent, and thoughtful.* But *I'm* not ready. As they grow up, they move away. In the school's hallways, when the first-graders whom I taught the previous year catch sight of me, they jump up and down; they shout to the others who were in my class—"It's Julie!" The second-graders are still excited, they wave and smile, but more sedately. By the end of second grade, I've receded into the past; I'm far away, and am undoubtedly smaller. I see the older children in the hallway, in their new bulkier bodies, and miss what's gone, their selves at age five.

One afternoon in the spring, a boy of fifteen or so appears in the classroom: tall, nice-looking, agreeable, solid, thoroughly teenage. Given a break from his high school, he was visiting his elementary school. Somehow, this being had developed out of the winsome, independent-minded boy of five, with his unnervingly direct gaze, who'd been a marvelous writer and drawer. To see him grown up unnerved me more. How could this boy, almost a man, be the person I'd taught? Where was the other boy? And who are we after all, what's the intrinsic self that makes us one person? *Is* there a core that's not mutable, that stays the same, whatever the role of chance and circumstances? And how do we—teachers and parents—let go of the person we thought we knew?

It's a question that occupies me sometimes as the parent of a grown-up. One afternoon, during a teaching break, Arshea and I talked about our own families. *The mixed feelings we have—her feelings about her son, who's fourteen. She wants him to be an adult but also doesn't want him to be an adult. I talk about my feelings when my daughter is mad at me—about how hard it is for me to admit it when she's right. We have to, I suppose, accept the ambivalence, the conflict we feel about who we want them to be, about what we want from them. Grow up, but depend on us. Move out, but not too far. Know your own mind, but don't use it to criticize our behavior.* Children grow up, say good-bye; I know it's a good thing, yet I experience a pang, the price of a changed relationship.

In those days at the end of the year, time seems to stretch out, stop, and then suddenly snap. *Memorial Day in one week. June will, as always, whiz by.* The contradictory nature of time seems inescapable: the absolute end of things seems to sneak up, unadvertised. On lazy August afternoons, Labor Day feels hazily distant, then it's suddenly upon us. A more serious example: a friend—a parent—is terminally ill; we know it, but in the period before death, time feels suspended, as if the period might last indefinitely, as if death could be cheated. Folk tales are based on the human desire for continuation, for the prolonging of what we desire, the denial of a necessary end of things. With a magic word or phrase, the rice pot goes on producing rice, and the lucky peasant is never again hungry. Whether our hope is for food or love or life, human minds resist ends.

Children may feel less ambivalence about the end of the year, which for them, after all, holds not only vacation, but also the next grade, and being older. For kindergarten children, who in September were new to elementary school, June holds a specific promise: in the fall, they'll be *returning*—no longer new, no longer the youngest. Yet even for children, feelings are mixed, because *this* year is ending.

For teachers, the severing of these ties is complicated. My teacherly ambivalence about the end of the year is fueled by the intensity of the connections I've formed with a particular group of students. For ten months, I've spent almost five hours a day with these children, and thoughts about them occupy me at other times too. For teachers of young children, the ties are especially strong. We teach through our selves: through the *tone* in which we ask our questions, through our genuine interest in and responsiveness to the children as individuals. We teach through our ability to listen—an attribute that is both professional and personal.

We teach through the relationships we form with students, relationships we've fostered, and through our identification with them and theirs with us.

On those last days, everyone is busy. The children who wish to help are put to work washing dolls and plastic animals. Some children help make piles of work to go home. Some children draw or build with whatever materials are left out. I fold construction paper to make files in which to send their work home, and the children illustrate the covers: "My Writing, June, 2005." Everything goes home: science drawings, writing, math papers, pages of numeral writing, the patterns they drew, the outlines of their shoes measured in Unifix cubes. The files go into bags, and so do their name cards, the alphabet letters and room signs they'd made in the fall, and the drawings they'd made for their cubbies on the first day of school. I pack up their models of undersea animals. I add a present for everyone—a small magnifying glass. The bags go home two days before the last day.

I busy myself with packing; the emotions are there, below the surface. The last day is a half day, dismissal is at noon. We walk across the yard, together as a class for the last time, about to not be a class. I hold the envelopes with the report cards, to be handed out to parents. But when I'd gotten the envelopes ready the day before, I'd neglected to organize them: I didn't put them in alphabetical order, as I usually do, and didn't make sure they were all facing the same way. *I had to keep flipping the envelopes, as I said good-bye to kids and parents, hugging, shaking hands, as if I'd had to distract myself from saying good-bye.* When the parents came in the gate, the children started hopping around me, moving like bubbles in boiling water, and the parents were waiting to say their good-byes too, and all the good-byes seemed to happen at once, until kids and parents were gone, except for the after-school kids, whose company I was grateful for as we headed back into the building.

Packing Up

The end is my knowing them at this *moment, my seeing them produce this classroom (which I then take apart). The end is knowing Henry.*

When school was over—after the hugs, after the rabbit had gone to someone's home for the summer—I went through the room, taking everything off the walls, putting materials away in bags and crates. I found objects: puzzle pieces, Lego pieces, broken crayons, play coins, old T-shirts, the bag with Sam's work, left behind; I could interpret the year from these artifacts. Over the next two days, I returned the classroom to what it was before the year began—empty walls, piled up furniture. I knew how I wanted to find the room when I returned in August, and felt satisfaction in the process of packing.

As I put things away, I thought about things *not* accomplished, things not done. I remembered an observation I'd intended to add to one of the reports. I made notes for next year. *Take out the checkers boards and the geoboards.* I thought about new activities and materials. *Do more counting of things. It can be a job, they pick a number, and have to count out that many objects—color tiles, pennies, birthday candles. A "number of the day"—numbers in teens, in twenties, and the objects stay in a bowl all day.* I wrote about a weak area. *Time . . . how to be in control of it . . . I always think I can do more than I have time to do. It's a failure to be realistic about time, but also—I hate making choices!* I had lunch with Michael, another kindergarten teacher, and we talked about working together more next year.

I also thought about the children's accomplishments: Sam's drawing of Graham's block building of the Lincoln Memorial. His drawing was a great *visual* comment on Graham's construction, proof of his drawing ability and of his interest in things around him despite his difficulty with spoken language. I thought about the amazing jet plane Max built in the blocks—huge, incredibly complex—which had been accidentally destroyed twice, and which he'd reconstructed *twice*. The reward of his perseverance was this object that took up most of the space in the block area, a jet plane, which no one else would even have thought about making, and which everyone admired.

I thought about an incident with Denay, from early in the year, when she was uncertain of herself and her place in the class: *Denay came up and said, Sam called me selfish girl—she was upset. We were on line and leaving the room, it was the end of the day—no time to call him over and talk to them both. I said, Oh, Denay, you know that's not true, you're a great kid, you can ignore him, just go like this. And I showed her how to shrug and look disdainful. But she was still upset, so I told her to stay with me, and we walked out of the room together. Then I saw Lizzie and said, Lizzie, Denay's feeling bad, will you walk with her? And later, I looked back and saw a very happy Denay.* My words weren't enough to remove the sting of Sam's words, but Lizzie's generosity and kindness, her immediate and unquestioning acceptance did the trick. This was Denay, all year, her mix of sensitivity and responsiveness; her emotions were visible, whether hurt feelings, or self-possessed pleasure when things went well.

And Henry, initially so marginal to the business of the class, drawn in finally, to the extent that others copied his work. With him, what had made the difference? If I had to point to a shift in his functioning in the room, it would be when he and Amina had worked together to measure the rug. They weren't close, weren't friends, yet on that day, they'd done something together that neither could have done alone.

Out of these moments and others, the class had taken shape. This metamorphosis, the formation of a group made up of these twenty-four separate individuals, didn't occur only because of what the children learned from each other—e.g., the way that Amina's Cave Book appeared a few days after Hayley's Fish Book, and was clearly inspired by it. Children use what's around them, love copying, and will take an idea and apply it in different forms for their own purposes. But the growth of the class—its cohesion as a group—came about not simply as a result of specific shared ideas. Through conversation, through the pooling of what each of them knew and what they didn't know, through the very differences among them, their vulnerabilities and shared uncertainties, and through the process of looking and listening to each other—which depended, sometimes, on my insistence that they look and listen, even when they might have chosen not to—the class came into existence as an entity. The differences and similarities in children's thinking produced a mix of insights and perspectives; they became aware both of what made each of them unique and of what they shared with the others. Out of the joint projects and constructions, the mix of ideas and aptitudes, they produced a class, an "us." Far from representing a loss for the individuals, they created a context in which to be themselves.

Certain conditions were necessary: relative freedom of action and thinking, a range of acceptable opinions and roles, children's work being valued and made public, and my attitude both of acceptance and expectation. Because there were various ways of contributing, and contributions were actively valued, the group made use of each child's singular concerns and powers. The culture of the class, its values, allowed for individual expression and achievements, as well as group expression and achievement. Just as the individuals formed the group, the group permitted them to develop as individuals.

On the last day, as we sat on the rug for the last time, Francie at one point suddenly got up. Distracted and tense, I overreacted, speaking harshly: "Where are you going?" She said, "Julie!"— her teenage tone and pose exaggerated and exasperated—"I'm *getting* a tissue!" Jonathan, who had never played much of a public role, who stuck with his particular friends, whose discussion contributions were rambling, self-referential, and quite intellectual, took up an unexpected position as spokesman. "Lighten up!" he said to me, smiling. I had to laugh; he was right. Later, I thought about the exchange and Jonathan's comment. Jonathan would not have been so outspoken earlier in the year. And because he was a child who was generally shy and sweet-tempered, he could get away with admonishing me, in exactly that joking way. The class had become an organism, with different tasks assigned to different people, an evolving organism, able to protect and defend itself.

The end of the year is arbitrary, in a sense—ten months of school, then summer vacation. We'd come to the end, and that was that. That afternoon, as I walked along the halls, some classrooms were already dark. A number of teachers, those who'd packed up before the last day, were ready to leave after they'd said good-bye to the last child. They dropped off their keys in the office, said good-bye to the office staff, and were on their way.

I'm envious of their freedom, but have to do it my own way. In August, I'd taken time to set up the room; now I had to take time for the ritual of putting things away. I stacked plastic bins and containers and put materials away in bags, threw things out and organized. Packing up the room is *my* metaphor, it's how I say good-bye to the year, an acknowledgment that I've come to the end of my efforts with this group of children. With difficult classes, classes that seemed never to come together in a caring and productive way, the end would bring relief but also a sense of defeat, despite the effort to balance out the year's successes and failures. With these classes I'm left with a residual awareness of what I couldn't affect, didn't manage to set right.

Things undone, things unaccomplished: *The BFG*, the book I didn't finish, is one more metaphor, for unfinished business, lack of closure, endings that don't end. I can, perhaps, find positive meaning in the metaphor. There's a benefit to incompleteness; it incorporates possibility. Thus, the unended story is a reminder of the inevitable incompleteness of a teaching year. It's a metaphor for the children themselves, who straddle past and future, *becoming* who they will be. *Who will Michael be, with his quick thinking and sense of discipline, the intentness he brings to figuring things out for himself? I don't mean his career (computer scientist? physi-*

cist?). I mean, what are the possibilities inherent in his thinking, his insistence on understanding? In a poem titled "Leaving the Rest Unsaid," the British poet Robert Graves writes of "The . . . mystery of my progress." The last poem in one of his collections, its last line ends "At a careless comma," [2]

The sense of incompleteness, of actions reaching toward the unknown (and unknowable), is integral to teaching. Karen Gallas describes her task as teacher-researcher as the attempt to "grab onto fragments of the life streaming by me." [3] Our knowledge is necessarily partial and in flux for another reason, too: because teachers, also are transformed by time. This doesn't mean simply that I'll do something differently next year (remember to use the geoboards) but rather that my teaching is by definition never a finished thing. The *knowing* of children is what I learn to do differently each year, as a result of thinking about *these* children and their actions.

At the beginning of each year, not knowing who the children are, my anticipation about the year is mixed with uncertainty. At the end of the year, as I take the room apart, my sense of achievement is mixed with—to borrow Graves's word—what's left "unsaid." The phrase *what's left unsaid* captures the contradictory meanings for me of the end of the school year, the challenge of accepting it as both finished and unfinished. Packing up, I envy and appreciate Caroline's invention of a metaphor that contained, in one image, the children's conflicting feelings about the end of the year, and the inevitability of change—and perhaps even about the mystery of time itself. Wrapping paper around broken arms, the children concluded and demonstrated that breaks mend; writing names on one another's casts, they said hello as well as good-bye.

10

❧

Postscript: Being a Teacher

Choosing to Teach

What would I say I've gained from a life in the classroom?

Before I began teaching, I'd been working in the bureaucracy of the federal poverty program. I sat at a desk, talked on the phone, checked off items on checklists. The pace and formality of the work and the windowless rooms denied something about who I was. Later that year, when I began teaching in rural northern Georgia, whatever loneliness I felt there—as an outsider, a Jew, a Northerner, a city-dweller, a political liberal—was balanced by my feeling for the blue hills and back roads, by the red earth coloring my sneakers, and by my feelings about the people I got to know, adults as well as children. All of that got mixed together with the job of teaching; remembering the school, I picture the field outside, and the sky.

I loved the physicality of the job: moving around the room, bending to listen, taking the kids outside. I loved the noise, activity, and surprises. I came to care deeply about individual children. My parents had both been teachers, and I thought I'd never teach—but there I was.

I must admit something else: I liked feeling I was doing something important in the world, and that I mattered in the children's lives. This was especially true in relation to the children who seemed most troubled, the ones who swung unpredictably back and forth between anger and calm. I saw them as condemned by the region's poverty to hard lives. The families' problems were real: the teeth of several of the children were blackened stubs as a consequence of the common practice of quieting babies with bottles of cola. I see, now, some youthful self-indulgence in my sense of guilt for the world's ills, and some condescension in my attitude toward the families, although condescension was mixed with respect for them and gratitude for their kindness toward me.

Over the years that I've taught, I've continued to enjoy the noise and activity of classrooms: I love the seeming chaos as different things go on at the same time; I love the buzz, love listening in on children's spontaneous talk. I will admit something else: I value being valued. I enjoy knowing that amid all the classroom movement, I'm a constant point of reference.

I've outgrown the idea that I'm responsible for saving the world, but I remain sharply aware of the injuries that social and economic forces inflict on individuals. I have greater respect for the world's complexity; I see that adversity besets families in different ways and that families cope with adversity in different ways. Yet I continue to be motivated by a desire to do work that has social value, work I believe in; I continue to feel affection and concern for the children I teach.

The feeling of moral obligation is a characteristic of good teachers. This isn't—as the chapter on Henry makes clear—an abstraction, a generalized love of humanity. It is made up of varying emotions, including, sometimes, negative emotions; it includes the ability to be (or appear to be) *unmoved* at times. When people hear that I teach young children, they frequently say, "You must be so patient!" In fact, patience isn't my strong suit, but my genuine interest in children and loyalty to their growth usually trumps my natural impatience.

One essential piece of teaching—of wanting to do it year after year, of sticking with it so that you get better—is the will for connectedness, the determination to find out who these children are, which is not entirely separate from finding out more about oneself. It is in the *wish* to bend and listen, the meaning *to the teacher* of that motion. It is in my caring enough to watch two children who've just made up after a fight, to notice how they walk away. My interest is rooted in my identification with childhood's delights, industry, wonder, and fears. Good teachers remember the feelings of vulnerability *and* power; they honestly share children's curiosity and amazement; they remember the feelings of disgust (Hayley's refusal even to look at the fish's eye). I'm in the classroom as a teacher, but in a vestigial way, as a child.

My sense of connection with children—with the intensity with which they experience things—is compelling and joyful for me, an aspect of the job that I value. It is also something I bring to the job, the source of my responsiveness. The focus and presence that teachers gain from the act of identifying with children makes us more alert to the immediate reality of children's experiences. A good teacher has a child's awareness of detail, an attentiveness that spotlights encounters—what was said, what actually happened. The teacher *notices*, minute by minute, looks around, listens, doesn't miss anything.[1] That recognition of ourselves in them (or them in us) is not an indulgence as long as it serves an educational purpose, motivating us to plot a path *for them* toward further development. Further, the empathy that we show children helps them develop empathy for others.

Teaching depends upon more than sympathy and identification, however. We are adults, and children depend upon us to be adults. The emotional distance we're capable of makes it possible for them to trust us; it permits us to help them manage distressing emotions. For me, achieving that maturity was not automatic. There were many days when I "lost it," blamed myself, felt awful, and wanted to quit; there were hard years. Slowly, I learned to manage my own feelings when things went wrong. The struggle brought hard-won confidence in my own powers. Throughout the school day, I communicate—not perfectly, but well enough—a presence that they and I can count on. Teachers' predictability *and* flexibility, emotional resilience and resourcefulness, the ability to share children's sense of humor *and* to demonstrate firm

The activity of classrooms

Photo by David Vitale-Wolff

intent—these create a classroom in which children feel respected, safe, and able to learn.

I have found in the classroom a place for intellectual engagement, a place to exercise my curiosity about the meanings of things. Like students, teachers should have, in Eleanor Duckworth's words, "wonderful ideas." The words emphasize the intellectual *and* emotional dimensions of a teacher's involvement. The possibility of intellectual engagement has been, for me, another reward of teaching.

My favorite books about teaching, the ones I grab off the shelf when I want to lend something to a new teacher, take as their subject a teacher's curiosity about particular children and their actions. Frances Hawkins's *The Logic of Action* describes her weekly visits to a class of six deaf four-year-olds; she includes her wrong turns and puzzlement, intuitions and successes, her "beliefs, and mode of operating."[2] She conveys the texture of her search for the *logic* of children's actions.

Curiosity motivates the teacher-writers I've quoted in these chapters. They are students of children's choices, insisting on children's intentionality and seeking to understand what that intentionality demands from them. This book constitutes an account of what happens in that space between children's actions and the teacher's wanting to know; a description of the back-and-forth that permits children's curiosity to be tapped. Our intelligence about the children we teach—our thoughts, questions, and informed guesses—defines our ability to make room for *their* intelligence. We don't have to be smarter than the children we teach, but we have to honor their intelligence.

The richness of our scrutiny—the layers of associations and multiplicity of possible responses—adds to good teaching. This calls for teachers to be people with lively imaginations and lively intelligence. Our curiosity should concern itself not only with children and their actions, but with content—books, bugs, music, math. Adult knowledge and curiosity *together* lead teachers toward useful inferences. The link between them is made explicit by Reggio educators. Loris Malaguzzi, the educator who provided the intellectual base for the Reggio approach, speaks of the central educational importance of "the act of interpretation," which implies not only that teachers listen with attention, but also that they have "a basic knowledge about different content areas of teaching." [3]

Thus, teachers must be—*or become*—people with their own passions, who get carried away by enthusiasm and can honestly say to a child, "I never thought of that!" When I bring my own interests to the classroom—collecting honey-locust pods for the science table, introducing the class to printmaking—what I add is not a particular pursuit but the quality of personal involvement that becomes a norm. The classroom offers us, as teachers, additional meanings at the same time that it offers children a context for their own pursuits and honest appraisals of their achievements. When we are successful, the children's educational motives—their wanting to know, their desire to do things well and to communicate—take over a classroom.

Staying in the Classroom

An experimental attitude—what does that mean? What does it require? What are the resources that I bring to the classroom?

What allowed me to *stay* in the classroom, what lent me the requisite sense of purpose and stamina? The attributes that benefited me have both positive and negative sides. I have had to contend with their problematic consequences, but at times they've served me well.

I have a stubborn streak. When I was growing up, the adults in my family had strong opinions; I took it for granted that people were opinionated. Annoying as my stubbornness can be to others, it has stood me in good stead as a teacher. It kept me going through periods of utter exhaustion, through periods when I felt I was a terrible teacher.

My oppositional nature helped me to develop intellectual independence. This trait has been particularly useful recently, as education has become increasingly inhospitable to children's play, and educational goals have narrowed. I could accept being the only kindergarten teacher who insisted on a daily work time during which children could build in the blocks, paint, make constructions, draw, work together, argue; who resisted overly academic practices. I have tried to judge things in terms of their underlying principles and their impact on children, and to adopt what I considered valuable. On occasion, I have closed my classroom door and gone my own way. I am willing to balk, to take unpopular points of view, either privately in conversations in classroom doorways, or publicly at teachers' meetings. I believe in my autonomy. As educational goals have become more regressive, I have become more committed to the values I began with, more compelled to have my classroom demonstrate my beliefs.

Despite a strong commitment to these beliefs, I have had to work at gaining confidence in my teaching and in the capacities of the children I taught. I have a critical disposition; developing trust in myself and in children demanded an effort. Bank Street College provided me with a theoretical framework for trust in children's growth, but I started out far from understanding how to apply these principles in practice. Frequently, my student teachers pushed me: I remember student teachers who had more trust in children's abilities than I did, who led class discussions and let moments of silence go by until someone had something to say. I'd be uneasy and doubtful, certain the children couldn't handle what was being asked. Always, the children surprised me. Over time, in small steps, I gave up some of my control to children and made room for their ideas and goals. At the same time, I've come to recognize and appreciate my own strengths.

The capacity for self-criticism, when tempered by a sense of self-worth, is a necessary trait. It makes intellectual honesty possible, permits us to look back at what we said or did and examine our own actions and motives. Teachers need to make a habit of, in

Deborah Meier's words, a "self-conscious reflectiveness about how they themselves learn and (maybe even more) about how and when they *don't* learn." [4]

I've come to see mistakes as essential to learning. Uncertainty, *not knowing*, is part of the territory of the profession at every point in a teacher's life. It makes possible the flexibility we need when we examine and interpret children's actions and formulations. If we want students to take risks and be compassionate toward others' mistakes, we have to accept being vulnerable in relation to our own mistakes. Charney speaks of "the courage to admit failure," as essential to our being "accountable to ourselves." [5] Thus, it's imperative that when experienced teachers train student teachers or mentor new teachers, they are candid about questions and doubts, and demonstrate how good teaching often arises from uncertainty.

The Teaching Environment

How free are we to use what we know? What do we actually control? What sustains us?

Years ago, in late August, I walked to school in paint-stained work clothes, prepared to spend the day among dusty boxes, pushing chairs and tables around. Approaching the school, I noticed a small hill of school furniture on the sidewalk, waiting to be picked up as garbage. I recognized a set of shelves that had been made by a carpenter parent and a low bench that I'd used in the meeting area. I went to the principal's office: what was going on? He made it clear that I had no say in the matter; he and the custodian had decided over the summer that only standard-issue Board of Education furniture would be allowed in classrooms. There was no money to replace the shelf unit and bench.

Young teachers are almost invariably idealistic, but as this incident illustrates, a school environment can create obstacles and make teaching harder. The principal felt that the school was *his.*

His use of his power—without consultation—undercut my autonomy, the sense that I could make decisions about my classroom. There must, of course, be a balance of accountability and autonomy. Here, the principal's authority was absolute. Soon afterward, I became involved in starting an alternative school.

The context of the story is the material reality of urban public schools, which has been much documented.[6] The scarcity of furniture, equipment, and supplies produces a culture of deprivation: *I notice the veneer peeling off the block shelf. It will do for one more year. I'm a child of this system.* Scarcity turns teachers into scavengers, and making do becomes second nature.

Teachers take pride in their ability to scrounge and recycle. But the impact of inadequate funding is not only material. Chronic deficiencies color our perception of ourselves and the job we do. The result of schools' material deficits is neither material nor measurable; it is a spiritual loss, a decrease in the hopefulness and sense of purpose that should be at the heart of any school. It's not just that poor schools are "underprivileged." It would be more correct to describe a process of *deprivileging*. The discrepancies between what individual schools offer students send messages to students about their worth and expectations. The deprivileging of schools is a deprivileging of our students and of ourselves.

When we as a society accept these gaps between schools, the rich possibilities that some children are offered are seen as belonging only to them, not to all children. Behind the demoralization of teachers in poor schools is the knowledge that inequities in the schools could be addressed if powerful elements in the society cared to do so.

Teachers are also affected by the predominant ethos of the schools, one that grades children according to test scores, and grades teachers and schools relative to children's grades. When kindergarten children are tested, they don't yet know they're not supposed to peek at others' answers. They ask me, "Is that right?"

A fuzzy red apple puppet, included in the kindergarten literacy test kit, can ask the test questions, but the children are not fooled, and their feet jiggle with nervousness.

As the testing ethos has taken hold, school systems have increasingly pushed for instruction aimed at children's test success. Teachers, handed lists of "standards" and given scripted programs, are less and less present in classrooms as individuals. Our development of elasticity and responsiveness toward students, of *feeling* for their purposes, is cramped and diminished. We aren't encouraged to find diverse *ways in* to subjects, to make curriculum alive for students, to integrate cognitive and affective dimensions of growth.[7] These aims are sabotaged by the need to "meet" standards. A strong motivation for teaching—our active engagement with children's learning—is undermined. Ironically, at the same time that educational processes are being robbed of all that genuinely motivates students and teachers, those in charge of school systems are offering students, teachers, and principals monetary rewards for increases in test scores.

Standardization also buttresses hierarchical decision making within schools, as well as requirements that teachers follow inane rules. Decades ago, when I was beginning to teach, we were evaluated on whether our window shades were aligned. Now, in many schools, when student work is displayed, teachers are expected to label work with relevant "standards." In another school, I would have been reprimanded for failing to post, next to children's fish drawings, a caption such as "Students begin to observe and describe how specific animal and plant parts enable the plant or animal to survive. Kindergarten Standard for Life Sciences Concepts." New teachers may follow these directives to avoid battles with supervisors, but the result is a classroom environment in which the words that accompany children's work don't make sense to the children themselves. Such demands have no educational purpose; they function to remind teachers of the limits of their autonomy.

Standardized testing has been justified by demands for accountability. But to assure accountability by relying on standardized testing assumes that quantitative measurement is neutral and objective, which it is not. As the British educator Susan Isaacs wrote, "The act of selection is itself an act of judgment. . . ."[8] Numerous factors influence children's functioning as students: their relationship to content and to peers, their feelings for the adults they come in contact with, their feelings about themselves, and their belief that the entire business of school makes sense. Standardized tests don't reflect these vital aspects of who a student is. Scores also screen out the social and economic realities that mediate children's development of school selves: their access to health care and housing, and job opportunities and economic well-being in the communities that schools serve. Scores deny the role these factors play in achievement, in school and beyond.

Despite the fact that standardized tests distort our picture of student functioning and of the factors that affect it, school systems continue to depend on them. The result is that the culture of testing has fundamentally and adversely altered the educational environment. It has, I believe, contributed to the decision of many new young teachers to leave the classroom.[9]

While school environments may make teaching more difficult, they may also provide *resources* for teachers. The alternative school that I was involved with in the early 1990s didn't last, but the collaboration with colleagues Hollee Freeman, Ginger Hanlon, and Gwyn Kellam influenced me throughout my teaching life.[10] Teaching is generally an isolated endeavor. But we *were* the school, and we gave ourselves the opportunity to meet every week; we knew the children in each other's classes; we were in and out of one another's rooms. Our meetings focused on the day-to-day life of our classes. We looked for the points of contact between threads of activity, the "logic" of children's actions. We brought a wealth of ideas to each others' curriculum plans, and because of our different histories and personalities, we were forced to spell out assumptions. We could talk openly with colleagues we trusted about children's behavior, map out options of response, and explore the implications of decisions. Our meetings kept us intellectually engaged, and nurtured flexibility and tolerance of uncertainty. Talking together helped us know what we knew. Working together increased our sense of autonomy.

Collaborative processes are central to the functioning of many alternative schools.[11] In Reggio Emilia, too, collaboration is critical, providing "not only a set of professional tools, but also a work ethic." [12] In the Reggio preschools, teacher development is described as a *right*: "Professional development is a right of each individual teacher and of all those who work in the school. [It includes] the right to think, plan, work and interpret together in a collegial way." [13] The documentation that forms such an important part of children's learning in Reggio is the basis for detailed investigations, with colleagues, of teaching and learning.

When teachers collaborate, the qualities of good teachers aren't viewed as inherent but as traits that can develop with effort, over time.[14] In schools built on collaboration, leadership is characterized by an active receptivity toward others' thinking and purposes, which is similar to the receptivity that characterizes classroom teachers but radically different from the authoritarian stance of the principal who threw out classroom furniture. In many schools, the possibility of collaboration doesn't exist. Teachers may, however, be able to find colleagues in other schools, and build networks of teachers committed to working together.

Collaboration both demands and engenders a high level of openness and intellectual autonomy. It redefines who we are as teachers and as people. Teachers who participate in these processes gain a greater ability to articulate their thinking; they gain intellectual confidence. Historically, preschool and elementary-school teachers have had a low status: they are mostly women, and the profession has been viewed as a women's field, an extension of mothering, in which "caring" counts more than thinking. We tend to be former "good girls," girls who liked doing the right thing. We tend to be conciliators, which is not entirely a bad thing, but puts us in the position of being like children who ask permission and may be refused. The sexual division of employment—the fact that school administrators tended to be male—reinforced women teachers' lack of confidence and sense of low status. Collaborating, teachers learn to speak with conviction. As we make claims for our knowledge and capacities, there is an additional invaluable result: we are more likely to defend our own interests and the interests of the children we teach, to press for a more human and encompassing conception of teaching.

Parents, too, are resources for teachers. Teachers, however, must work to develop trust, because differences between home and school are potentially thorny—gaps of language, culture, values, and norms. When these are overcome, children are the first beneficiaries, since they move every day between what may be separate cultures. Yet teachers, too, benefit from these relationships. Over the years, parents' warmth, talents, humor, and hard work have added immeasurably to my classroom, often in unexpected ways. Their appreciation of their children's efforts and accomplishments and their appreciation of my efforts have been a significant reward.

The responsibility for creating friendly and open relationships lies with teachers and schools. Parents' sense of involvement—the feeling that the school is *theirs*—is an amorphous thing, but it can be planned for, in particular, by making the *border* between home and school more porous than it usually is.

In my school, kindergarten parents bring children to the classroom during the first part of the year. The practice eases children's transition from home to school and also provides a time and space in which parents' presence in classrooms is not just tolerated but welcomed. The relaxed atmosphere allows me to get to know parents in a way that would otherwise be impossible. As parents stop by to look at something, they become more comfortable in the classroom. A parent can let me know about something going on in the child's life, and if necessary, we can schedule a meeting.

The informality of exchange fostered by morning drop-off establishes a background of trust and an assumption of common purposes that inform all subsequent meetings. Equally important, the parents get to know each other and to know the other children in the class. The social network that parents create is a resource for them, for me, and for the school. Morning drop-off engenders a commitment to the school that goes beyond parents' concern for their own child.

In Reggio Emilia, the *physical* border between home and school—the entryways and hallways where parents and teachers naturally meet—is designed to sustain exchanges between parents and school. Photographs of children at work, exhibits of work and dictated text in these areas invite parents immediately into the life of the school. These are not commercial photos but images of their own children, and the words are their children's actual words. By sharing this work, schools reveal the learning that occurs when teaching is based on children's authentic purposes. Documentation thus demonstrates children's capacities, helps parents see the schools' valuing of those capacities, and underscores the school's commitment to parents' knowledge of their children's efforts.

Teachers can highlight children's work in other ways. The notices that I send home to parents are written and illustrated by children. These display an originality totally missing from computer-generated graphics. These notices serve legitimate purposes, but also display, to the children as well as their parents, the children's conceptual abilities and expressive flair. Curriculum projects can serve similar functions. When the children mailed valentines to distant relatives, their learning was communicated by the cards and by the messages and addresses that the children wrote (at the same time that children's learning was motivated by the meaningfulness of these activities). Weekly newsletters can document work: teachers can include drawings and transcripts of discussions. Class performances and exhibitions of work also communicate educational values when these showcase children's authentic efforts and decisions.

Families can also be unique educational resources for children's exploration and understanding of the world. In initiating a study of the post office with her first-grade class, my colleague Linda Kasarjian asks parents to ask their friends and family members to mail postcards to the class; the cards lead to a variety of curricular experiences. Thus, the diversity of families' social relationships is at the heart of the study. Also, when parents participate in the classroom as volunteers, their contributions can make curriculum more real.

These strong links between schools and families make the school environment more democratic. In Reggio schools, and in American alternative schools, the school's curriculum—thought of most broadly—*is* democracy; the school's day-to-day functioning is based on principles of participation by individuals involved with the institution and the community outside it.[15] I don't mean that schools should be parent-run, but that teachers and educators generally should see their work, in part, as the sketching out of understandings about children's learning and the development of educational meanings.[16] One consequence is the *broadening* of parent's commitment to children's education. Currently, parents often view children's educational success narrowly, in terms of grades and scores, and their anxious pressure can have deleterious effects. Alyssa, for example, who had attended a preschool that was inappropriately academic in orientation, had few social skills and was resistant to learning: *she can read, and write her name in beautifully formed lower-case letters, but grabs and pushes when she has a problem with someone. "I don't like books," she tells me.*

What do we want for our children? When educators enlist parents in proposing answers, they open up the process to a range of possibilities. One Chinese New Year, the mother of one of the children visited the classroom. Newly arrived from China, speaking almost no English, she showed the children how to draw Chinese characters. As the children used ink and brush to write their new year's greetings, their knowledge of the world and of each other increased exponentially. The children's gain was also mine: in welcoming that parent to my room, I enlarged the meaning of education and shared responsibility for it.

Ourselves as Resources

The arc of the year is the year with this class. Just as telling a story is what makes someone a writer, what he gets better at, knowing children—knowing a class, helping it become a class—is what being a teacher is.

Adults are responsible for teaching children in the widest sense, for equipping them with the knowledge and competence we believe they'll need. A sense of this responsibility is part of what drew me to teaching. There are educators who interpret this responsibility to mean that adults owe children only facts and skills. But when facts are taught in isolation, it is harder to see patterns. In addition, facts change: they occasionally change *as facts*, revealed as no longer true, and they often change in their value or in their position vis-à-vis other facts. Repetition is often needed in order for children to learn skills, but it helps when skills are learned in the context of goals that children recognize; when taught as rote skills, separate from any meaningful context, they are less easily transferred.[17]

Our job as adults is to help children build *relationships*— to people and things in the world and to the act of knowing. This point of view assumes that children—and teachers—are active agents. For me, activism *defines* teaching and learning: much teaching consists of the search for students' meaning. Malaguzzi's words ring true: "The central act of adults . . . is to activate, especially indirectly, the meaning-making competencies of children as a basis of all learning." [18]

Building relationships is what we do best as teachers: relationships with students, content, parents, colleagues. Relationships are a net that we produce, which in turn sustains us. We work with our personal resources—our listening, involvement, valuations, presence. The primary relationship, between teachers and students, is one of personal loyalty. When a relationship with a student is bad—when I feel at a loss with a student, unable to connect—I doubt my ability to teach.

At these moments, which come often enough, I look around the classroom at the work layered on walls and surfaces: loops of patterned necklaces made from dyed and strung pasta shapes; a sewing project, little drawstring bags; drawings of sea creatures, a seahorse with its tail wrapped around seaweed; saved Lego constructions, including Michael's with its label, SPAC SIP [space ship]—all the captured life of this group.

None of these things existed before this class produced them. The originality of children's representations, the uniqueness of the objects they produce, point to the creative nature of learning. For this reason—because learning is creative—imaginative processes such as dramatic play have a necessary role in the classroom; they introduce an infinity of possibilities, elements that are entirely individual. "There is that in learning which is immeasurable," writes Patricia Carini; yet it's visible, in the variety of work, work that's truly children's own.[19] The room is a collage, mixing media, layering experience, creating new combinations; it provides a million versions of knowledge. "The classroom," Karen Gallas says, "is like perishable art."[20] I love it for being both solid *and* ephemeral.

Our resources are our own capacities: Our capacity to observe, especially at moments when nothing seems to be going on. Our capacity to be surprised by something a child said or did or made. Our capacity to be puzzled, and to mine puzzlement, to see something that escaped us earlier. Our capacity to recognize whatever has deep personal meaning, for our students and also for ourselves (a colleague's class study of birds). Not least, our capacity for friendship—our searching out sympathetic people, who provide the human environment we need. I began the school year, after all, walking to school with a friend. These are the steps that teachers can take immediately, right now; these resources—the capacities for observation, surprise, puzzlement, and connection—are always present. "Education in its widest sense," Carlina Rinaldi says, is "a hope for human beings." [21]

In recognizing what matters to children and to ourselves, we develop a culture of teaching. The more years we teach, the more we understand what the work entails; and the more complex, colorful, and detailed the culture becomes. In choosing to teach, year after year, we *learn* to teach; we gain conviction and we discover again and again who we are as teachers. Going through old photographs, I see themes: a bunch of children at a table, looking over

The class rabbit
Photo by Julie Diamond

each other's shoulders at photographs of themselves—as I'm waiting to write down their comments. In another photo, Max squats alone at the rabbit's cage, staring in, wearing on his head a pair of the doll's pants like a jaunty cap, while in the background, Laurel and Francie stretch out on the rug, looking at a book. One photo has no children, just a long train of Unifix cubes set up on chairs. I remember the work on these trains: each day, starting fresh, the children had made the trains longer and longer until after several days the linked cubes circled the room a few feet off the floor, like one of those superfast trains. That absorption is what I aim for—that, and the quality of certain comments and questions, the questions that intrigue us, children and adults ("Is snow really real?"), and that we love considering together. These moments point to the classroom life that I want for the children I teach, that permits them to flourish, to take off in unexpected directions, to live fully as children.[22] In considering children's involvement—in listening to their talk, watching Max watch the rabbit—*I've* lived fully, as a teacher and as myself.

NOTES

Introduction

1. Caroline Pratt, *I Learn from Children* (New York: Harper & Row, 1948), 9.

2. George Dennison, *The Lives of Children* (New York: Random House, 1969).

3. Materials produced by the Elementary Science Study of the Education Development Center (Newton, MA: McGraw-Hill, 1966–71) remain among the best curriculum materials available.

4. Charles Dickens, *Hard Times* (London: Everyman's Library, 1954), 1.

5. Eleanor Duckworth, "A Reality to Which Each Belongs," in *Holding Values*, ed. Brenda W. Engel with Anne C. Martin (Portsmouth, NH: Heinemann, 2005), 147.

1. August: Beginning the Year

1. Susan Isaacs, *Intellectual Growth in Young Children* (New York: Schocken Books, 1966), 17.

2. Isaacs includes lists of materials and activities that invited the children to draw conclusions from explorations of the world around them. For example, after the children had noticed that wax had melted on the school's hot-water pipes, they attempted to "melt other things in the same way—plasticine, chalk, wooden bricks, paper, scissors, etc." Ibid., 285.

3. Carlina Rinaldi, *In Dialogue with Reggio Emilia* (New York: Routledge, 2006), 207.

4. Patricia Carini, *On Value in Education* (New York: City College Workshop Center, 1987), 30.

5. Ibid., 31.

6. Ibid., 31, her emphasis.

2. Routines and Rituals: Making the Room Theirs

1. Ruth Charney, *Teaching Children to Care: Management in the Responsive Classroom* (Pittsfield, MA: Northeast Foundation for Children, 2002), 27.

2. Sylvia Ashton-Warner, *Teacher* (New York: Simon & Schuster, 1986), 101.

3. Hubert Dyasi, "Assessing 'Imperfect' Conceptions," in *Progressive Education for the 1990s*, ed. Kathe Jervis and Carol Montag (New York: Teachers College Press, 1991), 101.

4. John Dewey, *Experience and Education* (New York: Simon & Schuster, 1997).

5. Ibid., 58.

6. Ibid., 54.

7. Vivian Paley, *White Teacher* (Cambridge, MA: Harvard University Press, 2000).

8. Vivian Paley, *Wally's Stories: Conversations in the Kindergarten* (Cambridge, MA: Harvard University Press, 1981).

9. Vivian Paley, *The Boy Who Would Be a Helicopter: The Uses of Storytelling in the Classroom* (Cambridge, MA: Harvard University Press, 1990).

10. Paley, *Wally's Stories*, 21.

11. Dewey, *Experience and Education*, 54.

12. Ibid., 54.

13. Susan Isaacs, *Social Development in Young Children* (New York: Schocken Books, 1972), 452.

14. Isaacs, *Intellectual Growth*, 33.

15. Ibid., 33.

16. Ibid., 23.

17. Ibid., 33.

18. Charney, *Teaching Children to Care*, 234.

19. Ibid., 366.

20. Dewey, *Experience and Education*, 53.

21. Isaacs, *Intellectual Growth*, 157.

3. Collages: Making Art

1. Randy Kennedy, "Guggenheim Study Suggests Arts Education Benefits Literacy Skills," *New York Times*, July 27, 2006.

2. Pieces of mat board, called offcuts, can often be obtained free from frame shops; they're normally discarded, and are a valuable resource material for classrooms.

3. George Szekely, *Encouraging Creativity in Art Lessons* (New York: Teachers College Press, 1988).

4. Ibid., vii.

4. Finding Curriculum: A Study of Squirrels

1. Dorothy Cohen, *The Learning Child* (New York: Schocken Books, 1988).

2. Karen Gallas, *Talking Their Way into Science* (New York: Teachers College Press, 1995).

3. Ibid., 100.

4. Ibid., 100.

5. John Dewey, *The Child and the Curriculum* (Chicago and London: University of Chicago Press, 1969), 11.

6. Ibid., 11.

7. Eleanor Duckworth, *The Having of Wonderful Ideas and Other Essays on Teaching and Learning* (New York: Teachers College Press, 2006)

8. Ibid., 1.

9. Ibid., xii.

10. Ibid., 173–74.

11. Quoted in "The Role of the Teacher," in *The Hundred Languages of Children: The Reggio Emilia Approach to Early Childhood Education*, ed. Carolyn Edwards, Lella Gandini, and George Forman (Norwood, NJ: Ablex Publishing, 1993), 153.

12. Gallas, *Talking Their Way into Science*, 102.

13. See Vito Perrone, *What Should We Make of Standards?* (New York: Bank Street College of Education, 1999); Patricia F. Carini, *On Value in Education* (New York: City College Workshop Center, 1987); and Deborah Meier, *The Power of Their Ideas* (Boston: Beacon Press, 1995).

14. Maxine Greene writes, "Imagination may be the primary means of forming an understanding of what goes on under the heading of 'reality.'" "Texts and Margins," in *Arts as Education*, ed. Merryl Ruth Goldberg and Ann Phillips (Cambridge, MA: Harvard Educational Review, 1992), 5.

15. A Standards-Based Scope and Sequence for Learning: A Teacher's Framework for Standards-Based Planning (New York: Board of Education of the City of New York, 2000–2001).

5. The Uses of Literacy: Constructing Knowledge

1. Michael Chabon, *The Amazing Adventures of Kavalier and Clay* (New York: Picador USA, 2000), 119.

2. Mary Brown and Norman Precious, *The Integrated Day in the Primary School* (New York: Agathon Press, 1968), 59.

3. Education Development Center, *Insights: A Hands-on Inquiry Science Curriculum* (Dubuque, IA: Kendall/Hunt, 2004–8).

4. Gwendolyn Brooks, in *The Random House Book of Poetry for Children*, selected by Jack Prelutsky (New York: Random House, 1983), 120.

5. Certain books in a class library give evidence of their special relevance: by the end of the year, they are falling apart. These books may provide children, as individuals or as a class, with a vocabulary connected to their concerns. The books give teachers a language in which to address children's feelings and behavior. An example is given in Lynne Strieb's inspiring *A (Philadelphia) Teacher's Journal* (Grand Forks, ND: Center for Teaching and Learning, University of North Dakota, 1985). Strieb was reading Alice Dalgliesh's *The Courage of Sarah Noble* to her first-grade students. She had asked them about their fears: "Belinda has been afraid that her mother would not pick her up after school. . . . Later [she] was crying . . . and I said, 'Remember Sarah Noble. Try to be like her and say to yourself, "Have courage, Belinda Creighton, have courage!" She liked that.' " (20).

6. Leo Lionni, *Between Worlds* (New York: Knopf, 1997), 216.

7. Ibid., 234.

8. Board of Education of the City of New York, *Early Childhood Education* (New York: Board of Education, 1958–59), 51.

9. Molly Brearley et al., *The Teaching of Young Children* (New York: Schocken Books, 1969), 68.

10. Lillian Weber, "Comments on Language by a Silent Child," *Urban Review* 9, no. 3 (September 1976), 172.

11. Ibid., 175.

12. Ibid., 176.

13. Ibid., 176.

14. Ibid., 179.

6. The Uses of Literacy: Reading and Writing

1. Ashton-Warner, *Teacher*, 27.

2. Paolo Freire, *Politics of Education* (South Hadley, MA: Bergin and Garvey, 1985), 59.

3. Ashton-Warner, *Teacher*, 33.

4. Courtney Cazden, *Whole Language Plus: Essays on Literacy in the United States and New Zealand* (New York: Teachers College Press, 1992), 13.

5. Ibid., 5.

6. Karen Gallas, *Imagination and Literacy: A Teacher's Search for the Heart of Learning* (New York: Teachers College Press, 2003); and Anne Dyson, *Social Worlds of Children Learning to Write in an Urban Primary School* (New York: Teachers College Press, 1993).

7. Sue Bredekamp and Carol Copple, eds., *Developmentally Appropriate Practice in Early Childhood Programs* (Washington, DC: National Association for the Education of Young Children, 1996), 6.

8. Susan Radley Brown, director, Accelerated Literacy Learning (Houston, TX: 2004–5).

9. Weber, "Comments on Language by a Silent Child," 177.

10. Accelerated Literacy Learning, *Activating Background Knowledge to Build Schema, Grades K–2, 2005–2006* (Houston, TX: 2004–5).

11. Lucy Calkins, director, Teachers College Reading and Writing Project (New York: 2003–4).

12. Karen Gallas, "Arts as Epistemology: Enabling Children to Know What They Know," in *Arts as Education* (see chap. 4, note 14), 19, 26.

13. Radley Brown, Accelerated Literacy Learning.

14. Perrone, *What Should We Make of Standards?* 5.

15. Radley Brown, Accelerated Literacy Learning.

16. Karen Gallas, *The Languages of Learning* (New York: Teachers College Press, 1994).

7. Midwinter Doldrums and Quarrels

1. Charney, *Teaching Children to Care*, 404–5.

2. Ibid., 406.

3. Ibid., 407.

4. Ibid., 407.

5. Ibid., 363.

6. Dewey, *Education and Experience*, 46.

7. Ibid., 34.

8. John Dewey, *Democracy and Education* (New York: The Free Press, 1966), 359–60.

9. Carini, *On Value in Education*, 12.

10. New York City teacher Louisa Cruz-Acosta describes her quandary when the parent of a child in her class told that child not to play with a new friend because the friend was black. In thinking about how to respond, she found herself called on to "examine my beliefs in a

real situation," including her sense of obligation to the "classroom community," and her trust that children can find solutions to difficult problems when supported in doing so. Louisa Cruz-Acosta, "Friendship and Social Justice in a Kindergarten Classroom," in *Holding Values* (see chap. 1, note 5).

11. Ruth Charney, personal correspondence.

12. Carini, *On Value in Education*, 7–8.

13. Edwards et al., eds., *The Hundred Languages of Children*, 152.

14. Rinaldi, *In Dialogue with Reggio Emilio*, 102.

15. Perrone, *What Should We Make of Standards?* 9.

8. Welcome to the Aquarium: Knowing One Child

1. Gallas, *Languages of Learning*, 2.

2. Harriet Cuffaro, *Experimenting with the World* (New York: Teachers College Press, 1995), 14.

3. Don Dinkmeyer and Rudolf Dreikurs, *Encouraging Children to Learn* (Englewood Cliffs, NJ: Prentice-Hall, 1963), 207.

4. Some educators and psychologists have recently suggested that teachers use observational checklists in order to individualize management of behavior; see, for example, Eileen S. Flicker and Janet Andron Hoffman, *Guiding Children's Behavior: Developmental Discipline in the Classroom* (New York: Teachers College Press, 2006), chap. 3. Special educators have also recommended the use of detailed observational checklists that will yield clues about the function of children's behavior ("functional behavioral assessment") and thereby produce "effective" interventions. For me, observation is an integral part of the attempt to know the *entirety* of who the child is—and I use observation to see children in a broad, integrated way. The risk of more narrow assessments is that they develop inventories of pathology. I make observations in a systematic way, carrying around a clipboard with a class list on which I continually make notes of children's choices of activities and companions, work style, etc. I interpret notes separately, copying them over on pages for each child.

5. Dewey, *Education and Experience*, 62.

6. Patricia Carini, *Starting Strong: A Different Look at Children, Schools and Standards* (New York: Teachers College Press, 2001) and *From Another Angle: Children's Strengths and School Standards: The Prospect Center's Descriptive Review of the Child* (New York: Teachers College Press, 2001).

7. Rinaldi, *In Dialogue*, 63.

8. Ibid., 126.

9. Ibid., 63.

10. For a thorough discussion of how cultural norms play out in schools, see Lisa Delpit's *Other People's Children*, 2nd ed. (1995; New York: The New Press, 2006).

9. June: Meanings and Metaphors at the End of the Year

1. A.A. Milne, *Now We Are Six* (New York: E.P. Dutton, 1988), p. 101.

2. Robert Graves, *Poems Selected by Himself* (London: Penguin Books, 1961), 214.

3. Karen Gallas, *Sometimes I Can Be Anything: Power, Gender and Identity in a Primary Classroom* (New York: Teachers College Press, 1998), 146.

10. Postscript: Being a Teacher

1. See Ruth Charney's statement to her class, "I see everything." Charney, *Teaching Children to Care*, 27.

2. Frances P. Hawkins, *The Logic of Action: Young Children at Work* (Boulder, CO: Colorado Associated University Press, 1986), 8.

3. Loris Malaguzzi, "History, Ideas, and Basic Philosophy," in *The Hundred Language of Children* (see chap. 4, note 11), 66–67.

4. Deborah Meier, *The Power of Their Ideas* (Boston: Beacon Press, 1995), 142.

5. Charney, *Teaching Children to Care*, 406.

6. See Jonathan Kozol, *The Shame of the Nation: The Restoration of Apartheid Schooling in America* (New York: Crown, 2005), *Savage Inequalities: Children in America's Schools* (New York: HarperCollins, 1991), and *Letters to a Young Teacher* (New York: Crown, 2007).

7. As a result of pressure to produce "good" data, schools bump "soft" subjects—the arts, physical education, social studies. A *New York Times* article quotes the Center on Educational Policy to the effect that "almost half of the nation's school districts have significantly decreased the daily classroom time spent on subjects like science, art, and history as a result of the federal No Child Left Behind Act's focus on annual tests in reading and math." Sam Dillon, "Focus on 2 R's Cuts Time for the Rest, Report Says," *New York Times*, July 25, 2007. Teaching for the test is imperative because of everything that hangs on the scores (promotion, admission to better programs, school success).

8. Isaacs, *Intellectual Growth in Young Children*, 2.

9. The National Commission on Teaching and America's Future, a nonprofit group, "has calculated that nearly a third of all new teachers

leave the profession after just three years, and that after five years almost half are gone." The cost of replacing these teachers, according to the organization's estimate: "some $7 billion annually." Sam Dillon, "Schools Scramble for Teachers Because of Spreading Turnover," *New York Times*, August 27, 2007.

10. We were encouraged and supported by the Center for Collaborative Education, a network of New York alternative schools, and the Coalition of Essential Schools, a national organization of progressive schools. For these groups, collaboration was a central value.

11. See in particular Patricia Carini, "Prospect's Documentary Processes"; Leslie Alexander, "Time, Trust, and Reflective Thinking in a Teacher Collaborative"; and Rhoda Kanevsky, Lynne Strieb, and Betsy Wice, "A Philadelphia Story," in *Holding Values* (see introduction, note 5).

12. Quoted in Malaguzzi, "History, Ideas, and Basic Philosophy," 85.

13. Rinaldi, *In Dialogue with Reggio Emilia*, 133.

14. Marilyn Cochran-Smith connects the problem of teacher retention with the issue of how teacher development is viewed: "Teachers are much more likely to stay in schools and to be successful when teacher development is understood as a learning problem and not a training problem where the point is simply to be sure teachers can follow scripted materials and pacing schedules." Marilyn Cochran-Smith, *Stayers, Leavers, Lovers, and Dreamers: Why People Teach and Why They Stay* (New York: Bank Street College of Education, Occasional Paper Series 16, 2006), 16.

15. School-community links are described in detail by Vito Perrone in the chapter "The Community and the School," in *A Letter to Teachers: Reflections on Schooling and the Art of Teaching* (San Francisco: Jossey-Bass, 1991), 38–44.

16. Loris Malaguzzi notes that this enlarged relationship between schools and families requires teachers to "leave behind an isolated, silent mode of working that leaves no traces" and develop "skills to talk, listen, and learn from parents." Quoted in "History, Ideas, and Basic Philosophy," 63.

17. Repetition is required in the learning of many skills—certainly, for example, when children learn to write numerals and letters. I teach these in fairly standard ways: I write the numeral 5 in the air, the children copy and chant, "down, down, across," and they write the numeral on wipe-off boards and practice papers. Correctness counts in certain activities, and teachers learn to distinguish these topics. But much of what we want children to learn are things they must understand and be able to apply, and these are not best learned in standardized ways.

18. Malaguzzi, "History, Ideas, and Basic Philosophy," 75.

19. Carini, *Starting Strong*, 176.

20. Gallas, *Sometimes I Can Be Anything*, 146.

21. Rinaldi, *In Dialogue with Reggio Emilia*, 197.

22. The exemplary document *Children and Their Primary Schools, A Report of the Central Advisory Council for Education* (London: Her Majesty's Stationery Office, 1967), 188, summed up the "aims of primary education" in this way: "The best preparation for being a happy and useful man or woman is to live fully as a child. . . . Children need to be themselves, to live with other children and with grown-ups, to learn from their environment, to enjoy the present, to get ready for the future, to create and to love, to learn to face adversity, to behave responsibly, in a word, to be human beings."

CHILDREN'S
BOOKS CITED

Arnold, Tedd. *No Jumping on the Bed*. New York: Dial, 1987.

Brown, Margaret Wise. *The Runaway Bunny*. New York: Harper, 1942.

Burningham, John. *Hey! Get Off Our Train*. New York: Crown, 1989.

Dahl, Roald. *The BFG*. New York: Farrar, Straus & Giroux, 1982.

Feiffer, Jules. *Bark, George*. New York: HarperCollins, 1999.

————. *The Daddy Mountain*. New York: Hyperion, 2004.

Galdone, Paul. *The Three Billy Goats Gruff*. New York: Houghton Mifflin, 1973.

Grimm, Brothers, and Paul Zelinsky. *Rumpelstiltskin*. New York: Dutton, 1986.

Hyman, Trina Schart. *Little Red Riding Hood*. New York: Holiday House, 1982.

Jonas, Ann. *The Quilt*. New York: Greenwillow, 1984.

Joyce, William. *George Shrinks*. New York: Harper & Row, 1985.

Lionni, Leo. *A Color of His Own*. New York: Knopf/Random House, 1975.

————. *Alexander and the Wind-up Mouse*. New York: Knopf/Pantheon, 1969, 1974.

————. *Fish Is Fish*. New York: Random House, 1970.

————. *Little Blue and Little Yellow*. New York: HarperCollins, 1959, 1995.

————. *The Biggest House*. New York: Knopf, 1968.

London, Jonathan. *Baby Whale's Journey*. San Francisco: Chronicle Books, 1999.

MacDonald, Suse. *Alphabatics*. New York: Bradbury Press, 1986.

Milne, A.A.. *Now We Are Six*. New York: Dutton, 1927, 1955.

Scott, Elaine, *Twins!* New York: Atheneum, 1998.

Shannon, David. *No, David!* New York: Blue Sky Press, 1998.

Steig, William. *Sylvester and the Magic Pebble*. New York: Simon & Schuster, 1969.

————. *Amos and Boris*. New York: Farrar, Straus & Giroux, 1971.

————. *Brave Irene*. New York: Farrar, Straus & Giroux, 1986.

————. *The Amazing Bone*. New York: Farrar, Straus & Giroux, 1976.

Young, Ed. *Lon Po Po*. New York: Philomel, 1989.

White, E.B. *Stuart Little*. New York: Harper & Row, 1945.

Wood, Audrey. *Heckedy Peg*. San Diego: Harcourt Brace Jovanovich, 1987.

INDEX

THE NEW PRESS TITLES
OF RELATED INTEREST

BEING WITH CHILDREN
A High-Spirited Personal Account of Teaching Writing, Theater, and Videotape
Phillip Lopate

Lopate's classic account of his relationship to his writing craft and to his young students, with a new introduction by Herbert Kohl.

978-1-59558-337-6 (pbk.)

BEYOND THE BAKE SALE
The Essential Guide to Family-School Partnerships
Anne T. Henderson, Karen L. Mapp, Vivian R. Johnson, and Don Davies

A practical, hands-on primer on helping schools and families work better together to improve children's education.

978-1-56584-888-7 (pbk.)

THE CASE FOR MAKE BELIEVE
Saving Play in a Commercialized World
Susan Linn

From the author of *Consuming Kids,* a clarion call for preserving play in our material world—a book every parent will want to read.

978-1-56584-970-9 (hc.)

CITY KIDS, CITY SCHOOLS
More Reports from the Front Row
Edited by William Ayers, Gloria Ladson-Billings, Gregory Michie, and Pedro A. Noguera

This new and timely collection has been compiled by four of the country's most prominent urban educators to provide some of the best writing on life in city schools and neighborhoods.

978-1-59558-338-3 (pbk.)

CITY KIDS, CITY TEACHERS
Reports from the Front Row
Edited by William Ayers and Patricia Ford

A classic collection exploding the stereotypes of city schools, reissued as a companion to *City Kids, City Schools*.

978-1-56584-051-5 (pbk.)

CONSUMING KIDS
The Hostile Takeover of Childhood
Susan Linn

"An exhaustively researched picture of a $15 billion industry [child marketing] in near-total denial about the effects it has."

—Publishers Weekly

978-1-56584-783-5 (hc.)

FIRES IN THE BATHROOM
Advice for Teachers from High School Students
Kathleen Cushman

This groundbreaking book offers original insights into teaching teenagers in today's hard-pressed urban high schools from the point of view of the students themselves. It speaks to both new and established teachers, giving them firsthand information about who their students are and what they need to succeed.

978-1-56584-996-9 (pbk.)

FIRES IN THE MIDDLE SCHOOL BATHROOM
Advice for Teachers from Middle Schoolers
Kathleen Cushman and Laura Rogers

Following on the heels of the bestselling *Fires in the Bathroom*, which brought the insights of high school students to teachers and parents, Kathleen Cushman now turns her attention to the crucial and challenging middle grades, joining forces with adolescent psychologist Laura Rogers.

978-1-59558-111-2 (hc.)

HOW KINDERGARTEN CAME TO AMERICA
Friedrich Froebel's Radical Vision of Early Childhood Education
Bertha von Marenholtz-Bülow

An enchanting 1894 account of the inventor of kindergarten, introduced to a new generation of educators and parents by Herbert Kohl.

978-1-59558-154-9 (pbk.)